122:3 · July 2023

Feminism's Bad Objects

Jennifer C. Nash and Samantha Pinto, Special Issue Editors

AGAINST the DAY

Abolition Politics
Marquis Bey, Editor

Jennifer C. Nash and Samantha Pinto

Everybody's Maybes:
Reproducing Feminism's Bad Objects

Contemporary feminism loves bad objects. It so often operates by identifying and disavowing the values that the bad object seems to certainly hold, be it a so-called Karen's angry tirade or a "gender critical" tweet. Decrying the bad object allows feminism to perform its striving goodness, its ethical orientation toward an ever further-off completeness. If only it can expel the bad and embrace the newly minted good. We are reminded of Naomi Schor's diagnosis: "What I mean is simply this: at any given time, within the carefully policed precincts of the academy, some critical objects are promoted to the status of good objects (say, not so long ago, dead authors) while others are tabooed (say, in the old days, experience)" (Schor 1995: xv).

But this is both too flip and too presentist, born from an exhaustion as scholars, editors, and teachers of the post-Obama, post-Trump, long pandemic, Black Lives Matter moment—scholars who work on Black feminism and note its status in both the academy and popular feminism as something approaching an article of faith, a program that, if everyone adheres to it, will bring justice across the board. While we note with excitement the move from earlier eras marked by the difficult inclusion of "Black feminism" and women of color

The South Atlantic Quarterly 122:3, July 2023
DOI 10.1215/00382876-10643945   © 2023 Duke University Press

(WOC) feminism into the academic feminist program, we also find in the contemporary moves the structural and discursive haunt of earlier moments and movements in the field (Lee 2000).

Feminism's long struggle with its "proper objects," then, comes to the forefront of our 1990s-trained minds, its various tensions with gender, sexuality, difference feminism, dominance feminism, queer studies, transnational studies, and transgender studies, to name a few in its academic genealogy. At each turn, though tense, the "winning" side seemed foregone, righteous, a new good object to include in the pantheon of things feminism would claim responsibility and moral accountability for. These good objects necessitated the coproduction of bad objects—those demonstrating attachments to "women," but also to other passé objects, including, among others, motherhood, lesbians, and radical feminists.

To make an object "good" for feminism, it needs to be radical, subversive of the normative that old feminism's bad objects represent. The naming wars—the endless transformation of women's studies programs and departments into gender, sexuality, and feminist studies programs and departments—may have stuck us with various solutions to the conundrum of objects in feminism, but they also leave us with the trail of feminism's attachment to narratives of itself as inclusive, capacious, ethical, and ever-approaching completion of its moral mission. They also, of course, leave a trail of disposed objects for us to mull over as a defining feature of the field.

We mention these genres of feminism's objects—their orientations toward the past, present, and future of the field, and the life cycle of feminism as a concept and how we narrate it being "born" and "coming of age"—as a way to highlight the reproductive metaphors and labor that hover over our conceptualization of what objects animate feminist research. By struggling with and sometimes disavowing its origins in bad objects, feminism performs not its surety but its own ongoing uncertainty about its projects, its attachments, and its use. These *maybes*, rather than a weakness, represent a different version of a script of Hortense Spillers's own terms in her canonical "Mama's Baby, Papa's Maybe: An American Grammar Book" (1987), the matrilineal "belonging" of the Black child to the mother, in enslavement under *partus sequitur ventrem* and its afterlives, becomes the locus of tragedy and pathology for even and especially liberal interpretations of slavery's social effects on Black life. The baby that belongs exclusively to mother and isn't tethered to the paternal line is destined to be a social bad object in a field of relations that demands white paternal claims and resources for life paths to normative success, in the Moynihan-era moment that Spillers writes in, and against.

To claim the Black maternal is to argue for the possibility to reclaim risk as knowledge production, and to critique the systems that hold Blackness in constant negative relation to white forms (like the patriarchal nuclear family), and all genders and gendered expression in constant comparative relation to those forms, genres, and narratives of white ideal normativity. Here, the bad object becomes feminism's imagined old forms and attachments themselves, which as feminism revises, it leverages different claims against and revaluations of to narrate its coming into the present. Good and bad feminisms—not surprisingly in this moment narrated as Black and white feminisms—contest, contact, counter, and seem to ask us to take sides.

We work from the displacement that Spillers hints at when she talks of a grammar book of American—key for her—race that locks in not just systemic but symbolic, linguistic, and epistemological understanding of Blackness in relationship to whiteness as we approach bad objects in feminism. In this introduction, we reconsider how we can tell the stories of Black feminist thought and institutional feminist study through uncertainty and incommensurability rather than clear reproducibility of good and bad objects. We then consider the speculative place of reproductive history, metaphor, and technology vis-à-vis intersectionality as a foundational object of worry for and in feminism. Taking seriously the sustained focus on white women and white feminism as the quintessential bad objects and actors in the present of US feminism, we engage how the reproductive in Black feminism has been both an occluding and elucidating genre to refract Black women as subjects of a "white" field of feminism and the academy at large. We pay particular attention to the social reproduction of race in analyses of gestation, birth, and motherhood and the opportunities these sites represent for disorienting intersectional analysis rather than shoring up its contours. By challenging feminism's critical attachments to self-evidently ethical objects, this introduction, and this issue, offers a way forward in feminist study that imagines uncertainty as a core method and value of feminist inquiry.

All the Things a Bad Object Could Be Right Now, Because Feminism Is Its Mother

In the book chapter "Owning the Self in a Disowned World," Patricia J. Williams (1991) begins a career-long investment in studying the futures of reproduction. Williams spins a story of various limit cases that test speculative futures of race, gender, embodiment, belonging, and legal rights and injury through scandalized claims of the womb, including its speculative dimensions as both an engine of legal innovation when a white woman who claims to have been "wrongly" impregnated with Black sperm claims wrongful birth harms in witnessing and managing racism against her mixed race daughter, which Williams then imagines as a reparations strategy for her own mother. Williams then does a witty, hilarious written dance, claiming in the next few paragraphs a manifesto on bringing the deep uncertainty and lack of choice in the paternal history of Black women's maternity in the United States to assisted reproductive technology (ART) through a secret war of drafted white sperm donors "smuggling in vials" of Black sperm:

> I suggest guerilla insemination to challenge the notion of choice, to complicate it in other contexts. . . . What happens if it is no longer white male seed that has the prerogative of dropping noiselessly and invisibly into black wombs, swelling ranks and complexifying identity? . . . the symbolically sacred vessel of the white womb will bring the complication home to the guarded intimacy of white families. . . .
>
> I suppose I'd better disclaim this as a serious exhortation, lest . . . I get arrested in this brave new world for inciting reproductive riot. But it is interesting to examine the image it evokes, the visions of white mothers rushing to remedy the depreciation of their offspring in suits about the lost property of their children's bodies . . . I am overwhelmed by this image: the vault of sperm banks. The clean container of white wombs. The swift messenger, the hermetic fire of white phallic power. The materia principas of semen, sperm, paternity. From dross into capital. The daughter's born blackness as accident, as awful, as "fault" that must be rehabilitated and deterred by adequate compensation. (Williams 1991: 188)

More of these cases have come true, as white women's "wrongful birth" of Black children shows that Williams was prescient in her speculative rumination on the future of rights and repair through the legal, and the thorny multidirectional question such questions of the reproduction of race and racial reproduction launch into the world as it is. Her playful language around retributive vision slides into the absurd realism of racism as it stands and haunts the Black feminist self. Williams's analysis of the reproductive takes up the legal aspect of Spillers's now lauded flesh, the stories others have told about the Black woman's body that "confirm the human body as a metonymic figure for an entire repertoire of human and social arrangements . . . in a constant opposition of binary meanings. Apparently spontaneous, these 'actants' are wholly generated, with neither past nor future, as tribal currents moving out of time. . . . Although one would be unwise not to concede its dangerous and fatal effects" (Spillers 2003: 205).

As Spillers's point is to become leery of repetition and what it culturally and ethically reproduces in its abstractions, we'd like to put these stories together—those of intersectionality as tension, as conflict, as vulnerable opening—in considering the object of reproduction, and the particular ways that it can feel easy to tag landmark cases of supposed racial mis-production in ART as bad objects easily understood through the paradigm of "white women's tears" that so often accompany the campaigns for remuneration, restitution, and tortuous wrong. In doing so, we hope to think on the limits of invoking dominant paradigms like intersectionality as feminist constants that represent only the diagnostic and curative, rather than what either as a starting point might generate, which is a state of *less* understanding across difference. What else might feminism be and become, if we highlight its own focus on uncertainty and not the individual objects and subjects it might designate as its proper domain?

In the late 1990s, Richard and Donna Fasano's story electrified popular media. A white couple was implanted with embryos from their own genetic materials as well as one from a Black couple, the latter erroneously. They were informed about a possible mix-up before the birth of the children. The white couple was sued for a DNA test and then was forced to relinquish the child, Akiel (whom they called Joseph), to his "biological" parents four months after the birth. They did so, but only after establishing a contract for visitation rights over their Black "birth son" and to recognize their birth children as brothers, with a court later severing this contract after the Rogers, Akiel's (Black) biological parents, sued to have the visits terminated. Donna Fasano's insistence on referring to the two children as twins and referring to them as "two healthy, normal boys" was roundly critiqued by critical race theorists as racial color blindness at its worst, most propertied pitch: I don't see race, I see what's mine.

Potential unease loomed, though, over reifying categories of biological belonging and biological racial identity as immutable, as well as issues of gestational labor, even through weaponizing the legal system against an African American family. A cascade of research around the fallacies of reproductive choice and the dismal maternal and infant health outcomes for Black women from scholars including Dorothy Roberts, Camisha Russell, Deirdre Cooper Owens, Dana-Ann Davis, and Robyn Wiegman (who reads the Fasano case in her 2002 article "Intimate Publics: Race, Property, and Personhood" and her subsequent chapter in 2012's *Object Lessons*) followed.

But our own rehearsal here belies the fact that this case might *feel* obvious, but it was not, necessarily, from a legal or an intersectional feminist standpoint. Why does it feel like we—feminists, anti-racists—already know the stakes? Donna Fasano represents what we now call a Karen, an easy target, a bad (faith) white feminist object. The Rogerses, and Akiel, were her clear victims, taking her own understanding of her pregnancy with twins and her feelings around being disenchanted from normative notions of biological ownership and kinship after being alerted late in the pregnancy that there was a likely error, and holding on through the birth and the first four months to the performance of her expectations, of the normative, in a situation that factually and visually cued her and the world that it wasn't, in fact, "normal" at all to have one Black and one white child with two white parents. Donna Fasano's laying claim to Akiel, those feelings of white ownership on her part and on the mainstream white media's coverage, traffic in both white womanhood's claim to maternal care and protection unafforded to Black women's bodies in the history of the Americas and chattel slavery and in the disownment of Black children from their families during chattel enslavement to the whims of white owners. This is all in the shadow of *partus sequitur ventrem*, which, of course, claimed blood-belonging to Black mothers absolutely, while bestowing none of the custodial rights to keeping or claiming or caring for family. For African American life, then, the separation of biological parentage and custodial parentage is nothing new, and the specter of this hangs over the Fasano case.

But it is also a case about the reproduction of intersectionality itself, its spiky meeting points at intimate, tangled, embodied experience where historical experience meets physiological experience meets cultural-social experience in the wider context of infrastructure, structure, and institution (Wiegman 2002). The media circus around the Fasano case was always about what we might now call "white women's tears," yes, but like the "switched at birth" stories about white girls mixed up in a hospital that were made-for-TV movies in the 1980s, they are about a culture confronting the unthinkable that is, of course, eminently thinkable if one studies African American women's history and other histories of radical dispossession: that what one *knows*—love, blood, kinship, race, belonging, property—is not at all certain or stable. Identity, even self and intimates' identity, is not a given but a shifting set of identifications made legible by visual, genetic, social, emotional, and legal cues. Mama's babies become everybody's maybes, and engender many think pieces and an academic industry on the social and legal ramifications of ART, the future of Blackness in a world where one can "choose" their child's traits (which of course mate selection and patterns in "mate value" that reflect social segregation already produce), the ethics of medicine but also sociolegal practices such as trans-racial adoption and surrogacy that deeply implicate race and colonialism, and the social construction of gender, parentage, motherhood, and family writ large. Questions about whether sperm donation should be race-blind—and for whom—butt against calls for respecting cultural specificity and heritage as points of pride.

It is the 2014 Jennifer Cramblett case—where two white lesbians were inseminated with the "wrong" sperm—sperm they did not choose, and which they could identify as an error since their child was mixed race Black and white—that opened a(nother) floodgate of scholarship, including from Williams herself. Cramblett claimed that their neighborhood, their white families, and their community barely countenanced them as lesbians, let alone could set aside their racism in the mostly white suburb. She said that her own experience growing up in rural Ohio and with "limited cultural competency" made raising a biracial child particularly challenging. Her lawsuit described the trauma of "an unplanned transracial parent-child relationship for which she was not, and is not, prepared." As Cramblett filed tortious claims for their biological kin as wrongful, it's easy to see them as bad intersectional objects for a nonetheless obvious error from the sperm bank/insemination doctors. And again, the fascination and the swift condemnation of their claims lays bare not just the "threat" of racial mixing in engineered reproductive futures, but also the threat these structural claims expose for the left around what constitutes just antiracist life and practices in the US, in a structural system that at every turn denies a thriving cohabitable life or social reproductive autonomy for Black and white and other citizens. The figure of Cramblett, weeping as she describes how she was not prepared to raise a Black-identified child in her white, anti-Black, homophobic community is one of Williams's images that overwhelm, after the fact, but not where she, or intersectionality, stops.

And here, in a post-BLM world, we have the latest celebrity case of mixed embryos—here where two couples were each inseminated with the other's egg, and both resulted in live births. Here, too, racial "appearance" was the motivation for suspicion around biological belonging, but is delicately articulated by the white family, the Crambletts, choosing to go public (while, again, the brown family remain unidentified, seemingly by choice) even as they must articulate a fiduciary harm. This time, they cannot be articulated through wrongful birth and hardships of racism on a white family, but instead through the grief over the lost experience of birthing one's "own" child. Pictures accompany this new case's story, with their previous biological child in full view in a picture with a blurred out baby face, replete with black hair visible and darker baby skin. Again, the urge to mock here the subtext of whiteness is great, and easy. It also elucidates the great fear of uncertain connection, by which the appearance of phenotypic racial characteristics is the only "way" to make visible the medical error or intimate deception.

This then is another legacy of Williams's call to expand selfhood in a "disowned world" and Spillers's articulation of Mama's Baby—that the designation of blood-belonging to a fixed identity to and through the mother is no salve, no promise of embodied subjectivity or personhood, nor is "achieving beyond all measure," as Spillers powerfully articulates in "Mama's Baby, Papa's Maybe," about the demographic statistics of Black women in the United States in regard to education and jobs.

More Objects, More Problems, More Feminism

These stories of reproduction aren't easy for feminism, not just because they appear to pit bad white actors against good and often silent Black subjects as victims, but because they unveil the thicker injuries of systemic, structural uncertainty and unbelonging that characterize late-capitalist life, and that feminism cannot have definite or universal answers to as it might seem to promise. It, too, has a will to reproduce itself as sure, as outraged, as clear. But reproduction and its thorny publics offer bad objects that produce beautiful, incommensurable, difficult questions around the limits of individual choice and "good" political action, and of right legal, historical, and social interpretation around embodied acts from radically different standpoints, and differential and even competing solutions. These are limit cases, spectacular failures and exceptions that fascinate as they expose the instability of intimate lives, the degree to which they are shaped by promises (Owens 2023), by fictions (Holloway 2014), by the law and culture that surround us at that moment, but that may not be always or forever right in their orientation.

These ARTs and their afterlives cases pivot feminism as not an endlessly capacious and reproducible paradigm that offers interpretative and ethical certainty, but as what performance scholar Diana Taylor calls a scenario—a replaying of a script with a difference from the archive, the material history, that creates the context for its reception. The grammars of these spectacles of racial reproduction align with Spillers's psychoanalytic articulation of their making, but also pivot, change and shift the "maybe," and the bad object of property, the child—who must be authored, born, cared for in some capacity, who goes on, beyond the acute "situation" of their birth—to suggest the ways even feminism clings to its interpretive certainty rather than its potential to open up maybes that its constant revisions of its proper objects suggests.

Academic feminism, then, as it stands, is an ongoing, tense, and uncertain set of negotiations that are temporal and unstable. Embracing the "maybe" of feminism—uncertainty, complexity, the unfixed—doesn't mean giving up on the important histories of the field that have already been and are still being told. But what we hope to have traced here is feminism's potential as a site of naming incommensurability and vulnerability that is open-ended, unable to be completely resolved by an interpretive, conceptual, or analytic orientation.

This is an interpretation of feminism that is always self-implicated and interrogative of its attachments, to the difficult balance of holding on and letting go of the stories we have about ourselves as scholars and about the field of feminism as a political actor. Feminism must constantly grapple with bad systems writ large and bad objects in its academic homes. But it has other hard stories to tell about itself alongside these grammars, as Rachel Lee imagined even in 2000 around the "haunt" of WOC feminism to the constant articulated center of white feminist canon (Lee 2000). These are grammars of intra-Black, transnational, multiethnic, and intra-field conflict and difference, stories that have histories with the field as well from activism, labor, and social life, that might leave whiteness decentered, not the metaphorical referent. Feminism might speculate on difference, differently, and see what risks and questions and futures come to play when we insist on expanding its objects' temporalities and forms, rather than disciplining its reproduction into the latest objects that cast it as triumphant and salvific.

This issue is filled with essays that confront what the author's themselves, not just the field, cannot, will not, or do(es) not know. Feminism allows them, and us, to contemplate other objects, not "ourselves," to encounter both those objects and ourselves beyond ethical sorting. We remain awed at the many genealogies one can tell of feminism, and of its objects, and the affects and attachments they can yield beyond what we might think of as the proper objects and affects of "good" politics, and we find joy in tracing feminism's work on itself as an always potentially bad object. We want to end on the possibilities of that openness to imagining feminism's lineage as encompassing and including misunderstanding, uncertainty, and misinterpretation at its core. We imagine those feminist bad feelings as an alternate way of narrating the field, as it narrates itself, as ongoing and evolving, rather than preoccupied with a reproduction of itself in the same grammars we already think we know.

References

Holloway, Karla F. C. 2014. *Legal Fictions: Constituting Race, Composing Literature*. Durham, NC: Duke University Press.

Lee, Rachel. 2000. "Notes from the (non)Field: Teaching and Theorizing Women of Color." *Meridians* 1, no. 1: 85–109.

Owens, Emily A. 2023. *Consent in the Presence of Force: Sexual Violence and Black Women's Survival in Antebellum New Orleans*. Chapel Hill: University of North Carolina Press.

Schor, Naomi. 1995. *Bad Objects: Essays Popular and Unpopular*. Durham, NC: Duke University Press.

Spillers, Hortense. 2003. *Black, White, and in Color: Essays on American Literature and Culture*. Chicago: University of Chicago Press.

Spillers, Hortense J. 1987. "Mama's Baby, Papa's Maybe: An American Grammar Book." *Diacritics* 17, no. 2 (Summer): 64–81.

Wiegman, Robyn. 2002. "Intimate Publics: Race, Property, and Personhood." *American Literature 74, no. 4*: 859–85.

Wiegman, Robyn. 2012. *Object Lessons*. Durham, NC: Duke University Press.

Williams, Patricia J. 1991. *Alchemy of Race and Rights*. Cambridge, MA: Harvard University Press.

Durba Mitra

Sisterhood Is X:
On Feminist Solidarity Then and Now

"I confront the frustration of trying to begin writing, the worry that I will not find words to say what needs to be said; that I daily lose the capacity to speak in writing" (hooks 1986: 125). bell hooks opens her 1986 article "Sisterhood" by narrating her struggles to write a renewed call for feminist sisterhood. Over the course of the essay, hooks insists that feminists must not abandon the concept despite conflicts about racial difference that felt increasingly insurmountable in the American feminist movement of the early 1980s. For hooks, solidarity in sisterhood was about the affective possibilities of feminist collective and the moving power of mutual care. Even as she critiqued white women's reductive visions of sisterhood that equated women through a common experience of oppression, hooks insisted that more inclusive visions of feminist praxis must be diligently pursued as a radical pedagogy of democratic struggle united across social difference and geographies. Global sisterhood was for hooks "a training ground" (127) where there was no need "to eradicate difference to feel solidarity" (138). hooks's vision of sisterhood animated a uniquely feminist vision of political solidarity that confronted overlapping structures of gender, class, and racial domination.

The South Atlantic Quarterly 122:3, July 2023
DOI 10.1215/00382876-10643959   © 2023 Duke University Press

Challenged by the vexed labor of writing in today's alarmingly authoritarian moment, I see in hooks's reflection on the project of sisterhood an invitation to reflect on the possibilities and failures of feminisms past and present. What are the stakes of taking up hooks's project of sisterhood today? Sisterhood seems out of sync for the politics of our present. Much like bell hooks, I am struggling to write, not finding the words to adequately express how we think solidarity in our moment almost four decades later. Yet, in the current moment of vaccine imperialism, climate catastrophe, and gender policing, truly transnational feminist solidarity feels more necessary than ever.

Today, the notion of sisterhood appears more romantic, nostalgic, and naively optimistic than politically useful. It seems almost impossible to imagine how one might convincingly argue for feminist unity through sisterhood in these alarmingly authoritarian times, when the vocabulary of womanhood and family has been so effectively repurposed by gender-policing advocates to unjustly exclude trans and other gender nonconforming people from political and social life. The urgency of bell hooks's pleas feel distant, the fury of her demand for collective action wholly unconvincing.

Rather than solidarity through global collectives, more often, in a time of endless pandemic, political protests for racial justice, and violent majoritarianism across the world, the refrain one might hear from a feminist today is "I am tired." Tired of false claims to equivalence between forms of oppression, fatigued by expansive carceral state institutions that seem irredeemable, exhausted by reactionary politics that propagate biological determinism, racial inequality, and religious majoritarianism for authoritarian ends. It is a time of exhaustion produced by unrealized promises of women's equality half a century after global movements for women's rights and continued frustrations with the persistent failures of political and social institutions to sustain childcare, health care, state services, and fair wages. Collective visions feel incompatible with the tiring temporality of never-ending crisis that organizes today's politics of precarity.[1] This exhaustive mode of feminist critique converges with increasingly pessimistic conceptual visions of minoritized lives that produce "no futures" and few viable alternatives to the failed project of liberal humanism, a melancholia that has dominated much of critical theory since the 1990s.

Yet the 1970s concept of *sisterhood* was a wholly different mood. Sisterhood offered an optimistic foundation for new internationalist feminisms, an ideal concept that envisioned real widescale structural change for women through the possibilities of collective action that reached across borders. Sisterhood was a vision of an explicitly *feminist* solidarity, an international feminist coalition that went above and beyond the masculinist politics of solidarity of the international Left to fight against masculinist authoritarianism. These new feminist imaginaries sought to build a complex infrastructure that linked autonomous women's movements to policy change at the level of states, nongovernmental organizations, and international governance structures like the United Nations. Feminist sisterhood emerged in this moment as a critical language of alliance, friendship, coalition, collectivity, and liberation based in aspirations for ideals of women's equality and gender justice that shaped a new agenda for feminist internationalism.

What was imagined in the global sisterhood of the 1970s and 1980s? What are the enduring effects of these definitive projects of global sisterhood from the era of women's liberation? And what is the place of a politics of transnational solidarity fifty years later? Situating the vexed history of global sisterhood and its fate as a "bad object," this essay meditates on the history of global sisterhood to imagine the limits and possibilities of feminist solidarity now.[2] I trace this vexed genealogy to evaluate the modes of feminist solidarity made possible and foreclosed by the concept of sisterhood. Revisiting coalition in our moment now, fifty years later, may offer new avenues for feminist sisterhood for the twenty-first century through the subversion of normative kinship and biologically deterministic ideas of cis womanhood. Perhaps, instead of treating sisterhood as the relic of an exclusionary past, we might reimagine a politics of sisterhood for today.

The Promises of Sisterhood

The politics of sisterhood gained momentum in a time of uneasy optimism as people struggled for civil rights and decolonization and mobilized under the promise of a novel global egalitarianism. Sisterhood was part of a new lexicon of anti-imperial internationalism that began to flourish in the shadows of world war, colonialism, and segregationist politics around the world. Internationalism offered a new vocabulary of possibility, of future unity in "one world" that transgressed national, linguistic, and economic divides and reflected a new horizon of decolonization. As Toni Morrison beautifully renders this moment in her critical essay reflections from the 1990s on global politics, the language of alliance across decolonizing geographies was "less like categories of historical trends than *yearnings*" (Morrison 2021: 6). Yearnings for a new world order based in aspirations for international equality and novel political possibilities for civil rights and true democratic participation, where the darker peoples of the world, newly liberated, would rise together and imagine the world anew.[3] The language of longing for international alliance would "corral the earth into some semblance of unity" (6) and reimagine "human destiny" (6) through radically equitable futures.

The idea of sisterhood in global feminist movements was part of this broader aspirational vocabulary of solidarity. In this new vision of global rights, political movements appropriated the language of the family to make an argument for collectivity, from the lexicon of kin terms that became the grounds for anticolonial nationalism to the intimate idioms of family in the Civil Rights Movement. It was reflective of a longer tradition of feminist critiques of the masculine language of "brotherhood" in the international left from the time of the French Revolution's *fraternité* to the domain of men's politics in the Communist International. In the term "sisterhood," women allied the feminist movement with larger left politics of collective action and claimed an essential place in the global political family.

Yet, even as it grew in popularity, sisterhood was vigorously debated in the emerging global feminisms of the 1970s. In feminist speeches, protests at conferences, and a flourishing world of feminist writing, minoritized activists and intellectuals from around the world questioned the often reductive and romantic language of sisterhood of the new global feminisms promoted by American women. Notably, in spaces like the UN International Women's Year conferences and international feminist collaborations, international women critiqued American activists, including Betty Friedan, Gloria Steinem, and Robin Morgan, who imagined themselves as the sole bearers of an enlightened vision of global sisterhood.[4] At the first UN conference in Mexico City, Betty Friedan declared America to be the origins of the global women's movement and proclaimed white American feminists to its primary leaders to the *New York Times*: "We are our sister's keeper."[5] As Nima Naghibi (2007: 83–84) recounts, Friedan's visit to Iran the year before in 1974 was equally fraught, turning into something of an Orientalist dream of sisterhood where Friedan proclaimed her love of Iranian caviar and basked in the adoration of elite Iranian women and the shah himself. The discourses on sisterhood through the universal oppression of women were met with animated critiques built on long-term resistance by women of color and colonized peoples to white feminist collusions with British and American imperial projects.[6] The history of sisterhood had long been entrenched in a troubling colonial imaginary that utilized the language of kinship to fortify racial domination and the gender policing project of empire.[7] For women of color, the sisterhood of the 1970s bore the marks of this racist colonial history.

Despite their critiques of its use, women of color feminists did not reject the idea of sisterhood itself. Rather, they saw radical possibilities in new structures of social practice and theory that looked to collective sociality to undo overlapping structures of oppression for women. Sisterhood was reimagined through organizations of writers like "The Sisterhood" with members like Toni Morrison and Alice Walker, feminist political organizing against gender violence and women's deaths culminating in the Combahee River Collective, and the extensive writings of Black women and women of color in anthologies and women of color collections.[8] Indeed, sisterhood was the basis of that bridge of mutual care across communities among women of color. Cherríe Moraga, in the 1981 preface to *This Bridge Called My Back*, narrates her personal journey across the racist geography of Boston, into the *underground*, and her refuge in Barbara Smith's home, where Smith declares that they are sisters. For Moraga that sisterhood was a profound and ongoing labor of care: "I earned this with Barbara. It is not a given between us—Chicana and Black— to come to see each other as sisters" (Moraga and Anzaldúa [1981] 2002: xlv).

Audre Lorde extends this line of thinking in her vision of sisterhood, proclaiming sisterhood to be the work of explicit alliance across oppressed Indigenous, colonized, and Black women to sustain the possibility of *living*: "we are sisters, and our survivals are mutual" (Lorde 1986: 7). Women of color feminists like Lorde saw in the concept of sisterhood the radical potential of social autonomy for women of color to persist in the face of authoritarianism perpetuated by structures of patriarchal and state violence intent on disappearing and killing women. While they offered trenchant critiques of white sisterhood's complicity in systems of racism and global class subordination, women of color saw in minoritized sisterhood the possibility of survival. In this line of thinking, sisterhood was an orientation toward one another other as women of color feminists, based in a chosen sociality of people who had explicitly built a set of shared values. The sisterhood across Black and other women of color offered a radically different imaginary for worldmaking as these activist intellectuals continued to invest in the political concept of sisterhood as a radical vision of social liberation based in a radically alternative sociality against white heterosexual patriarchy.

These diverse, often contrasting visions of feminist alliance and internationalism through sisterhood have been largely disappeared from today's political movements. As Morrison mourns, the "globalization" of the 1990s obliterated the possibility of the unifying internationalisms that shaped political imaginaries from the 1960s. Even as the 1990s saw the flourishing of transnational women's organizations that utilized a rhetoric of sisterhood, the material possibility of autonomous feminist movements across borders became increasingly tenuous.[9] Globalization cynically appropriated the language of aspirational global unity and repackaged the ideal of "one world" for capitalist ends in the form of new transnational markets, the global expansion of multinational corporations, and an increasingly dominant sector of internationally funded nongovernmental organizations. As these rapid changes unfolded in the 1990s, transnational feminist theorists extensively documented globalizing labor economies and gendered migration that increasingly fortified systems of labor exploitation for migrant and Third World women through the guise of egalitarian internationalism.[10] Demands for solidarity transformed in the early 2000s as political movements for rights faced new challenges in endless wars, the retraction of state social services, the growth of the transnational NGO complex, and the rapid increase of private for-profit ventures in the domains of public health, education, and labor.

The Anthology of Sisterhood

Perhaps the most prominent feminist to utilize the language of sisterhood from the early 1970s was the writer and radical feminist Robin Morgan, whose anthologies on sisterhood shaped an era of feminist publications in the 1970s and 1980s. Morgan's sisterhood represented a decisive shift in the global politics of feminist solidarity. Morgan declared over three volumes and more than three decades that sisterhood *is*, in the present tense, powerful (1970), global (1984), and forever (2003). Sisterhood, in Morgan's formulation, was a universal concept with endless potential, endowed with political potency, reaching an all-encompassing geography, and, in her estimation, a project spanning all of time. Morgan, through her projects on sisterhood, fortified an exclusionary politics of global sisterhood in three ways: first, she positioned America and American women in a position of epistemic authority on global women; second, she proposed that women were a political idea predicated solely on demographic, biologically essentialized difference; finally, she insisted sisterhood was a project of equivalence based in the universalist, comparative study of women across races, classes, and geographies.

Robin Morgan's sisterhood volumes began in 1970 with the first edited anthology, *Sisterhood Is Powerful: An Anthology of Writings from the Women's Liberation Movement*. The 1970 volume, a compilation of prominent women's writings from the movement, was a key text for the emerging American women's movement of the late 1960s and early 1970s. Most significantly, the anthology launched Morgan's career as a feminist writer and editor of the *Sisterhood* series, a speaker at radical feminist rallies and conferences, and a leading public voice who eventually came to edit *Ms.* magazine.

Morgan's introduction to the *Powerful* volume, "The Women's Revolution," is striking for its declarative tone, beginning with the opening sentence: "This book is an action" (Morgan 1970: xiii). In the framing remarks, Morgan paints a picture of her own radicalization and growing consciousness to the oppression of patriarchy, which she links to the experience of giving birth to a child and her own growing sisterhood in women's liberation organizations that showed her the truth of women's oppression of women through statistics. These *facts*, she says, opened her eyes to the truth of the condition of women in all of history (xv). As Morgan declares, she, herself, was the culmination of a whole history of women's oppression, the origins of her rage: "I couldn't believe—still can't—how angry I could become, from deep down and way back, something like a five-thousand-year-buried anger" (xv). Consciousness was an epiphany realized through the knowledge brought by sisterhood, and those who denied the fact of women's oppression colluded with patriarchy to sustain their own oppression: "To deny that you are oppressed is to collaborate in your oppression. To collaborate in your oppression is a way of denying that you're oppressed—particularly when the price of refusing to collaborate is execution" (xvi).

Through these condemnations of women's complicity with their own oppression, Morgan narrated the triumphant history of the new movement for women's rights in the late 1960s, women who had attained true consciousness. And as she told the triumphant story of early women's liberation, Morgan posited women's movements as the sole site for truly revolutionary politics. In the first *Sisterhood* anthology, Morgan introduced a theme that emerges again and again in her personal papers and publications, the moral certitude that her visions of sisterhood and her position as a primary leader in the movement was the only way to save the world: "More and more, I begin to think of a worldwide Women's Revolution as the only hope for life on the planet" (Morgan xxxv).

The introduction to *Sisterhood Is Powerful* is filled with triumphant language about Morgan and her position as a symbol of women's new revolutionary consciousness. Even as she insisted on the transformative power of sisterhood, Morgan's framing is striking in the clear absence of any definitional language to explain what constituted this essential term of sisterhood. It was a given for Morgan. It would continue to be treated as a given in Morgan's

Sisterhood anthologies that followed. Indeed, over the course of three anthologies, Morgan never states what exactly sisterhood is. From the introductions of the volumes, we can infer it is a relationship solely based in a biological notion of cis women and their common history and experiences *as* women. She asserts and reasserts the biological nature of womanhood by linking biological motherhood to sisterhood. Her perspective on sisterhood as the biological reproductive capacity of women is animated in the long poem that closes the introduction to the *Sisterhood Is Powerful* volume: "Our sister earth/Our children that we made in Our own holy Bodies/at last we are beginning to be shrill as banshees/and to act" (xxxix). Sisterhood names the sociality of women's solidarity and was formed through the rage of a new collectivity in pursuit of women's liberation.

From the first *Sisterhood* volume, Morgan gained a following and key position as a speaker and writer in the American women's movement. Yet with her visibility came more publicity for her hostile vision of feminist politics. In a now infamous event cited as the origins of contemporary trans exclusionary feminist visions of women's rights, Morgan, a heterosexual cis woman married to a cis man, delivered an explosive speech in 1973 at the West Coast Lesbian Conference where she condemned and decried the participation of a transgender woman singer, Beth Elliot, who Morgan called "an infiltrator, a destroyer with the mentality of a rapist."[11] Morgan's speech came just a few years after the publication of the *Powerful* anthology, which quietly, in poetry and self-narrative, manifested Morgan's biologically deterministic understanding of the subject of women's liberation. Morgan's condemnatory speech in 1973 caused profound discord in the audience, with dozens of women walking out of the performance, while organizers condemned Morgan for her hostile position and dangerous condemnation of gender nonconforming people as outsiders to the movement.

Morgan was one several prominent American women in the 1970s who soon took their feminist projects global, utilizing new international platforms like the United Nations conferences to position themselves as the sole leaders against women's universal subordination. By going global, feminists like Morgan found a new domain to insist on the common oppression of women. Through global women's issues, American feminists projected the urgency of their vision of women's rights in novel culturalist arguments that condemned the pervasive presence of gendered violence, labor exploitation, illiteracy, and postcolonial patriarchy and positioned American transnational feminism as the hallmark of a new era in global rights. It also provided cover for a set of white women who faced increasing scru-

tiny for their biologically deterministic understandings of women as subjects and insistence on negative understandings of women's victimhood as
the sole basis of rights-based advocacy.

The global in this renewed fervor for feminism provided fertile ground
for extending the project of sisterhood to be a vast comparative project that
extended across geographies. Fertile, because Morgan's turn to global sisterhood sought to explain women's oppression through the metrics of global
demography and population that assessed women's worth in and through
their fertility that expanded rapidly in the early 1980s. In the introduction of
Morgan's *Sisterhood Is Global* (1984), the influence of demographic measures
is clear, with Morgan's introduction framing the project of global sisterhood
through the utility of the quantitative demographic studies by country that
organized the chapters in the volume. Each woman author represented her
nation-state, and each nation's women were enumerated in statistics about
women's status. *Sisterhood Is Global* exalted the structures of knowledge of
quantitative social science that had gained currency at the time through new
programs on women in international development. Her introduction was a
clear display of the crude comparative work of American feminists who used
the shock and awe of global statistics of women's deaths and suffering to
convince audiences of their unique role as global leaders in combating the
oppression of women in the rest of the world.

The *Global* anthology was voluminous at over eight hundred pages
with chapters from seventy countries. Each of the authors was made to represent their country in a comprehensive, representative project for "worldwide freedom for female human beings" (Morgan 1984: xiv). Each country's
chapter was framed by a "Statistical Preface" with "usable" demographic
information and key statistics from each country to be used by everything
from "women's studies, international affairs, development and population
issues" (xvi). The preface sections focused on a comprehensive overview of
"key stats," including the sex ratio of the population and other demographic
information, including birth rates, death rates, infant mortality rates, life
expectancy, and a section on "economy" on women's labor and economic
roles. The sections that followed included "Gynography," which offered mea-
surements and qualitative data overviews on marriage, divorce, contraception, illegitimacy, rape, prostitution, and "traditional/cultural practices" in
each country (xx–xxi). The following sections, "Mythography" and "Herstory" offered the history and cultural myths that demonstrated the oppression of women in each nation-state. Morgan later credited herself as the first
person to use the term "herstory" as a critique of the androcentric nature of

history: "I coined this word half-jokingly in 1968. . . . Now that the United Nations and NASA have adopted the use of 'herstory' in official documents, it's probably time to reclaim it (smiling)" (Morgan 2003: xxxixn37).

In Morgan's view, her visionary work of global sisterhood could only be realized in a large-scale project that compared the demographics of women worldwide. Solidarity, in other words, was a project of equivalence through data collection. The popular language of population offered proof of the political urgency of the project of sisterhood: "women constitute not an oppressed minority, but a majority—of almost all national populations, and of the entire human species" (Morgan 1984: 3). This global comparison would offer an omniscient view of all the world's women, a universal comparative perspective that Morgan regularly deployed in her own writings and speeches to demonstrate the generalizable condition of all women's oppression. Demography served as the ultimate commensurate object in Morgan's sisterhood, shaping knowledge that delimited the project of feminist solidarity to research on measurable equivalencies of women's oppression across the world.

For Morgan, biopolitical quantitative social scientific measures, what would soon be called "indicators" in gender and development language of the late 1980s—everything from sex ratios, marriages, birth rates to life expectancy—were essential to the project of sisterhood between women from across the world. Demography, rather than political coalition or mutual care, was the dominant connective tissue for global feminist research between nation-states in the global condition of women. In a summary sheet in her papers offering "facts on women around the world" from the introduction to the *Sisterhood Is Global* volume, Morgan cites random statistics from different regions to show the urgency of the global project of sisterhood and the cultural problem of non-West patriarchy. These pages of bullet points offer dramatic facts that would bring attention to the condition of women through their shock value: "Fifty percent of all women in India gain no weight whatsoever during the third trimester of pregnancy, due to poverty. Two out of five women in Latin America work as domestic servants. Ninety-four percent of women in the Sudan are nonliterate. . . . Seventy million women alive today are genitally mutilated . . . " and on and on.[12] In this vast factsheet, Morgan demonstrates her omniscience about the common oppression of women, arguing for the necessity of this performative game of comparative oppressions. And the intention was clear: as Morgan asked in a rejoinder to Black and Third World feminist critiques of racism, classism, and social differences in the feminist movement at the end of her *Sisterhood*

Is Global introduction: "Are we then really so very different?" (Morgan 1984: 36). For Morgan, there was kinship in common experiences of gender oppression, a sisterhood based in the *sameness* of women.

Morgan's *Global* project of sisterhood as a praxis of data collection was realized in the Sisterhood is Global Strategy meeting, what Morgan declared as the "first feminist think tank," which took place at Hunter College on November 18 and 19, 1984, following soon after the publication of the volume.[13] Morgan raised over $50,000 (a value that today would be nearly $135,000) for the 1984 institute and more money after for the continuation of the project from a range of donors, including prominent women philanthropists, the United Methodist Church, the Skaggs Foundation, and the Ford Foundation.[14] In her project summary, Morgan declared the Sisterhood Is Global Institute would "develop women-defined tactics" to "improve the situation of female human beings cross-culturally."[15] The institute brought together authors from the volume, inviting women from across the world to New York City to conceptualize a long-term intellectual project of meetings that continued in the "sisterhood is global" cause. The twenty-five women who were to attend were diverse (ultimately, some did not make it to New York, including an ill Simone de Beauvoir). Women were to represent the nations and regions of Belgium, Brazil, the Caribbean, Colombia, Finland, France, Greece, India, Israel, Kenya, Mexico, Nepal, New Zealand, Nigeria, Norway, the "Pacific Islands," Palestine, Poland, Portugal, Saudi Arabia, Spain, Sri Lanka, Thailand, Yugoslavia, and Zambia.[16] Yet, while women served as representatives of different nation-states (i.e., the list offered both nation-state and representative names; e.g., "India—Devaki Jain"), Morgan insisted in her opening statement for the meeting that the gathering was unlike any other conferences global women attended. It was not "a UN conference, an international agency seminar" but instead a "unique and autonomous gathering of international women who come together in the *sisterhood of our pain* . . ."[17] Each of the respective entries in the published volume offered a country report of the region the author represented. Morgan declared that the *Global* volume and conference represented all cultures and types of "development," from the First to Third World.

In this vast project of commensurability, Morgan, the editor and curator of the *Global* volume and global institute, would play the leading role in the sisterhood. No document makes Morgan's understanding of her role in this vision of global sisterhood through her Sisterhood Is Global Institute clearer than a note that Morgan wrote to herself as a motivational saying to be hung on her office door:

ADACIOUS AND HUBRISTIC SYLLOGISM OF THE DAY:

Women are the saving force on the planet.

The International Feminist Movement is the saving force of women.

This visionary team is the saving force of the International Feminist
    Movement.

Ergo: This team is the saving force on the planet.[18]

The anthology *Sisterhood Is Forever* (2003), published almost twenty years
after the *Global* collection, fortified the triumphant vision of Morgan's project of the sisterhood anthology as the primary guiding documents for the
feminist movement. As Morgan describes the massive impact of her own
anthologies, the *Sisterhood* volumes were still in demand decades after their
production. They were "goddesses, demanding sacrifice on their altars"
(Morgan 2003: liv). *Forever* built on Morgan's insistence that her version of
sisterhood would be essential to the freedom of humanity, retrospectively
assessing her contributions to the women's movement as timeless. As Morgan proclaims in the introduction, the anthology was to be the sole guidebook for the fate of the planet: "The book that rests in your hands is a tool for
the future" (lv). As she closes the volume, Morgan declares that *"feminism is
the politics of the twenty-first century.* In that sense, New World women have
just begun" (lv).

Morgan's sisterhood projects promoted cis womanhood as the singular premise of global feminisms. It saw sisterhood as a vast comparative project based in new structures of social scientific knowledge. This knowledge
economy naturalized the nation-state as the foundational category of all
global research and analysis on women and foregrounded comparative
oppression, as measured in quantitative demographic data, as the primary
method to create this global sisterhood. By never offering a definition of the
term "sisterhood" across the volumes and treating women solely in terms of
biological reproduction and demographic fact, Morgan made clear that sisterhood was to be taken as a self-evident term reserved for biologically cis
women and them alone. Morgan's demographic argument for a feminist politics saw feminism as a project for cis women by cis women. There is a clear
through line from Morgan's public insistence that trans women were not
women to her biopolitical understanding of women as population. Women's
rights, Morgan declared again and again, shaped the fate of the planet
because women were "more than half of the world's population."

The Limits of Sisterhood

bell hooks's 1986 essay "Sisterhood" was published soon after Morgan's *Sisterhood Is Global* volume. It offers a clear departure from Morgan's project of sisterhood as commensurability. In her pleas for a return to radical sisterhood, hooks recognized how the sisterhood of white American feminists offered commonality as the sole justification for global solidarity politics. Sisterhood in this paradigm of global feminisms was based in the comparison of women's oppression and promoted solidarity through the social science of comparative development. In critiquing the false and often superficial nature of feminist solidarity politics, hooks distinguished her vision of sisterhood across difference from the language of commonality staged by so many feminists who claimed leadership on the stage of global feminism. As hooks argues in her essay, in line with the labor of sisterhood of Cherríe Moraga in *Bridge*, "We must define our own terms. Rather than bond on the basis of shared victimization or in response to a false sense of a common enemy, we can bond on the basis of our political commitment to a feminist movement that aims to end sexist oppression" (hooks 1986: 129). In her critique of women as solely subjects of victimization and men as the false "common enemy" of women, hooks builds on key feminist critiques that questioned feminist visions of liberation invested in separatism and state punitive governance that produced women solely as victims and subjects of harm.

Solidarity in sisterhood for hooks required radical inclusion of sexual practices that were explicitly anti-homophobic, aware of class exploitation, and open to other ways of being in one's body: "To build a politicized, mass-based feminist movement, women must work harder to overcome the alienation from one another that exists when sexist socialization has not been unlearned, e.g. homophobia, judging by appearance, conflicts between women with diverse sexual practices" (hooks 1986: 130). Sisterhood in this vision was a practice of intentional ethical consensus, not an epistemological project of equivalence. Nor was sisterhood a superficial declaration of support, a circulated petition with signatures with little public action, or an empty gesture of appearing on the side of good politics. Sisterhood was political praxis, sustained through long-term mutual care. hooks emphasizes the commitment required of such a project: "Solidarity is not the same as support. To experience solidarity, we must have a community of interests, shared beliefs and goals around which to unite, to build Sisterhood. Support can be occasional. It can be given and just as easily withdrawn. Solidarity requires sustained, ongoing commitment. In feminist movement, there is need for diversity, disagreement, and difference if we are to grow" (138). In 1986, despite the failures of the project of global sisterhood to be radically inclusive, hooks reinvested in sisterhood the potential for a vision of feminism shaped by the possibilities of social difference.

Yet, despite hooks's best efforts, by the early 1990s, sisterhood was no longer redeemable as a concept for feminist organizing. In a 1995 essay entitled "Sisterhood and Friendship as Feminist Models," feminist philosopher and activist María C. Lugones differentiated white women's use of the term *sisterhood* to obfuscate difference from histories of sisterhood in civil rights organizing among Black women. As Lugones argues, sisterhood was a metaphor for a model of egalitarianism based in the Anglo-American family, a term deployed by white feminists uncritically despite feminist critiques of the patriarchal family. She argued that the use of sisterhood by white women obscured the origins of the use of this term in feminist movements of the 1960s and 1970s, where white women borrowed from the language of civil rights activism but were unwilling to acknowledge the complicated inclusion of Black women in mainstream feminisms.

Why use a kinship term for feminist social alliances between that had never achieved any sense of equality across racial difference? The use of the concept proved "burdensome to women of color" (Lugones 1995: 137) because the use of sisterhood erased difference under the pretense of inclusion. For Lugones, sisterhood was not viable across regions and cultures, giving the example of the equivalent term in Spanish, *"hermana"* (138), which she argued had no political weight, unlike terms that implied friendship and companionship. Lugones juxtaposed sisterhood to the concept of friendship, which she argued was more egalitarian and agentive in possibility. Lugones argued that friendship should be the new conceptual framework for solidarity. Friendship offered a kind of "practical love" based in "pluralism" (141) forged by people that was not unconditional but based in a shared ethos of feminist responsibility and mutual care. Yet friendship was not often thought of as a political concept, and few took up the idea of feminist friendship as political praxis in the years that followed Lugones's call.

The pathbreaking feminist theorist Oyeronke Oyewumi took the argument that sisterhood was a failed project even further in the introduction to the volume *African Women and Feminism: Reflecting on the Politics of Sisterhood*, insisting that sisterhood could never be a term for cross-cultural alliance because of its formation as a relationship of the Anglo-American nuclear family. Oyewumi asks, why should we desire a cultural idea that is not our own as African women? As she describes, "We must question the very foundation of sisterhood, both as a concept and as a desirable relationship. Undoubtedly a cultural understanding is expressed in the choice of 'sisterhood' over other terms to describe relations between white and black women. Race was the first border it had to cross before sisterhood went global" (Oyewumi 2003: 5). White women enforced kinship structures on Black American women and then took that project around the world.

Sisterhood was a false imposition of affective connection, antithetical to what Oyewumi described as African kinship based in motherhood and generational power. She differentiated the sisterhood of Black women in the diaspora from that of African cultures. Providing a different genealogy for sisterhood, Oyewumi insisted that sisterhood symbolized the "(dis)connection" (Oyewumi 2003, 10) between African cultures and the diaspora. Instead, any use of the term among Black women was the result of the history of *gendering* that was essential to enslavement: "The languages that many of the enslaved West Africans brought to the Americas did not contain linguistic equivalents of the kin terms 'brother' and 'sister' because many African languages do not express gender-specificity in sibling designation. Though one is unable to establish the exact moment at which the enslaved Africans started to address each other in these terms in the Americas, it is clear that such usage evolved with the experience of slavery and acculturation" (10). Extending this argument about the fundamental difference of gender in the diaspora, Oyewumi critiqued African American feminists like Audre Lorde who romanticized ideas of African social egalitarianism and sexual diversity.

Oyewumi offers a key argument against the gender essentialism of white feminist sisterhood. The problem with sisterhood was the way that it imposed gendering as the premise of political alliance. Oyewumi offers a generalized argument against the biological determinism of sisterhood: "In African societies, the question of organizing to attain a political goal speaks to the issue of forming political alliances, and not sisterhood, since group identity is constituted socially and *is not based on any qualities of shared anatomy popularly called gender*" (19, emphasis added).

For feminists like Lugones and Oyewumi in the 1990s and early 2000s, sisterhood was an irredeemable project. It represented the way that feminist movements had long obscured the problem of racism through universalizing and biologically essentialist language of women's oppression. Beyond its implicit racism, sisterhood, uncritically wielded the negative obligations of kinship, a western vision of the family forced onto other women around the world as a tool of hegemonic political organizing by white American and

European women. Perhaps most powerfully, in Oyewumi's analysis, sisterhood was bad because it symbolized a broad failure of political organizing as a gender deterministic project, equating political coalition with alliance through a biological notion of woman. These projects of sisterhood, like the ineffectual international circulation of Eve Ensler's *Vagina Monologues*, posited the American feminist vision of universal sisterhood as the sole avenue to women's freedom around the world.[19] In their critiques, Lugones and Oyewumi insisted that sisterhood was a failed project, one exhausted of any of its previous political value. Sisterhood obscured more than it described and offered little intrinsic affective meaning for most of the women in the world. Yet Lugones's idealized friendship and Oyewumi's ideas of alliance through motherhood did not seem to offer a durable political alternative with viability across borders. There appeared to be no effective term to name global feminisms. "I am your friend" did not carry the same conceptual weight as "we stand together in sisterhood."

As Lugones and Oyewumi cautioned against, imperial sisterhood reemerged once again at the turn of the twenty-first century, this time in the powerful use of gendered language of normative familial roles that would come to play an essential role in the US War on Terror. In 2001, First Lady Laura Bush's radio address in November of 2001 on the Taliban's oppression of women invoked the role of women in the family to argue for what was to become the longest war in history: "We may come from different backgrounds and faiths, but parents the world over love their children. We respect our mothers, our sisters, and daughters" (Bush 2001). Sisterhood's past as a space of possibility for chosen family, for a politics of mutual care, was perhaps forever lost in that moment. Its place as a desirable object for imperial, western, racist feminism was enshrined in US policies of perpetual war.

Sisterhood Is *Yearning*

So, is sisterhood all bad for twenty-first-century feminisms? Sisterhood was certainly not forever, however much Morgan declared it so just after 9/11 in her 2003 anthology. Today, more than twenty-five years after the largest global gathering of women in Beijing and over fifty years after Morgan's first use of the concept for women's liberation, the moral invocation of sisterhood as powerful and global is almost inconceivable. Sisterhood presents new problems for an inclusive feminist agenda, most glaringly in its long shadowy history as a term of cis enforcement, epitomized in Morgan's biologically essentialist demographics of global feminist solidarity, critiqued by

Oyewumi as the Western enforcement of a politics of sexual difference, and later invoked again as Muslim women's victimhood became a primary justification for the US War on Terror.

Yet, in the focus on sisterhood as a failed rhetoric, feminist scholarship may have lost sight of material conditions that did make a moment of yearning, imagining, and debating feminist collectivity possible in the 1970s. These conversations took place in the form of global conferences, feminist anthologies, and the many global networks of collaboration across borders. For almost three decades, there were expansive opportunities for feminists to physically be together, to travel and meet one another, and to engage in unruly international exchanges where tensions and difference took place on a global stage. From her writings and her personal papers, we learn how Morgan's vision of sisterhood was primarily an avenue for her own (exclusionary) vision of leadership, not unlike many of her American peers. But the curated anthology and institute of *Global* did make possible an international debate about the nature of solidarity like the many UN conferences and workshops at Wellesley College, Barnard College, and more. In thinking sisterhood solely in terms of its universalizing discourse and rhetorical complicity in imperial projects old and new, we may lose sight of critical *material* shifts that emerged in the 1970s and the massive material retraction of resources from feminist projects that followed this era in the late 1990s and early 2000s through the new global War on Terror. Through the appropriation of the language of sisterhood for governance feminist projects of anti-trafficking and war, the funding structures that underwrote the women of color and global feminist anthologies, the international conference of feminist intellectuals and activists, and the flourishing of feminist publishing houses have been almost completely hollowed out.

Today there is a dramatic a shift away from the wide-scale funding for projects of women's solidarity that shaped the expansion "sisterhood" in the 1970s and 1980s. We might take the example of the Ford Foundation. There is much to be said about the complicated work that the Ford Foundation has done in relation to feminisms of the 1970s until the 1990s, from mandating social science research reports on the status of women, to exploitative agricultural development programs, to restricted funding for the first women's studies centers around the world.[20] Yet the central place of Ford in the making of many different women's organizations, educational programs on women's studies, and feminist publications cannot be denied. As we saw, the Ford Foundation facilitated the making of Morgan's Sisterhood Is Global Institute. It also underwrote the publication of a wide range of books, including a number of feminist anthologies and publishers that promoted sisterhood from publication houses like The Feminist Press. Ford funded the training and travel of Black women, women of color, and Third World feminists to global venues including the International Women's Year and Decade conferences in Mexico City, Copenhagen, and Nairobi, as well as the Fourth World Conference on Women in Beijing in 1995. Ford created scholarships and fellowships to fund the education of underrepresented scholars and students, including the establishment of Asian and African women's centers, Black and Latinx scholars in the US academy, as well as Dalit scholars from India who pursued international PhDs.

With rising authoritarianism in the Global South especially, international funding aid has become increasingly suspect, making the feminist internationalism of 1970s and 1980s sisterhood all but impossible. For example, in Modi's India, the Ford Foundation was named a national security risk in 2015 and was forced to exit the region. The accusation of corrupt foreign funding has been a key tool for authoritarian regimes in places like India and Pakistan to critique transnational feminist and rights organizations that fund projects for minority and sexual rights, monitor human rights violations, and protect free speech. No critique is leveled more regularly against sexual rights movements across the world today than the accusation of taking foreign funding or being fed "foreign" ideas of gender and sexual liberation, whether it be with women's marches in Asia, Latin America, and eastern Europe, or the new surge of laws against homosexuality and the criminalization and expulsion of organizations supporting sexual minorities in sub-Saharan Africa.

Today, there is a radically different material world supporting transnational or global causes of gender and women compared to what might have been found thirty or forty years ago. The rapid expansion of NGO sector work has permanently shifted the terrain of feminist organizing. With the Global War on Terror, the Bush administration ended all funding to the UN Population Council in 2001, one of the largest funders of social scientific research on women and a major source for research that used the language of sisterhood and solidarity. Radical feminist causes across borders lost the funding machinery of the 1980s and 1990s from foundations, replaced instead by deeply reactionary privatized anti-trafficking coalitions that promote carceral policies established through a dangerous alliance of American conservatives and women.[21] We live in a time of profound retrenchment of policy and transnational funding for feminist work. Even with the many shortcomings of NGO feminist efforts, and there are many, there is no doubt that solidarity feminisms have been in retreat for some time with profound material effects for people and organizations across the world.

In this alarming time of authoritarianism, there may be space for a reinvented sisterhood. Maybe, as Morgan declared, sisterhood *is* essential for twenty-first-century politics, but in a vision of sisterhood that is antithetical to Morgan's gender essentialist vision. This sisterhood would not be nostalgic or recuperative of the universalisms of yore that utilized a developmental language of commensurable oppressions to argue for feminist solidarity. Rather, perhaps the twenty-first-century sisterhood could reflect hooks's challenge to see solidarity as an ethics based in mutual exchange, in Lorde's desire for a sisterhood based in survival, in the affective dimensions of the *yearning* envisioned by people like Toni Morrison, reflected in the political praxis of hooks, Lorde, Chandra Mohanty, Cherríe Moraga, Gloria Anzaldúa, M. Jacqui Alexander, and so many others. Sisterhood in our moment now might offer a powerful political platform, one that intentionally reimagines normative kinship structures and explicitly *subverts* biological deterministic ideas of feminism to uphold transgender and queer living as a key priority in the twenty-first century feminist project.

Or maybe the term *sisterhood* is unnecessary for today's solidarity politics, a limiting paradigm for movements of marginalized people in the face of inhumanity. Maybe sisterhood, with its checkered past, is officially too bad to be good. Even still, I am left to meditate on hooks's opening lines, struggling to put words on the page, wondering how we are to write in our time of authoritarian violence around the world. I turn again to these debates of solidarity and sisterhood because there is a need in this moment for reflection on a twenty-first-century language of solidarity. For however pessimistic much of our contemporary critical thinking is, that feeling of yearning persists. We see it the undeniable aspirations in political mobilizations now that utilize the banner of feminism to question authoritarianism and make broad demands on the state for minoritized rights across communities. The diversity of these demands can be found in the manifestos of the Aurat Marches in Pakistan, demands of the #NiUnaMenos campaigns that originated in Argentina and spread across Latin America, and in the claim of citizenship itself at protests from India to Sudan. These movements make broad demands through new visions of inclusive democratic participation for the twenty-first century. These movements seek to undo an authoritarian biopolitics of life and death that has so easily objectified and disappeared women, queer, trans, nonbinary people. Instead, they seek to imagine a collective ethics of living.

Perhaps people are no longer moved to collective action with the invocation of sisterhood today. Maybe many never were. Perhaps in the twenty-first century, our yearnings reside in the increasingly narrowing space between "lives" and "matter," in the declaration of feminist strikes, of mobilizations against the murder of women and trans people where masses proclaim, "not one more," and in the resonances of Lorde's sisterhood as mutual survival against authoritarian violence. It may very well be that our material, social, and political solidarities were never meant to have one name. Yet let us remember, from this complicated history of sisterhood, there have been, and continue to be, fierce collectives who fight for the possibility of living.

Notes

1   For a critical reflection on short-term cycles of crisis and the structural failures of crisis policymaking for Black mothers, see Nash 2021.

2   Indebted to the foundational work of Robyn Wiegman, whose *Object Lessons* (2012) has offered essential critical tools for reflective thinking on the moralism of feminist and queer diagnostics of good and bad objects.

3   This optimism for radical egalitarianism is what political theorist Adom Getachew describes as the utopian project of worldmaking in *Worldmaking after Empire* (2019).

4   Jocelyn Olcott maps these conflicts at the first United Nations Conference on Women in Mexico City. See Olcott 2017.

5   *New York Times*, June 4 1975, as cited in Olcott 2017: 120.

6   See Shehabuddin 2021.

7   See for example the use of the language of daughters and sisters in racialized colonial campaigns around prostitution and British and American feminist missionary transnationalism in the work of early women promoting policing and empire, as epitomized in the life of white supremacist Katherine Mayo. See Burton 1994 and Sinha 2006.

8   On the organization "The Sisterhood" and a longer genealogy of the novel political organizing of Black women as Black *feminists*, see the research of SaraEllen Strongman (2018).

9   Many feminist organizations of the 1990s continue to utilize a language of religious sisterhood, like the Black Muslim women's organization, Women in Islam, founded by Sister Aisha Al Adawiya in 1992.

10   For a reflection on this early 1990s moment and the place of transnational feminisms today, see Tambe and Thayer 2021.

11   On Morgan's explosive speech and dissenting voices including Black women and other key feminists who critiqued Morgan following the conference, see Finn Enke (2018: 9–29). On this moment and Morgan's role in inciting transphobic positions in the feminist movement, see Samek 2016: 232–49.

12   Morgan, "Facts on Women around the World," 1–2. Folder "Doubleday meeting, 1984 and undated," Box W9, Morgan Papers, Duke University.

13   Morgan, "The Sisterhood is Global Strategy Meeting" Conference Statement, 1. Folder "Conference, 1984 Folder 3 of 3," Box S11, Morgan Papers, Duke University.

14 See Morgan, Folder "Ford Foundation 1981–1987 and n.d. Folder 2 of 2" Box S12, on funding from the MacArthur Foundation, see Box S13; on the Skaggs Foundation, see Box S14, Morgan Papers, Duke University.

15 Morgan, "The Sisterhood Is Global Strategy Meeting Conference Statement, 1. Folder "Conference, 1984 Folder 3 of 3," Box S11, Morgan Papers, Duke University.

16 Morgan, "Sisterhood Is Global Strategy Meeting Participants Attending," 1. Folder "Conference Materials, 1984," Box S11, Morgan Papers, Duke University.

17 Morgan, "An Agenda-of Atmosphere," 1. Folder "Conference, 1984 Folder 2 of 3," Box S11, Robin Morgan Papers, Duke University; emphasis added.

18 Morgan, "Audacious and hubristic," 1. Folder "Personal notes, drafts, undated," Box S12, Morgan Papers, Duke University.

19 See for example this failure in the context of Hong Kong, in S. L. Cheng, "Vagina Dialogues? Critical Reflections from Hong Kong on The Vagina Monologues as a Worldwide Movement," *International Feminist Journal of Politics* 6, no. 2 (2002): 326–34.

20 The epistemological implications of the funding infrastructures for social scientific research on women and gender built between international governance and foundations like Ford were profound, permanently shifting the trajectory of women's studies around the world. See Mitra (2023).

21 See, for example, the collusion of evangelical movements and radical governance feminists in Bernstein 2010.

References

Bernstein, Elizabeth. 2010. "Militarized Humanitarianism Meets Carceral Feminism: The Politics of Sex, Rights, and Freedom in Contemporary Antitrafficking Campaigns." *Signs: Journal of Women in Culture and Society* 36, no. 1: 45–71.

Burton, Antoinette. 1994. *Burdens of History: British Feminists, Indian Women, and Imperial Culture, 1865–1915.* Chapel Hill: University of North Carolina Press.

Bush, Laura. 2001. "Taliban Oppression of Women." Presidential National Radio Address, November 17. https://www.washingtonpost.com/wp-srv/nation/specials/attacked/transcripts/laurabushtext_111701.html.

Enke, Finn. 2018. "Collective Memory and the Transfeminist 1970s: Toward a Less Plausible History." *TSQ* 5, no. 1: 9–29.

Getachew, Adom. 2019. *Worldmaking after Empire.* Princeton, NJ: Princeton University Press.

hooks, bell. 1986. "Sisterhood: Political Solidarity between Women." *Feminist Review* 23: 125–38.

Lorde, Audre. 1986. "Conference Keynote Address: Sisterhood and Survival." *The Black Scholar* 17, no. 2: 5–7.

Lugones, Maria, with Pat Alake Rosezelle. 1995. "Sisterhood and Friendship as Solidarity Models." In *Feminism and Community*, edited by Penny A. Weiss and Marilyn Friedman, 135–146. Philadelphia: Temple University Press.

Mitra, Durba. 2023. "The Report, or, Whatever Happened to Third World Feminist Theory." *Signs: Journal of Women in Culture and Society* 48, no. 1: 557–84.

Moraga, Cherríe, and Gloria Anzaldúa, eds. (1981) 2002. *This Bridge Called My Back: Writings by Radical Women of Color.* Berkeley, CA: Third Woman Press.

Morgan, Robin. 1984. *Sisterhood Is Global: The International Women's Movement Anthology.* New York: Anchor Press.

Morgan, Robin. 2003. *Sisterhood Is Forever: The Women's Anthology for a New Millennium.* New York: Washington Square Press.

Morgan, Robin, ed. 1970. *Sisterhood Is Powerful.* New York: Vintage Press.

Morrison, Toni. 2021. *The Source of Self Regard: Selected Essays, Speeches, and Meditations.* New York: Knopf.

Naghibi, Nima. 2007. *Rethinking Global Sisterhood: Western Feminism and Iran.* Minneapolis: University of Minnesota Press.

Nash, Jennifer C. 2021. *Birthing Black Mothers.* Durham, NC: Duke University Press.

Olcott, Jocelyn. 2017. *International Women's Year: The Greatest Consciousness-Raising Event in History.* New York: Oxford University Press.

Oyewumi, Oyeronke, ed. 2003. *African Women and Feminism: Reflecting on the Politics of Sisterhood.* Trenton, NJ: Africa World Press.

Robin Morgan Papers, Duke University, Durham, NC.

Samek, Alyssa. 2016. "Violence and Identity Politics: 1970s Lesbian-Feminist Discourse and Robin Morgan's 1973 West Coast Lesbian Conference Keynote Address." *Communication and Critical/Cultural Studies* 13, no. 3: 232–49.

Shehabuddin, Elora. 2021. *Sisters in the Mirror: A History of Muslim Women and the Global Politics of Feminism.* Oakland: University of California Press.

Sinha, Mrinalini. 2006. *Specters of Mother India: The Global Restructuring of an Empire.* Durham, NC: Duke University Press.

Strongman, SaraEllen. 2018. "The Sisterhood: Black Women, Black Feminism, and the Women's Liberation Movement." PhD diss., University of Pennsylvania.

Tambe, Ashwini, and Millie Thayer, eds. 2021. *Transnational Feminist Itineraries: Situating Theory and Activist Practice.* Durham, NC: Duke University Press.

Wiegman, Robyn. 2012. *Object Lessons.* Durham, NC: Duke University Press.

Robyn Wiegman

Feminism and the Impasse of Whiteness;
or, Who's Afraid of Rachel Doležal?

Let's face it: no one really *wants* to think about
Rachel Doležal. Her fifteen minutes of fame were
declared exhausted about fifteen minutes after she
was "outed" as being "born white" by journalists
in June 2015, thereby setting off a media storm
about *transracialism*, a term that had largely been
confined until then to describing families with
white parents and adopted children of color.[1] By
the time Netflix released the documentary *The
Rachel Divide* (Brownson 2018), popular interest in
the story had evaporated even as the mainstream
media—the *New York Times*, *The New Yorker*,
Forbes, *Vogue*, *The Guardian*, *Vulture*, etc.—used
the occasion to try to squeeze a few more ounces
of revenue from the spectacle of a presumed white
woman still insisting, as she does today, that she
is Black. In 2020, when I first picked up a copy of
Doležal's 2017 autobiography, *In Full Color: Finding My Place in a Black and White World*, the hard-
back remainder, originally priced at $24.95, was
selling for $8.32. If I had waited a year I could have
gotten it for $1.99.[2]

If you have been living under a rock or in a
cave or writing your dissertation you may be
thinking "Who's Rachel?" but afraid to ask. The
popular media story is the most spectacular one

The South Atlantic Quarterly 122:3, July 2023
DOI 10.1215/00382876-10643973   © 2023 Duke University Press

and it begins on TV. As president of the NAACP chapter in Spokane, Washington, Doležal was being interviewed by a local reporter ostensibly about anti-Black hate crimes in the region.[3] But when the reporter went off script and turned the conversation to her racial identity, asking bluntly "Are you African American?" Doležal hesitated, face quivering, and replied, "I don't understand the question," before walking away (Moyer 2015). The refrain "I don't understand the question" became a meme on social media as commentators tried to figure out what precisely Doležal didn't understand about racial identity in the United States, where, since the earliest years of slavery, having a mother designated as Black was the propertied condition in which one *was* Black. Doležal's mother, Ruthanne, it would soon be widely known, was self-described and phenotypically "white," and while she would mother four Black adopted children in addition to her two "natural" (and naturally white) ones, she and her equally self-defining white husband Lawrence never described their family as an experiment in US racial formations even if it absolutely met the criteria as a "transracial" one. They were driven instead by pro-life evangelical Christian commitments. (Think Amy Coney Barrett.) In their various media appearances in the days after Doležal's story went national, Ruthanne and Lawrence offered themselves as living proof of Rachel's racial nativity, assuring audiences of the interpretive narrative that was quickly taking hold: that if a woman "born white" claimed to be Black it was not just preposterous but an act of deception and cultural theft, a way of benefitting socially and financially from an identity she not only didn't live but didn't earn (Kim 2015). For Ruthanne, the matter cut even deeper: "Rachel is desperately trying to destroy her biological family," she explained (*Good Morning America* 2015).

This sentence is worth remembering, as the rivalry between mother and daughter is a central part of the Doležal story, especially given the fact that Rachel would come to adopt one of her mother's adopted children and make a home for a second. Rachel also birthed her own children and talks about herself in her autobiography and in interviews as both a Black mother and the mother of Black sons (see Harris-Perry 2015). While there is no evidence to say that she imagines the constitution of "Black family" in a reverse of the historical institutional racial script—such that Black children make the mother Black—there is much to contemplate about Doležal's insistence that the breast she offers to her children, metaphorically and literally, has no relationship to that of her white mother's. Add to this the accusation by Doležal and her Black sister Esther that Ruthanne turned a blind eye to the sexual abuse and violence inflicted on the children by both white men in the family, Lawrence and his white son Joshua, and we have a story both more typical and more complicated than what "Rachel Doležal" has come to represent. Here, the knots of race and sexuality are entangled in the fraught intimacies that characterize the family as both a political and pedagogical institution, compounding not only the charged affective terrain of secrecy and deception that enfolds Doležal as a media spectacle but the very character, both moral and ideological, of the transracial adoptive family itself. Riven from within by accusations of violence and sexual trespass, the Doležals fractured into two family units over primal scenes asserted and denied, and two mothers emerged into public discussion, each with different claims of providence over the meaning and form of transracial filiation.[4]

But let me not get too far ahead of myself, especially when I have work to do to convince you—and myself—that there's something important to be gained for feminism and its anti-racist commitments by approaching the media spectacle around Rachel Doležal without relying on the litigating language of the law, as much popular commentary has done, which prioritizes judgement and sets us on a path to prosecute or defend. Nor am I going to consider her race-trading as emblematic or even symptomatic of a trend of born-white imposture, no matter how much the proximity of her "outing" to that of Jessica Krug, CV Vitolo-Haddad, and Satchuel Cole, among others, has underwritten a discourse in popular media commentary about a seeming contagion of white women pretending to be Black.[5] It may sound strange to say, but Doležal is actually more interesting and more difficult to contend with than these other figures who used the off-ramp of "white women's tears" and the moral mea culpa of confession to forward their seemingly self-negating but otherwise self-aggrandizing apologies (Hamad 2019; Phipps 2021). Doležal, on the other hand, is to a large extent unrepentant, and while her craving for publicity and celebrity has fueled her ongoing acquiescence to scenes that everyone knows in advance will entail some measure of her humiliation, her story, as Marquis Bey and Theodora Sakellarides (2016: 35) write, *"does* warrant a discussion—albeit one that significantly differs from current popular discourse." For these scholars, "what ought to be of greatest interest is how Dolezal's actions speak to the volatility—and the fugitivity—of race, and what can come to be known of Blackness because of her racial inhabitation" (35).[6] Their project inspires my own, but as you will see, my destination is not toward arguing with or against their final insistence that Doležal's "Blackness undoes rigid racial logics" (2016: 44). I'm more interested in what is so troubling about Doležal's *whiteness* and the kinds of pleasure she seeks in trying to be completely done with it.

As Bey (2020: 207–8) suggests elsewhere, "I actually do not like [Doležal]. . . . And yet, I cannot . . . not think about . . . what she forces us to think."[7]

My project aims to open up the space identified here between the feelings that Doležal arouses—Bey (2020:207) also calls her "annoying"—and the analytic work that grappling with her public presence and persistent claim to Blackness evoke. To paraphrase Bey, I cannot not think about what she forces people to feel: anger, contempt, condemnation, pity, embarrassment, but never as far as I can tell identification, recognition, sympathy, or even real (as opposed to feigned) indifference. To get at these matters, this essay proceeds more or less psychoanalytically, which forgoes the attempt to render a binding decision about Doležal in order to consider the work done by and to all of us with fictions of personhood, including those that have been written directly into the law to naturalize self, family, and race. In leaning into the psychoanalytic, I should be clear, I am not interested in it as a tool for locating mental disorder, though there are no shortages of diagnoses that characterize Doležal as not simply disturbed or crazy but clinically delusional, dissociative, or borderline. But any move from the law's discourse about bodies and blood to the idea of the poisoned mind would simply mean stepping from one toxic brew of biopolitical management into another. When it comes to Doležal, it seems to me, there is danger on all sides. I seek instead to begin thinking about *the problem of thinking about* Rachel Doležal for feminism's anti-racist agenda by using some of the interpretative habits that psychoanalysis offers, including three of its foundational convictions: that self production is never divorced from fantasy; that the work of analysis begins, methodologically and ethically, with listening to the revelations and obscurities of first person speech; and that there is much to learn by reading between the lines, especially when one is confronted by unreliable narrators in contexts awash in ambiguity and contradiction (which is to say in every context, with every narrator). Add to this the transferential complexity of all relations and it becomes clear that attending to the incapacities of Doležal's speech about race and identity requires attention to the faith feminist scholars put in what we consider our own.

This aim arises in part from the invitation to this special issue of *SAQ*, which asks contributors to "sit with feminism's 'bad objects'" in order to consider the affects and desires that continue to define and enliven academic feminist practice. This "sitting with" is of course a rather tall order. It asks us not to condemn and certainly not to try to rehabilitate the bad object but to risk our implication in it, perhaps even to risk being read as *no different* from it. In the usual scenarios, let's remember, bad objects make the critic politically good by way of critique and negation, through the force of disavowal and disidentification. And Rachel Doležal is the kind of bad object that can make a white girl critic like me good (or at least better than expected) because I can use her as a vehicle for defending myself against the charges of deception, betrayal, appropriation, ignorance, and yes sheer racism that follow her insistence that "I wasn't passing as Black; I *was* Black" (2017: 148).[8] In fact, I would wager to say, because the editors of this issue have already done so, that there is nothing more powerful today in feminist critical practice than taking the figure of the white woman as "the bad object of feminism," she who must be "cast off from the corpus of feminist theory and politics, in order to save feminism itself" (Nash and Pinto 2021: 884, 887). For white feminist critics, the performance of solidarity with Black women and Black feminism entails "internaliz[ing] and enact[ing] White women as an object of feminist rage" (896). Hence the lure for the white feminist critic, keen to perform an auto-correction to generate her anti-racist credentials, to join the widespread critical and cultural admonition: Rachel, stop. You *were* passing; you *aren't* Black. *To sit with.*

In what follows I am going to take this instruction as both a guide and a caution. As a caution it means trying to rustle up some patience for actually bearing the discomfort of the indeterminacy my dual training in cultural studies and poststructuralist theory taught me was more—much more— than academic luxury. As Stuart Hall (1997: 58) insisted, "There is absolutely no political guarantee already inscribed in an identity." To love or hate Doležal, to condemn or defend: these bipolar reactions, as an end, do little to illuminate the affective and critical complexity of what she has come to evoke. As a guide, *sitting with* points me toward engaging what I might otherwise allow myself to ignore. Here I am thinking of all the ways that Doležal enacts a number of distinctly feminist pedagogies. For starters, she relies on personal narrative and self-description as the epistemological ground of her identity claim, which aligns with one of feminism's most cherished axioms: that drawing from and remaking the personal is a key component to social transformation, being both a source of political agency and a profound indication that social categories of identity and psychical processes of identification are not, conceptually or experientially, the same things. In addition, Doležal's rejection of whiteness, the very fact that she refuses to *be* white, reiterates decades of left leaning anti-racisms, underscoring the political imaginary that seeks, in a world made by white supremacy, for white people to renounce their privilege in being white. No matter how much, in the instance of Doležal, we might want to see her as a violator of these axioms, not their adherent—on the basis, say, of the liberalism of the self-made subject or the structural impediment to white transcendence of a world made to privilege us—the fact remains that this bad object is bad in part because of the ways that she seeks to be good. A woman born white who refuses to be white. A woman born white who uses her body to reproduce Black life. A woman born white who repeats, to the point of literalization, the feminist demand to "internalize and enact White women as an object" of her rage. When Shoniqua Roach (2021: n.p.) dramatizes "the provocation" she finds at the heart of Rafia Zakaria's (2021) influential new book *Against White Feminism*, no one would suggest that Rachel Doležal answers the call for "*everyone* and anyone who claims to be a feminist . . . to dispense with whiteness . . . and to become women of color."[9] And yet, no matter how incoherent and unpalatable her attempt, from one perspective, this is precisely what Doležal has done.

To sit with. Here, then, is my strategy for approaching the bad object that organizes this paper. I begin by attending to the story Doležal tells in her autobiography, *In Full Color: Finding My Place in a Black and White World* (2017), which, as Nathan Rabin (2021: n.p.) remarks in a rare review, is a failure not just of self-explanation but of genre. In his terms, the narrative moves confusedly between "fairy tale" and "superhero origin story," but reads most tellingly as "dark comedy and . . . a tragedy of self-delusion." Rabin is surely right about the crisis of genre, but this raises the question of what genre, if any, *is available* for the story of an ex-born-white woman that not only can amass the power and epistemological privilege that feminism has long given to first person speech but hold in check the authority readers garner in refuting or correcting it. This is not a question aimed at rescuing Doležal's reputation, as I take her to be a perfect example of what Naomi Schor ([1987] 2007: 155) calls a "failed interpretant," which refers to unreliable narrators or protagonists who misread the "signs" and "signals" they receive, overemphasize details (often by focusing on the wrong ones), and ignore information that is easily available to them.[10] But it does call forth the possibility that there's much more at stake for feminism in paying attention to Doležal's rendering of the story than we have considered it useful to explore.

That "more" lives in my essay's title, which offers the language of impasse to configure the contradictions and conceptual limits that attend anti-racist feminist pedagogies aimed at dismantling whiteness today. By impasse I mean something quite other than a stalled conversation or argumentative deadlock, those colloquial uses that bear with them the idea and ideal of a breakthrough that generates consensus and progress. As I see it, the impasse of whiteness is not about disagreements, whether political or theoretical, especially not when the discourse that sets out to parse the failures of "white feminism" circulates so widely *as* a set of agreements—about historical narration, citational practice, critical affect, organizational form, and racialized subjectivity—that carries the promise to fulfill feminism's emancipatory agenda to finally speak to and for the needs of all women.[11] Nor does impasse serve here to reference an interregnum, that time-space of suspension when movement between one organization of life is ending and a new one has yet to emerge into affective or analytic legibility (see Berlant 2012). As I use it, impasse is not a holding space for enduring a present whose potential we cannot possibly know, but a means to evoke how the power and privileges constituted by the structural organization of white supremacy are maintained through incommensurability and incoherence. Think, for instance, of how corporeal schemas write racial identity as a visual logic on the skin even as whiteness is not singularly beholden to an essentialist logic, being available as a political attachment, social norm, or psychic mode of identification to everyone. Or how the theoretical deconstruction of whiteness as a social fiction offers little force when it comes to disrupting its everyday affective and institutional materializations.

In this quicksand, where whiteness operates through the both/and of identification at the same time that its formal legal logic is driven by a history of identitarian either-or's, the imperative to unseat the hold of whiteness on feminism runs into the contradictions that have long sustained it. These contradictions are multiple, but my itinerary in this discussion will lead us primarily to two: the analytic disjuncture that comes from reading white supremacy as an ontological feature of social structure while insisting that the privileges that accrue to whiteness can be self-consciously known and politically undone; and the affective disjuncture that rejects white feminism's fantasies of cross-racial sisterhood in order to forge a liberatory and distinctly reparative vision of an intersectional feminism that eliminates the threat of internal racial antagonisms altogether. In both of these cases, amelioration—real or imagined, theoretical or affective—comes at a fantastical cost, offering white women an impossible agency founded in self-conscious disidentifications with whiteness and the tantalizing specter of not being an object of feminist rage, while situating social antagonisms and structural materialities in feminism as correctable errors. For reasons that I hope will become clear, I take these contradictions as related to the hermeneutic conundrum that Rachel Doležal both embodies and represents. To unravel these matters, let's start by following this bad feminist object to her autobiography's interpretative dead ends.

For many observers, Doležal's story begins with a lie, but I'm inclined to say that it begins with the media's revelation of a lie, which opens up a distinction between who Doležal takes herself to be and the truth-driven narratives of identity that are written into law and lore as biogenetic family. In the clash between subjective assertion and heredity as genealogical commonsense, Doležal's now famous lie is split into two temporal frames, *before* and *after* her media descent into public whiteness. In the "before" times, which some commentators cast as nearly a decade long, she lived in Black community as a Black woman, produced Black art, fought for Black political emancipation, and taught Black studies; as Bey (2020: 213) notes, "thousands of people" took Doležal as Black, "from various black laypersons to National Association for the Advancement of Colored People (NAACP) members to white racists." In these times, the lie for which she would later be accused was effected largely through substitution and omission: adding a check mark to the option of Black along with white on an application form or providing none at all; designating a chosen father to replace the white one she refused to call her own; and always trusting everyone to draw the conclusion she wanted, without having to say so, based on the political and social communities she assembled around her. As she writes in her autobiography about her chosen father, Albert Wilkerson Jr., "Nobody ever asked me if [he] was my biological dad. They just assumed that he was. . . . Visually, we made sense" (2017: 154). With the media's revelation, Doležal was catapulted into the "after" times or what we might call the era of the alibi, which is our ongoing present. Here she has been asked repeatedly to come clean, admit the lie, confess her privilege, and offer atonement by performing white shame. But she won't. Instead, she insists in interview after interview that "I feel Black," and "I identify as Black"—an insistence underscored by her main line of defense: "nothing about whiteness," she writes on page 1 of the autobiography, "described who I was" (1).

Doležal's dual emphasis on feeling and identification is consistent across the different media platforms in which her self-narration appears, but I am especially struck by how the autobiography, as a genre devoted to the task of first person exploration and enunciation, has no interest in delivering a developmental narrative to ground her self-identification as Black. This is the case in part because the structuring alibi Doležal offers is a stubborn anti-narrative one; she does not *become* Black but *is* Black, and her Blackness is asserted in the opening pages in a way that offers no argument to dispel the doubting reader's disbelief. "Whenever it came to shade in the skin," she writes about her childhood, "I usually picked a brown crayon rather than a peach one. . . . I could see that my skin was light, but my perception of myself wasn't limited to what my eyes could take in. The way I saw myself was instinctual, coming from some place deep inside me" (9). What emerges across the next several hundred pages is a recounting of events in which this *felt* identity is manifested in increasingly literal ways, not as a discovery but as a matter of turning the inside out in order to create both a socially perceived self and a life that coheres with "who I really am" (9; 226).[12] As she puts it, "I wasn't trying to be anyone else. I wasn't copying someone else's life as a way of escaping my own. All I wanted was to be the most beautiful shade of myself I possibly could" (155). The language of the visual here is arresting, as it links Doležal's self-declared identity to the tableau of bodily signs that have long comprised the toxic components of race and its fetishizing handmaiden, racial stereotype. But note that she calls her skin tone "light" not "white," and configures her self as a "beautiful shade," which points to Doležal's ongoing refusal to accept the discourse of racial being and biological belonging that converge in her parents' charge that she was "born white." "Yes," she says in turning the tables on their authority right from the start, "my parents weren't Black, but that's hardly the only way to define Blackness" (4). A page later, she double downs on her refusal of white family belonging: "We don't get to choose our parents" (5).

In giving an account of herself as Black (or more aptly in failing to), Doležal's story quite strikingly begins and ends in the same place, with a description and defense of an inner truth whose revelation into confident self presentation is the main message the autobiography seeks to sell. As such, the narrative leans heavily into the discourse of possessive individualism that posits an ego driven, internally consistent, and wholly knowable self as the autobiographical narrator who speaks both for and as the author herself. In this mode, the work of self narration proceeds as description, not as a self-consciously engaged construction, even as readers will never be unaware of how desperate Doležal is to deliver a story about being Black that can be believed. At the same time, Doležal's Blackness is absolutely dependent on the sustenance of the Black gaze and the relational affirmation it delivers. Narratively, this relationality is routed initially through the use of familiar mythic tropes about Africa as the birthplace of human life, literally presented as imaginary projections, but as the autobiography moves forward it is sedimented in intimacies with specific Black people. These include Doležal's Black siblings and sons, and less obviously but perhaps most potently in her own self-styling of a visible "look" that conforms, as she tells it, to the Blackness she feels. Think here of how, in the daily ritual of refashioning her blonde whiteness into an image of Black femininity, it will always be her own Black(ened) face that offers *its* gaze to her in the styling mirror.[13]

Given these conceptual contradictions in which the "I" is both already constituted as Black and in need of Black recognition, the project she promises in the prologue—to document "the evolution of my identity"—has no coherent emplotment. In fact, we might say that in terms of the theoretically useful distinction between identity (as social designation) and identification (as psychic process) there is no "evolution" to be found (246, 4). The text does not trace a transformation in consciousness—how could it if she always saw her body in her mind's eye as brown? Nor does it formulate pleasure in reversing racist logics by making whiteness the inadequate antecedent, not the destination, for humanity and personhood—how could it if "nothing about whiteness described" her to begin with? In the breach between the language of self possession she draws on and the developmental narrative she fails to tell, the autobiography turns toward the therapeutic discourse of self-help and survival, which presents self-acceptance and self-love as the necessary alchemy to overcome the traumas of physical and psychological abuse along with the guilt and shame that so often accompany them. Here aspiration toward personal freedom is coupled with that of inspiration in order to stage a story that models courage and self-determination for others to follow. This makes *In Full Color* a totem to suffering, as the narrative is driven by a repetition of scenes that depict abuse and betrayal, first within her family, then in a series of relationships including her marriage to a Black man who wanted her to "act 'whiter,'" then in a society that rejects her for "who I am" (115, 217).[14] The culmination is a charge against a social world that "tried to strip me of my identity" alongside a hope to live someday "as a whole person" and "to solve the many problems emanating from racism and the racial divide" (277). In the end it is the racist fixity of ideas about race that Doležal tags as the source of her social rejection, the faulty agency that catapults her into the media spotlight where she loses friends, jobs, and the continuity of living her life as a Black woman. "If my story can advance dialogue," she writes in the autobiography's concluding line, "and provide some measure of comfort to those who find themselves drifting somewhere between Black and white, or with no category at all, I'll consider the struggle I've endured simply for living as my true self to be entirely worth it" (277).

I've thought a lot about the way *In Full Color* is drawn to popular cliché and what it might mean—as opposed to how excruciating it feels—for a literary critic to closely read a text so definitely disinterested in language as a medium of thought or communication. But the autobiography's narrative and explanatory failures, no less than its aesthetic ones, are crucial not only to thinking about the problem of thinking about "Rachel Doležal" but why calling her a failed interpretant requires that we do more than luxuriate in our critical ability to expose her impoverished formulations. For as Schor explains, when it comes to the power relations that reside in critical practice, a failed interpretant is often *too* easy a mark, allowing the critic to build their interpretative castle without attending to the broader implications of what the interpretant's failure means. In the case of *In Full Color*, this meaning is less about the rigidity of racial categories per se, as Doležal wants us to believe, than about the contradictions that reside in their animation and inscription as material fictions. As is now widely understood, the anti-essentialist intervention of social constructionist theory—which postulates that racial categories are social, not natural biogenetic truths—does little to explain how the fictions of race materialize a social and psychical reality in what Lauren Berlant (2012) has taught us to call the genres of everyday living. For Berlant, genres are not literary forms available to a sovereign subject to express their already constituted self but pedagogical modes of social and psychic organization through which the very experience of lived experience comes to be registered, narrated, and re/composed. While Berlant's interest, as readers of *Cruel Optimism* (2012: 6) well know, is in the way the genre conventions of the "good life" fray under the historical conditions of neoliberalism, the approach they offer to understanding genre has a much wider applicability, allowing us to consider how racial fictions take material form through the repetition of conventions and, when conventions fail, through the improvisations that people devise to invent new worlds or to rummage incoherently through the ruins of existing ones.

To read *In Full Color* along these lines is to pay attention to how genre conventions both shape and distort Doležal's effort to market her story as a model for others, which is to say to improvise a genre she can call her own. Rabin (2021) begins to get at this when he describes Doležal as an autobiographer who cannot figure out which genre her story lives in: fairy tale, black comedy, superhero, tragedy—we can add others—melodrama, fantasy, horror, murder mystery. This is part of what makes her a failed interpretant: the stories she tells—or more aptly the snapshots she offers—recycle a wide range of genre conventions without ever fully digesting them. Indeed, I think of the autobiography as bulimic; it takes up (or takes *in*) a multiplicity of familiar formulas but delivers mostly messy regurgitations. I don't use this language arbitrarily. In chapter 3, "Oatmeal," Doležal describes the punishment rituals to which she and her siblings were accustomed—"spankings that could push into the double digits"—and recounts an episode when she tried to fulfill the golden rule of cleaning her plate but the consistency of a large bowl of oatmeal made her gag (2017: 16). "When I tried again, I threw up in my bowl," she writes, before telling us that her father forced her to finish the now regurgitated breakfast later that day (17). "In the Doležal household, discipline and obedience were to be learned," Doležal writes, "no matter what the cost" (18). This scene and others like it sketch a childhood of intense labor, strict religious indoctrination, corporeal abuse, and ultimately creative resistance. In chapter 5, "Hustling to Make a Dollar," Doležal describes how her parents would wring "as much labor out of each child as possible" as predicate for turning the suffering of others toward her own struggle: "I empathized with those whose free labor helped build this country," she writes in referencing chattel slavery (25). "Punishment for even the most trivial offenses was often decided on a whim" and survival required "inner fortitude and day-to-day resourcefulness. . . . I developed a similar resourcefulness" (26).

In staging analogies of this kind, Doležal seeks to forge a kinship between the cruelty of her evangelical patriarchal home and the white supremacist regime of racialized slavery. In doing so, the empathy she expresses toward the enslaved, recognizable as the very stuff of sentimental fiction and its white liberal affects, acts as a transferential mechanism for establishing her *felt* identity according to the stock conventions of trauma, struggle, emancipation, and pride that have been framed as the national multicultural narrative of Black American experience—a framing that reached its apex during the Obama presidency (2017: 9).[15] The autobiography also draws on, with an important twist, the structural conventions of the slave narrative, with a named ghostwriter, Storms Reback, a white man, playing the part of amanuensis, and a foreword by her chosen dad, Albert Wilkerson Jr., who offers testimony to the autobiographical integrity of the text to come. Using his own story of growing up in the segregated South, Wilkerson is able to authenticate Doležal's Blackness by establishing his own. "I was born in 1938 in Birmingham, Alabama," he writes at the outset, before recounting a racist incident with a white cop that forces his family north (xiii). Once north, he describes continued discrimination and his growing appreciation for the work of others—he names Frederick Douglass, Martin Luther King Jr., Malcolm X, and his own father—"who, by example and by the power of their convictions, fought racial bias and prejudice" (xiv). Rachel Doležal, he tells us, is "such a person" (xiv). In celebrating Doležal's anti-racist activisms, Wilkerson dismisses her parents' revelation—"What she was accomplishing was much more important to me than what color she was"—and affirms that "she looked Black and her vibe felt Black. . . . Yes, I saw her as Black" (xv). Through the voice of her chosen dad, the foreword performs the role of the text's Black father: Doležal "became like a daughter to me," he writes, while collecting her Black children, Franklin and Izaiah, into his paternal embrace as well (xv).

As a story of Black paternity—first of fathers and sons and then of fathers and chosen daughters—the foreword is most interesting for what it *doesn't* say about mothers, especially given the priority of the maternal line in US histories of racial identity. In describing his family's need to leave Birmingham on "the midnight train to Chicago," Wilkerson uses a royal "we"—"we had to leave town"—but offers no indication whether his mother participated in the exodus or was already gone from the family scene; her existence is narratively absent (xiv). Much the same is true of Wilkerson's wife, Amy, who appears in the autobiography's photo gallery but has no role to play in the foreword and is mentioned only twice in the text, neither of which refers to her as part of Rachel's chosen family (154, 265). While Wilkerson's absent mother is Black, the mother of his children, Amy, is white, and Doležal's comments about her point toward the autobiography's aggressive need to refuse any manner of identification with the figure of the white mother. Remember, Doležal affirms her felt family relation to Wilkerson as her "dad" by noting that no one ever asked her if he was her biological father. "They just assumed he was, based on my appearance and his," she writes. "Visually, we made sense" (156). And then, quickly, she acknowledges the point that must be brushed aside, because Wilkerson is actually rather dark-skinned. "The fact that his wife Amy was white may have lent even more credibility to the idea, although . . . I never referred to her as 'Mom,' and she never called me her daughter" (154). Ditto for Nancy, the white wife of another Black man, Spencer Perkins, whom Doležal also refers to as a chosen father. "I truly felt part of [the Perkins] family, and as a way of expressing this love I called Spencer "Dad," his older sister "Aunt Joanie," her husband "Uncle Ron," Spencer's father "Grandpa Perkins," and Spencer's mother "Grandma Perkins" (100). In a note on the bottom of the page, Doležal seeks to clarify her omission: "I did not, however, call Spencer's wife Nancy 'Mom.' That she was white may explain why neither one of us was comfortable adopting that level of familiarity with each other" (100).

This last sentence, "That she was white," demoted to the foot of the page, is both an admission and a diversion—or better yet what we could call an under-thought. On the face of it, Doležal wants to posit that she and Nancy are nothing alike: her Blackness and Nancy's whiteness don't mix or, rather, in the language that Doležal uses, aren't conducive to "adopting" the familiarity of affectionate family names. At the same time, of course, Doležal is confessing her proximity to Nancy through negation, offering an explanation that turns against itself through the other word that has gone missing, not "Mom" as Doležal would have it, but *"also"*: "That she was *also* white may explain . . .," or "That she was a white woman *also* adopted by Black family may explain . . ." By casting Nancy's whiteness as the prohibition to "adopting" (such an important word choice) familiarity, Doležal extends her natal alienation from her birth mother, Ruthanne, to the other white mothers who appear in the text. This extension is aided by the "born Black" perspective of Wilkerson, whose paternal voice in the foreword authorizes Doležal's status as chosen daughter, establishes her as a mother of Black sons, and casts the autobiography as "a unique opportunity to reflect on the complex social construct of race and racism . . . from the perspective of a young woman who has personally experienced their profound effects from both sides of the color line" (xvi). "Both sides," Wilkerson says, but Doležal never talks about *being* white on the white side of the color line; on the contrary, the entire effort of the autobiography is to establish that she was Black in self conception no matter which side she was supposedly on. For this reason, every instance of proximity to a white mother requires some form of negation, even if, as Doležal admits, the acceptance she receives as Wilkerson's daughter is due in large part to the fact that his white wife Amy is assumed to be her mother.

To see how the white mother's eradication serves as the autobiography's primal scene, let's return to the first chapter, which, you might remember, opens by taking aim at family origins as the locus of racial belonging. "We don't get to choose our parents," Doležal writes as preamble to the story of her own birth that, she tells us, lived in family lore as an attempted murder (5). "I would continually be reminded throughout my childhood just how difficult my delivery had been for my mother. That I'd nearly killed her weighed me down with a sense of guilt I could never fully shed" (6). The guilt Doležal confesses here is caught up in a grammatical no-man's-land, as the sentences use various verbs in their past tense—would, had, could—but offers the narrator no present tense in which the expressed emotion remains true. Not then "a sense of guilt I *have* never fully shed," but a far more distanced account, one that becomes overtly disingenuous as Doležal turns from the story of her mother's near death to a near death experience of her own. This experience involves an accident Doležal had before she was two years old when, "unsupervised in the house, I fell down the stairs that led to the unfinished basement . . . breaking my collarbone and several vertebrae" (7). Rather than rushing the child to the hospital, Doležal's parents maintained their religious belief in prayer and natural healing, which, Rachel tells us, led to ongoing neck pain. "To Larry and Ruthanne, my neck pain wasn't a consequence of their negligence," but was "God's way of punishing [me]" for being a stubborn child (8). In moving from the specter of matricide to that of infanticide in just a few paragraphs, chapter 1 reinterprets Doležal's anti-maternal aggression into evidence of her second class citizenship, all while casting her white parents as guilty of causing a bodily affliction that would become life-long. "I've lived with chronic neck pain ever since" (8).

We are surely not surprised that Doležal fails to make the interpretative moves that are readily available here: that for Ruthanne and Larry she *is* and has always been a pain in the neck or, just as pertinently, that her parents and the whiteness of unchosen kinship they represent are for her a pain in the neck. Either way, the opening chapter offers an image of a body that remembers somatically what Doležal's autobiography will consistently refuse, refute, or revise: that the social construction of race as a mode of corporeal inscription and biological belief begins with the mother. Understood in this way, it becomes clear quite quickly that Doležal's proclamation about whiteness in the prologue harbors a specific charge if only we can read between the lines: "nothing about [*my mother's*] whiteness described who I was" (1; emphasis added).

Nowhere is Doležal's effort to reject the social and psychic meanings of being "born white" more pronounced than in a series of fantasies recounted in chapters 2 and 5. These fantasies, mixing the conventions of fairy tale, captivity narrative, and ethnographic travelogue, simultaneously erase her white skin and deepen her attempts to forge analogies between her incarceration in the Doležal family and trans-Atlantic slavery—all while working to eradicate the figure of the white mother. One such fantasy takes place in the garden where she was often required to work. Covering her arms and legs in mud, she writes, "I would pretend to be a dark-skinned princess in the Sahara Desert or one of the Bantu women living in the Congo I'd read about in copies of *National Geographic*. In my fantasy, Larry and Ruthanne had kid-napped me, brought me to the United States, and were raising me against my will in a foreign land" (11). A few chapters later, Doležal doubles back to this fantasy but offers a key addition: "My previous fantasy about being a Bantu woman living in the Congo returned. I imagined I was an only child, and *my mother was ill or dead*, and I had to dig up enough cassava to feed my entire family" (emphasis added, 29). This death dream is the second—and last time—that Doležal will use the language "my mother" (the first I cited in the birth story discussed above). While its use here is not meant to refer to Ruthanne, the shift from being a "woman" to being "an only child" is an important temporal regression, as the adult Doležal is recounting how as a child she would escape "the oppressive environment I was raised in" by call-ing forth an "imaginary world" (11). This imaginary world features a child whose mother is ill or dead, which enacts Rachel's most robust wish to be rid of the mother whose racial identity is other to the one she invents for herself, while also clearing the space for Doležal, the Bantu princess, to become her imaginary family's new and decidedly Black mother, the one who would "feed my entire family." Stunningly, in 2010 Doležal manages to convert her fantasy of maternal replacement into living reality when she actually adopts one of Ruthanne's adopted Black sons, Izaiah, thereby turning him from her sibling into her son.

In terms of the conventions of genre, Doležal's murderous relation to the white maternal is a far cry from the sentimental tradition she otherwise draws on to generate analogies between different forms of (predominantly) female suffering. Here we have something more akin to a psychological thriller (without the thrill) or a murder mystery (without the mystery), which does the work of cutting the umbilical cord to whiteness by symbolically erasing the white mother as predicate for Doležal's own claim to Black maternity. This cut is absolutely foundational to the story Doležal tells and it is not surprising that it is performed without a self-reflective engagement with what her fantasies, depictions, and refused identifications with Ruth-anne, Amy, or Nancy mean. How could it be otherwise? To succumb to the accusation that she has lied about her born-white nativity would require con-ceding to what her detractors take to be true: that like her own mother, Rachel Doležal is a white woman who mothers Black children. This recogni-tion is intolerable to Doležal, which makes it difficult to disagree with Ruth-anne's assertion that "Rachel is trying to destroy her biological family." But I've no interest in adjudicating the conflict at the center of the Doležal's fam-ily melodrama. After all, there are a lot of reasons to be in favor of the destruction of the white biological family, just as there are a lot of reasons to sit with the twists and turns of the autobiography's attempt to sever all ties to whiteness by undermining or refuting the reproductive agency of white women. What's more, in her aggressive rejection of the idea of racial identity as a genetic inheritance—touted at various points in the autobiography on the grounds that race is a "social construct"—Doležal goes all the way toward refuting family resemblances (she once looked a lot like Ruthanne) by cultivating a bodily presentation that can help erase the once unmistakable impression that she is white (85, 147, 236, 246, 275).[16] With the help of makeup, skin toner, wigs, weaves, and braids modeled on styles long associated with Black women, she crafts the kind of visual image that "made sense" to her chosen kinship relations, thereby forging a link between seeing herself as Black and being seen as Black (156).

Still, we must ask, because so many people have asked it, why Doležal's insistence on not being white manifests itself in being Black in the visual domain. Why, if race is a social construct, as Wilkerson and she both tell us, and if identity is an inner knowledge not an outer sign, as she maintains, does she nonetheless work so hard, indeed incessantly, to be *seen and to see herself* as a light-skinned Black woman? If Doležal has a direct (let alone satisfying) response to this issue, she does not offer it, even as the cultivation of her body's racial signs figure quite prominently in the autobiography's depiction of the need to "embrace my true self" (91). Here again we see how "the evolution of my identity" that Doležal promises at the outset was never meant to refer to an evolution in her racial identifications. The cultivation of the visual evokes instead her growing determination to let her body speak what she takes *feeling* Black to mean (4). Over time, as she puts it, "I allowed the little girl I'd colored with a brown crayon so long ago to emerge" (91). Hence, in her early twenties, Doležal takes a comment by a Black female friend that "'to copy is to compliment'" as Black "permission" to begin "to embrace the exterior expressions of my feelings," which entails copying Black women's hairstyles and adding bronzer and suntanning to her daily routine (91). Doležal is quite cognizant that these practices can easily be leveraged into charges of cultural appropriation, as no entry into the visual register of hair and skin can outrun associations with the racist stereotyping at work in blackface. But she assures her readers that *her* self construction as Black passes the moral test. "Cultural appropriation is a tricky subject," she writes, which is why "I dedicated no small amount of thought and reflection to . . . examining my life to ensure that I was making authentic choices, not offensive or insincere ones" (92). Nearly every instance in the autobiography that verges on the matter of ethical conduct is resolved through such declarative assurances of authenticity and sincerity; she has looked inward and no intention to harm has been found. As she puts it, "I wasn't passing for something I wasn't but identifying with something I was" (239).

Doležal is quite clearly, and frustratingly, a literal not an interpretative thinker, which might be an aspect of her inheritance as the child of evangelical parents that she can never shed. What it yields, as I have suggested, is a descriptive flatness, not only anti-metaphorical and humorless, but narratively non-psychological as well. And yet it marries the therapeutic with an effort at prophecy, as Doležal positions herself as a messenger with a story to deliver to aid those who have found themselves misrecognized and socially rejected. Add to this her insistence on a perception that "wasn't limited to what my eyes could take in" and it is not such a leap to say that her Blackness is wrapped in a certain kind of theology, one that is more self-help than religious, more narcissistic than cosmological (9). But she is no theologian, even of the talk show kind. Still, I have to argue that she is not performing blackface, at least not in its historical function as a means to manage racial anxieties by offering white audiences a collective experience in which white bodies "master" Blackness through the intimacies of imitation as ridicule.[17] To my mind it is more accurate to say that Doležal mimics corporeal Blackness in order to pass *from copy to original*. Look again at the quote above: "I wasn't passing for something I wasn't but identifying with something I was" (239). Here Doležal cancels herself twice—"I wasn't . . . I wasn't"—before arriving into a positive grammar of self-affirmation—"I was." This is a fascinating tongue twister, inviting (as all double negatives do) a reading of the sentence in reverse: I *was* passing for something I *was* but identifying with something I *wasn't*.[18] This seems to me to be a far more apt depiction of the psychical ligaments of Doležal's story. It renders her commitment to copying aspects of Black feminine style as part of a pursuit of the authenticity of Blackness, an authenticity she seeks as the counter truth of social definitions of being "born white"; i.e., she "wasn't passing for something I wasn't." She is thus not passing *through* Blackness as a way to shore up the security of whiteness, but imitating Blackness to recover what she calls "the essential essence of who I am" (271).

In the end, Doležal's literalist interpretations are no match for the fantasies that enable and subtend them, as social construction becomes a way to tag all racial categorization as the product of malignant cultural fictions while the autobiography resurrects a distinctly humanist discourse of inner truth—an "essence" no less—that finds expression in materializing the signs of

Blackness on born white skin. In this incoherence, Doležal's attempts to forge a genre of her own go nowhere. Even the gesture to model herself for others has no generative effect as the transraciality she claims gets configured in contradictory terms. On the one hand transitivity unsettles racial fictions about blood, biology, and the immutability of nature by disarticulating Doležal from assumed identification and belonging to her birth family, which opens the way for a born white woman to refuse her taxonomic classification and stake a claim to identity elsewhere. Race is rendered a "floating signifier," as Stuart Hall (2017: 64) described it in a now famous lecture nearly three decades ago, bound to histories of meaning making that are socially produced, not naturally given, and hence neither stable nor transcendent. On the other hand, because the social fictions of race are lived through visual economies that remain stubbornly in place—are lived precisely, as Hall notes, in practices that *signify* the flesh—Doležal's insistence on being read according to what she feels reverts to the body, that domain in which Blackness has been and continues to be scripted as corporeally real—even when, and this is key, Black identity does not always meet the measure of the visible's epistemic demand. In the contradictions that ensue, it is the aporia in the visual economy of race, generated by the violence of sexual bondage that underwrites the law of maternal descent, that enables Doležal to make herself readable as Black. And it is this readability that works, in turn, as the very condition through which Wilkerson and members of the Black community would come to "authenticate" her claim to being Black.[19]

For Jelani Cobb (2015: n.p.), the gut punch that Doležal's story delivers arises here, where the very experience granted to her by the material violences of the one-drop rule gives her access not only to knowledge that comes from living (as) Black but to the fact that, "at least among black people," she would be "taken at her word." In knowing "this ugly history," he writes, "she understands the exact nature of the trust she violated."[20] Cobb's reading underscores the idea that Doležal is a failed interpretant—a misreader of signs, including the signs that Black experience would have given her—even as it points to the way that race is itself an epistemological, economic, and biopolitical project founded on interpretative fictions that move ably between and around the contradictions that constitute them. Hall (2017: 37) referenced the double dealing at the heart of racial logics (which is to say their instabilities and fabrications) when he noted "how symptomatic it is of racial discourse per se that the physical or biological trace, having been shown out of the front door, tends to sidle around the edge of the veranda and climb back in through the pantry window!" To be sure, Hall's concern, speaking in

1994, was not about a born white girl being able to maneuver cross-racial identifications into a corporeal fiction but the reverse, the way that scientific knowledge of the fictivity of race was unable to defeat, indeed could barely counter, how it was mobilized ideologically to produce not just the idea of race or the racialized subjectivities that live its non-truth but the very structures that hold in place an anti-Black world. By reading Doležal's entanglement in what is symptomatic about racial discourse, Cobb draws attention to what Doležal's failed interpretations reveal. "In truth," he writes, "Dolezal has been dressed as we all are, in the fictive garb of race, whose determinations are as arbitrary as they are damaging. This doesn't mean that she *wasn't* lying about who she is. It means she was lying about a lie." Two lies then, utterly incommensurate with one another, and yet knotted together inescapably in the materiality of the fictions they draw on and reveal.

≡

The incommensurability that Cobb and Hall help us to see is at the core of what I am calling the impasse of whiteness, which I take as both a descriptive and an analytic formulation that links Doležal's failed attempts to refuse whiteness to some of the complexities and incoherences that accompany contemporary feminism's own anti-racist pedagogies. For as much as we might read Doležal's incapacities to secure a credible narrative to house her refusal—"nothing about whiteness described who I was" (1)—there is something illuminating, if unnerving, about the autobiography's insistence that the primal scene for not being white resides in subduing the authority of the white mother and crafting, in citational form no less, new origins grounded in identifications with Blackness. Certainly the book understands, intuitively or perhaps I should say performatively, that the dividing line between racialized fantasy and its social actualization is a thin and permeable one, and while much of what is taken as Doležal's grift is thought to reside here, in the born whiteness of her imagination of Africanist origins, in the curly wigs and braided hair designs, and in the dark(er)-skinned babies she births, Cobb's point is worth sitting with: Rachel should have known better not because she was white but because living as Black should have taught her otherwise. In turning the problem of thinking about Doležal from an emphasis on her essentialized born whiteness and its fantastical and hallucinatory theft of Blackness, Cobb's discussion locates her interpretative failure in the epistemology of having lived in Black(ened) skin.[21]

Here then is one configuration of the impasse of whiteness that haunts and taunts contemporary feminism, which as you will see leads rather quickly to others. It has to do with the way that whiteness, as we have come to understand it, poses an impediment to knowing much, if anything, about what constitutes it. Its construction is founded on an epistemological prohibition, one whose deconstruction has often led to a smorgasbord of sentimentalities that in liberal form are confession based, tear ridden, and narrated through apology and guilt, which is to say utterly inadequate in their narcissistic response (hello, Karen! Hello, Becky!) to a vast and violent racialized social structure. In academic and popular feminist discourse the recognition of this epistemological prohibition underlies a familiar pedagogy for white women to construct their otherness to whiteness from within. In hyperbolic terms we might describe this pedagogy as a competition in which white feminist scholars try to be less egregiously white than the next white woman, which is why I gestured at the outset of this essay toward the idea that there is no greater gift to the white feminist performing her anti-racism than a born white woman who can't read the cues (might we even call them the anti-racist norms?) of how not to sound or be like Rachel Doležal, the bad feminist object whose repudiation can help restore faith in feminism's capacity to transform the world. On this score, the road from Karen, Becky, and Miss Ann to Jessica Krug and Rachel Doležal, to the entire repudiated cast of feminism's own white (fore)mothers is paved with interpretative gold. And yet, no matter how much the critique of failed whiteness installs the disidentification with whiteness it seeks, its productivity always risks missing its mark. Why? Because the position being sought—to not *be* white, performatively, politically, or critically—meets its limit in the ongoing failure of consciousness and self-reflectivity to do all the necessary work of unbinding whiteness from the structures of the social that produce and protect it.

In this context, where the epistemological prohibition that defines the operations of whiteness comes to be challenged but not undone by the epistemological profit conferred on self-consciousness, it becomes easier to see why the discourse of "white feminism" in contemporary feminist scholarship offers both relief and anxiety for white feminists seeking to negotiate its pedagogical demands. Relief because the space of negation it enables gives white feminists the opportunity to perform, through the repetition of renunciation, a relation of otherness to the history of white political incapacity that is born in the definitional characteristic of the unself-consciousness of whiteness itself. Anxiety because such disidentifications don't in themselves deconstruct the white privilege that sets them in motion, as their, which is to say my, corporeal whiteness carries a potent specular power that resists my self-conscious resistance to being (taken as) symptom and agent of the production and reproduction of white supremacy. At the level of the signification of the flesh where racial fictions are written as ontological realities, whiteness as structuring condition is in fact *indifferent* to whether or not I pledge my allegiance or pronounce my disavowal. Or to put it this way, I benefit even if I politically don't want to, because not wanting to—no matter how valuable to anti-racist agendas—offers no embodied experience through which to measure the benefits I do or don't receive. On the contrary, what the impasse of whiteness delivers is precisely this inoculation against the material force of white disidentifications that on their own cannot render structurally real the conceptual and affective deconstruction of whiteness that drives them. This is true whether or not such disidentifications are made in psychical terms, as a mode of self-study that works to uncover the entitlements that whiteness delivers, or, importantly, in citational practices, through the dismantling of white feminist histories as the singular terrain for configuring the past and future of feminism (see Schuller 2021).

To talk about the structural conditions of white supremacy as nonnegotiable at the level of the subject is of course to confront one of the most coveted beliefs in US feminism, which tasks working on the self as the central scene and theme for any kind of social transformation. But this "working on" is asymmetrical in its pedagogical charge and political force, as what white women must seek is how *not* to be who we were taught/encouraged/indulged to think we are but its opposite, a deconstruction of self constitution and epistemological privilege. Embodied experience for women of color, on the other hand, is conceived in constructionist terms, as the conduit not only for self-making and social revision but as the perspective white women must adopt (but not co-opt) to configure their disidentification in legibly anti-racist terms. Embodied experience thus conditions the epistemological lack that white women must overcome, while it is configured for women of color as the epistemological ground, first, of self-knowledge and resistance against the false representations and discriminating assaults, both literal and metaphorical, that accompany racialized schemas of whiteness as the universal predicate of Being in an anti-Black world, and second, as a pedagogical model for unbelonging to whiteness itself. These asymmetries underlie the painful history in which the feminist anthem, "the personal is political," has repeatedly failed to produce the suturing effect for feminist solidarity that its citation and circulation intends, precisely because the ground on which the personal is constructed and performed is not, as the phrase is often taken to suggest, the same.

Doležal, for her part, is more than a little bit aware of the impasse of whiteness in the configurations that I outline above, as *In Full Color* has all the trappings of a failed attempt to configure a method to outmaneuver them. Think here of the way that her frustratingly literalist interpretations focus her disidentification with whiteness on the other within, designated as the white mother whose overnomination in the national story of biological kinship and racial belonging must be supplanted with narratives of new origins, albeit messy and off-putting ones, that render Blackness both psychically prior and the speculative condition of a self-enunciating wholeness. While disidentification initiates the work of white racial deconstruction, Blackness becomes the embodied origin of epistemological truth. In this face-off with the white mother—explicitly configured as those who craft their maternal desire to include mothering Black children—Doležal can tolerate no trace of similarity or sameness, which is why the autobiography's recollection of the scene of her own birth is inflected competitively through the prism of matricide on the one hand and retaliatory neglect and child abuse on the other. It is also why the autobiography does its best to erase all evidence of white mothers. But Doležal's intolerance goes farther, as she implicitly rejects disidentification as the destination of a racially conscious self, which is to say she rejects the very framework of self-conscious whiteness that promises to differentiate the ideological and political commitments crafted by self-consciously white women from their white others. Instead, Doležal transposes the conditions that lead to the impasse—the incommensurability of the impersonality of structure vis-à-vis first-person negotiations—by rejecting the project of trying to be *not* (unself-consciously) white in order to insist instead on feeling (self-consciously) *non*-white.

This transposition is what most frustrates many of Doležal dissenters, not simply because of the proliferation of lies that so infamously set it into motion. The matter cuts deeper, as Doležal is far too brazenly committed to securing a certain kind of bodily pleasure and political credibility in rejecting the anti-racist ethos to interrogate what it means, in the past and the present, to be racially white. The con she thus achieves, for those who think of it this way, is wrapped in an unforgivable audacity as she ferries her flat-footed literalism across the impasse of whiteness by seeking—and securing— identificatory pleasure in be(com)ing Black. In these terms, Doležal's most affronting transgression may well be the very literalism of her citational practice, the way she recycles the fictive signifiers of race as an end run around the ethical responsibilities of anti-racist whiteness, which must first see itself as white in order to disidentify with the power and privilege conferred on white skin. When Sophia Seawell (2018: 56) calls for Doležal to stay "with the trouble of being a white ally," she is clearly trying to help Doležal sort out all these citational mistakes. But I'm not convinced that everything that troubles feminism about Rachel Doležal would be settled if only she would learn to behave. On the contrary, the political desire for born white women to learn—or in some instances to choose (see Schuller 2021: 10)—how not to be unself-consciously white would remain. So would whiteness as epistemological deficit as well as the impossibility of its deconstruction from within the embodied experience that comprises it. And we'd still be drawn, because we already are, to the search for citational solutions that can displace the authority and centrality of white women's single-axis gender obsessions by generating new historical and analytic origins for feminism—origins that can reflect as well as found an emancipatory agenda for a sisterhood, imagined otherwise. As Kyla Schuller (10) puts it, "intersectional feminism articulates a planetary vision in which all have access to what they need to thrive in mind, body, and spirit."

Counter histories to the whiteness of feminism have existed, of course, ever since feminism became the name for describing and resisting gendered regimes. But my sense is that the very specification of "white feminism" generates new conditions for reconstructing feminism's political imaginary, one that opens to a transformed future by retrieving and institutionalizing an intersectional past that can carry the promise of surpassing the whiteness that has long threatened it.[22] In this promise, the problem of whiteness for feminism is negotiated through citational and analytic disidentifications, as the great white foremothers of the movement, no less than of the field, are repudiated for their historical complicity with white racial hegemonies, and the citational economy of the text is made to signify as Black even when its author is white. This is at least one of the ways we might interpret Shoniqua Roach's (2021: n.p.) characterization of the provocation of *Against White Feminism* as a call to "become women of color." Still, the metaphoric and the citational don't unwind the contradictions of the impasse so much as give hope for bypassing them. If there is something uncannily familiar in all this—in the pursuit of new origins and a kinship uncontradicted by white privilege—it is audible not because I've been sitting with Rachel Doležal so long that I hear strange permutations of her failed interpretations and disidentifications everywhere. The point is a little more difficult, as there is no single way to address the impasse of whiteness and no final clarity on how the knots—or as the case may be the *nots*—of whiteness as structure and lived experience can be materially overcome. Rachel Doležal—disconcertingly, tragically, laughably (take your pick)—sought recourse in a literalist escape, becoming a Black woman most fully when the Black community accepted the significations she wrote on her skin. The negotiations offered white feminists via the critique of white feminism are hardly comparable except at the level of the wish they repeat and sustain. If even this similarity is too much to digest, the option remains to stick to the belief that feminism's bad objects are bad for all the right reasons.

Notes

The author thanks Julien Fischer, Jennifer Nash, Jennifer DeVere Brody, Samantha Pinto, Zahid Chaudhary, and the audience at Princeton University's Humanities Council works-in-progress event for their generous feedback and edits. She is also grateful to Anne Brancky and Youna Kwak, who organized the 2021 ACLA session on "Bad Objects," which gave her a venue in the midst of the pandemic to think about Doležal with a community of committed interdisciplinary scholars.

1   The use of these terms is ubiquitous in the cultural discourse about Doležal. For "born white," see Svrluga 2015; for an instance of the language of being "outed," see McGreal 2015; and for "transracial" see Brubaker 2016 and Alim 2016. For the history and political culture of transracial as a referent for mixed-race adoptive families, see Briggs 2012.

2   In 2017, Doležal was charged with welfare fraud for taking public assistance without revealing that she had received over $83,000 in income since 2015, including an advance from BenBella Books for the autobiography that reportedly barely sold six hundred copies. She was ordered to repay $8,847 and to perform 120 hours of community service (see Arciga 2019). It was lost on nearly no one that being accused of being a welfare cheat is one of white nationalism's favorite stereotypes of Black women.

3   Among her other roles in Black political movement, Doležal worked at the Human Rights Education Institute, taught courses in African American cultural studies at Eastern Washington University, and served on the Spokane volunteer police ombudsman committee.

4   Of the four children adopted by Ruthanne and Larry Doležal, two, Ezra and Zach, now defend the parents against the stories that Rachel tells about the culture of work and punishment in the family. See Gayle 2015.

5   There's also Kelly Kean Sharp, a (now former) assistant professor at Furman University and African American history scholar, who self-presented as Chicana, wrote blog posts about her *abuela* in Mexico, but who grew up white in LA. On the rash of poseurs, see Flaherty 2020 and Lewis 2021 as well as Cherid 2021, who refers to the practice of whites passing as Black as "blackfishing" (359).

6   Doležal uses a caron, which is Czech in origin, for the spelling of her family patronymic in the autobiography and its byline. I am using that spelling throughout this essay except where work cited uses "Dolezal."

7   In what I think is the only book-length study that takes up Doležal as its primary case study, McKibbin (2021) offers a kind of metacommentary about the move that Bey makes here, where his dislike of Doležal is not an impediment to considerations of what her story reveals about the ideology of racial identity. "What is important to this discussion," McKibbin writes, "is not debating Doležal's character but rather what her claims can help us understand about our assumptions, beliefs, and practices with

regard to race and, consequently, how we are thinking about the possibility of transracial identities. Thus, my focus is not ascertaining the veracity of Doležal's claims or that of any other potentially transracial person's" (4).

8   To make matters worse for the critic tasked with "sitting with," Doležal offers this insistence after what many commentators take as a false and harmful analogy: "Just as a transgender person might be born male but identity as female, I wasn't pretending to be something I wasn't but expressing something I already was" (2017: 148). This line is repeated, with an important variation later in the text: "I wasn't passing for something I wasn't but identifying as something I was" (239).

9   As I read it, Roach is absolutely not endorsing a literalist interpretation of the provocation she finds at the heart of *Against White Feminism* but trying to underscore the inclusivity that Zakaria seeks in disarticulating whiteness as a political position and faulty feminist philosophy from the white women who routinely embody it. As Zakaria (2021: ix) puts it, "You do not have to be white to be a white feminist. It is also perfectly possible to be white and feminist and not be a white feminist. The term describes a set of assumptions and behaviors which have been baked into mainstream Western feminism, rather than describing the racial identity of its subjects. At the same time, it is true that most white feminists are indeed white, and that whiteness itself is at the core of white feminism." In these maneuvers, as Roach intimates, Zakaria evokes a universal—and universally progressive—feminism defined by its intersectional commitment to "women of color" as a political ontology.

10   I am taking enormous liberties in my use of Schor's concept of the failed interpretant. Apologies to the faithful.

11   The specification of white feminism as a specific historical political entity has of course been around for decades, but in referencing it as a "discourse" here I am attempting to engage the proliferation of scholarly and popular conversation organized around it, including its circulation in ways that exceed the citational through social media and in activist contexts. For some of the most prominent works at the time of this writing, see Beck 2021; Chaddock and Hinderliter 2019; Daniels 2021; Hamad 2019; Schuller 2021, and Zakaria 2021.

12   It is not possible to read Doležal's emphasis on materializing her felt Blackness without hearing echoes of the most familiar narrative tropes of transition in our times, that of transgender, even if what we might be hearing are simply the reductionist outlines of first person speech conforming to the dictates of a standardized self-representation. But the analogy between transracialism and transgender has been a persistent feature of the cultural maelstrom around Doležal, as Caitlyn Jenner came out as transgender within the same few weeks of the summer of 2015 that Doležal's story broke. In the culture war produced nightly by conservative media, with *Fox News* taking the lead, Jenner and Doležal were yoked together as comparable figures whose identity claims were being treated by the left in supposedly hypocritical ways, as Jenner was celebrated for her bravery in claiming who she really was while Doležal was critiqued for performing an elaborate masquerade. This controversy hit the academy especially hard when *Hypatia* published an essay by Tuvel (2017) with the provocation "In Defense of Transracialism," that led not just to mass editorial resignations but to adamant rejections of thinking transracialism and transgender together. For important interventions against the prohibition, see Green 2015 and Stryker 2015. See also Brubaker 2016. On the *Hypatia* controversy, see Winnubst 2017 and Bérubé 2018.

13   The Netflix documentary *The Rachel Divide* (Brownson 2018) is fascinated with the image of Doležal in front of the mirror and returns multiple times to the daily ritual of hair and makeup. See Corey 2018 for a review of the film.

14   It is important to note that Doležal's (2017: 118) discussion of her marriage to Kevin is the first time in the autobiography that she describes being instructed *into* whiteness: "Learning that a Black man could be, culturally and philosophically, as white as any white man was a painful lesson for me." The snapshots of her childhood experience feature no overt family discourse about race, other than in Rachel's depiction of Larry and Ruthanne's efforts to adopt Black children, which Doležal describes "as a way to avoid (or, at the very least, limit) paying taxes to a government they blamed for subsidizing abortions" (45). Kevin, who as far as I can tell has never spoken publicly about Doležal, is depicted not only as patriarchal and anti-Black but also prone to domestic violence. "Kevin grabbed the back of my hair and threw me across the room" (125). In chapter 16, titled "Emancipation," Doležal describes the end of her marriage. "The divorce was finalized in April 2005. . . . I was truly owning who I was: a woman who was free, self-reliant, and, yes, Black" (129).

15   The multicultural narrative of American democratic becoming was a main narrative in Barack Obama's presidential campaign and tenure in the White House (see Taylor 2016), and clearly a strong element in the current white nationalist reclamation of US history, which has been fueled most recently by the specter of the 1619 project by Nikole Hannah-Jones (2019), which re-narrates national history through slavery and its legacy. Importantly, Jones's language about the project gives slavery primal agency in the historical aspiration of national democratic completion. She writes, "Yet despite being violently denied the freedom and justice promised to all, black Americans believed fervently in the American creed. Through centuries of black resistance and protest, we have helped the country live up to its founding ideals" (n.p.).

16   In her historical study, *Miss Anne in Harlem: The White Women of the Black Renaissance* (2013), Carla Kaplan offers an important lens for understanding the different cultural narratives that accompany "reverse passing," as it is sometimes called. Doležal's autobiography both evokes these plot lines and diverges from them. Like Miss Anne, Doležal rejects her biological inheritance and seeks instead to be accepted into the Black community, but her story offers the interesting twist that the family she comes from is a transracial one. Like Miss Anne, Doležal is similarly committed to anti-racist politics and dedicated her labor to projects and organizations that sought to address white racism, but Doležal never did so as a white ally; her anti-racist work was part of her understanding of being Black. And finally, while she too was libidinally invested in Black men, marrying one and having a child with another, Doležal's most distinct racial fetishism was and is profoundly self-centered, as it is on her own body that she writes the identity she claims.

17   In his work on white minstrelsy, Eric Lott (1995) has diagnosed the affective labor that blackface performs for white audiences as white actors pass through Black stereotype to shore up whiteness not just as an identity but as a sensorium to be shared. See Taylor and Austen (2012) for a discussion of the Black minstrel tradition and the complexities of its performance and reception for Black performers and audiences alike.

18   Gates (2018) uses the language of the "double negative" to break through the long-standing debate about positive and negative images in the study of Black representation in popular culture. By "taking up Herman Gray's call to analytically shift discussions of identity

and media 'from signification and representation to resonance and experience,'" Gates argues for the critical value of "embrac[ing] the designation of 'negative'" (16).

19   In the year after the autobiography was published, Doležal changed her name to Nkechi Amare Diallo, meaning "gift of God," though she continues to use her birth name professionally. As Ann DuCille (2020: 168) discusses, the ghost that haunts this name change is Amadou Diallo, an "unarmed and minding his own business" Black man who was "blasted to death by nineteen of forty-one bullets nypd officers fired at him." In considering "Rachel Dolezal's appropriated namesake," DuCille points out how the racial profiling that gets "black men like Diallo killed actually aided and abetted Doležal in the racial ruse that enabled her to pass for a black woman."

20   The second lie, which undergirds the very structure of anti-Black racism, is to Cobb's mind "far more dangerous" than Doležal's. His point is not to eliminate the pressure on Doležal to address what he calls her "dishonesty" but to grapple with the "vexed criteria being used to exclude her," which risks homogenizing Black identity while leaving the most dangerous lie intact. In "Incorporeal Blackness," Bey (2021: 208) pushes this last point to its extreme, granting Doležal her cross-racial bona fides in order to argue for the speculative capacities of Blackness as a "modality of becoming [unmoored] from given ontologies." As Bey puts it, "Dolezal passes for black, sure, but so then does Cornel West, Toni Morrison . . . and any other 'black' person you can name. That is to say, maybe she wasn't 'born black'—but no one is" (218). The "incorporeal" of the essay's title answers the call to take social construction past its familiar insistence that race and gender are social fictions to the ground of the body itself. "We cannot wish for fundamental, radical change without also putting at imminent risk . . . our deepest tethers to our own bodies" (221).

21   For Cobb, the privilege that Doležal demonstrates is not found, as other commentators would have it, in the matter of her choosing to be Black as the epitome of white privilege, which Alisha Gaines (2017) tags in the title of her book as "being Black for a day." His analysis is more scathing, as my discussion here hopes to convey.

22   Schuller's book (2021: 124) is especially forceful on this point, describing Elizabeth Cady Stanton as "the inventor of white feminism" and offering, in a series of seven chapters, a genealogy of feminism that was intersectional from the beginning. Key figures for this retelling include Frances E. W. Harper, Harriet Jacobs, Zitkala-Ša, Dr. Dorothy Ferebee, Pauli Murray, Sandy Stone, and Alexandra Ocasio-Cortez.

References

Alim, H. Samy. 2016. "Who's Afraid of the Transracial Subject? Raciolinguistics and the Political Project of Transracialization." In *Raciolinguistics: How Language Shapes Our Ideas about Race*, edited by H. Samy Alim, John R. Rickford, and Arnetha F. Ball, 33–50. New York: Oxford University Press.

Arciga, Julia. 2019. "Nkechi Diallo, Formerly Rachel Dolezal, Reaches Settlement in Welfare Fraud Case." *The Daily Beast*, April 4. www.thedailybeast.com/nkechi-diallo-formerly -rachel-dolezal-reaches-settlement-in-welfare-fraud-case.

Beck, Koa. 2021. *White Feminism: From the Suffragettes to Influencers and Who They Leave Behind*. New York: Atria Books.

Berlant, Lauren. 2012. *Cruel Optimism*. Durham, NC: Duke University Press.

Bérubé, Michael. 2018. "The Way We Review Now." *PMLA* 133, no. 1: 132–38.

Bey, Marquis. 2020. "Incorporeal Blackness: A Theorization in Two Parts—Rachel Dolezal and *Your Face in Mine.*" *CR: The New Centennial Review* 20, no. 2: 205–41.

Bey, Marquis, and Theodora Sakellarides. 2016. "When We Enter: The Blackness of Rachel Dolezal." *The Black Scholar* 46, no. 4: 33–48.

Briggs, Laura. 2012. *Somebody's Children: The Politics of Transracial and Transnational Adoption.* Durham, NC: Duke University Press.

Brownson, Laura, dir. 2018. *The Rachel Divide.* www.netflix.com/title/80149821.

Brubaker, Rogers. 2016. *Trans: Gender and Race in an Age of Unsettled Identities.* Princeton, NJ: Princeton University Press.

Chaddock, Noelle, and Beth Hinderliter, eds. 2019. *Antagonizing White Feminism: Intersectionality's Critique of Women's Studies and the Academy.* New York: Lexington Books.

Cherid, Maha Ikram. 2021. "'Ain't Got Enough Money to Pay Me Respect'": Blackfishing, Cultural Appropriation, and the Commodification of Blackness." *Cultural Studies↔Critical Methodologies* 21, no. 5: 359–64.

Cobb, Jelani. 2015. "Black Like Her." *The New Yorker,* June 15. www.newyorker.com/news/daily-comment/rachel-dolezal-black-like-her.

Corey, Mary F. 2018. "The Rachel Divide." *Cineaste* 43, no. 4: 43–45.

Daniels, Jessie. 2021. *Nice White Ladies: The Truth about White Supremacy, Our Role in It, and How We Can Help Dismantle It.* New York: Seal Press.

Doležal, Rachel. 2017. *In Full Color: Finding My Place in a Black and White World.* Dallas, TX: BenBella Books.

DuCille, Ann. 2021. "'Can't You See I'm White?': Reading between the Sight Lines of Racial Difference." *differences* 31, no.1: 163–80.

Flaherty, Colleen. 2020. "Even More White Lies." *Inside Higher Education,* October 29. https://www.insidehighered.com/news/2020/10/29/unmasking-another-white-professor-allegedly-posing-person-color.

Gaines, Alisha. 2017. *Black for a Day: White Fantasies of Race and Empathy.* Chapel Hill: University of North Carolina Press.

Gates, Racquel J. 2018. *Double Negative: The Black Image and Popular Culture.* Durham, NC: Duke University Press.

Gayle, Damien. 2015. "Rachel Dolezal Accused of 'Blackface' by Adopted Brother." *The Guardian,* June 13. www.theguardian.com/us-news/2015/jun/13/rachel-dolezal-blackface-race-brother.

Good Morning America. 2015. "Father on Rachel Dolezal's Alleged Race Deception: 'It's puzzling to us,'" June 15. www.abc7news.com/rachel-dolezal-fake-black-is-or-white-naacp/785372/.

Green, Kai M. 2015. "'Race and gender are not the same!' Is Not a Good Response to the 'Transracial'/Transgender Question OR We Can and Must Do Better." *The Feminist Wire* (blog), June 14. www.thefeministwire.com/2015/06/race-and-gender-are-not-the-same-is-not-a-good-response-to-the-transracial-transgender-question-or-we-can-and-must-do-better/.

Hall, Stuart. 1997. "Old and New Identities, Old and New Ethnicities." In *Culture, Globalization and the World System,* edited by Anthony D. King, 41–68. Minneapolis: University of Minnesota Press.

Hall, Stuart. 2017. "Race: The Floating Signifier." In *The Fateful Triangle: Race, Ethnicity, Nation,* edited by Kobena Mercer, 31–79. Cambridge, MA: Harvard University Press.

Hamad, Ruby. 2019. *White Tears/Brown Scars: How White Feminism Betrays Women of Color.* Carlton, Victoria, Australia: Melbourne University Press.

Hannah-Jones, Nikole. 2019. "Our Democracy's Founding Ideals Were False When They Were Written. Black Americans Have Fought to Make Them True." *New York Times,* August 14. www.nytimes.com/interactive/2019/08/14/magazine/black-history-american-democracy.html.

Harris-Perry, Melissa. 2015. "Exclusive Full Interview: Rachel Dolezal Breaks Her Silence." Online video clip, June 17. www.msnbc.com/melissa-harris-perry/watch/rachel-dolezal-breaks-her-silence-465691715976.

Kaplan, Carla. 2013. *Miss Anne in Harlem: The White Women of the Harlem Renaissance.* New York: Harpers.

Kim, Eun Kyung. 2015. "Rachel Dolezal's Parents: We Taught Our Kids 'Always Be Honest,'" June 15. www.today.com/news/rachel-dolezals-parents-we-taught-our-kids-always-be-honest-t2614.1.

Lewis, Helen. 2021. "The Identity Hoaxers." *The Atlantic,* March 16. www.theatlantic.com/international/archive/2021/03/krug-carrillo-dolezal-social-munchausen-syndrome/618289/.

Lott, Eric. 1995. *Love and Theft: Blackface Minstrelsy and the American Working Class.* Oxford: Oxford University Press.

McGreal, Chris. 2015. "'Rachel Dolezal: I Wasn't Identifying as Black to Upset People. I was Being Me." *The Guardian,* December 13. https://www.theguardian.com/us-news/2015/dec/13/rachel-dolezal-i-wasnt-identifying-as-black-to-upset-people-i-was-being-me.

McKibbin, Molly Littlewood. 2021. *Rethinking Rachel Doležal and Transracial Theory.* Cham, Switzerland: Palgrave Macmillan.

Moyer, Justin Wm. 2015. "'Are You an African American?' Why an NAACP Official Isn't Saying." *Washington Post,* June 12. www.washingtonpost.com/news/morning-mix/wp/2015/06/12/spokane-naacp-president-rachel-dolezal-may-be-white/.

Nash, Jennifer, and Samantha Pinto. 2021. "A New Genealogy of 'Intelligent Rage'; or, Other Ways to Think about White Women in Feminism." *Signs* 46, no. 4: 883–910.

Phipps, Alison. 2021. "White Tears, White Rage: Victimhood and (as) Violence in Mainstream Feminism." *European Journal of Cultural Studies* 24, no. 1: 81–93.

Rabin, Nathan. 2021. "Exploiting the Joy of Trash: Rachel Dolezal's *In Full Color: Finding My Place in a Black and White World.*" *Nathan Rabin's Happy Place* (blog), December 31. www.nathanrabin.com/happy-place/2017/6/6/color-me-bad-case-file-87–rachel-dolezals-in-full-color.

Roach, Shoniqua. 2021. "Becoming Women of Color." *Signs* Short Takes. http://signsjournal.org/zakaria/#roach.

Schor, Naomi. (1987) 2007. *Reading in Detail: Aesthetics and the Feminine.* New York: Routledge Press.

Schuller, Kyla. 2021. *The Trouble with White Women: A Counterhistory of Feminism.* New York: Bold Type Books.

Seawell, Sophia. 2018. "Feeling Black, Reproducing Whiteness." *Junctions: Graduate Journal of the Humanities* 3, no.1: 45–58.

Stryker, Susan. 2015. "Caitlyn Jenner and Rachel Dolezal: Identification, Embodiment, and Bodily Transformation." *Perspectives on History* (blog), July 13. www.historians.org/publications-and-directories/perspectives-on-history/summer-2015/caitlyn-jenner-and-rachel-dolezal-identification-embodiment-and-bodily-transformation.

Svrluga, Susan. 2015. "Rachel Dolezal Admits That She Was Born White." *Washington Post*, November 2. https://www.washingtonpost.com/news/grade-point/wp/2015/11/02 /rachel-dolezal-admits-she-was-born-white/.

Taylor, Keeanga-Yamahtta. 2016. *From #BlackLivesMatter to Black Liberation*. Chicago, IL: Haymarket Press.

Taylor, Yuval, and Jake Austin. 2012. *Darkest America: Black Minstrelsy from Slavery to Hip Hop*. New York: W. W. Norton.

Tuvel, Rebecca. 2017. "In Defense of Transracialism." *Hypatia* 32, no. 2: 263–78.

Winnubst, Shannon. 2017. "Why Tuvel's Article So Troubled Its Critics." *The Chronicle of Higher Education*, May 8. www.chronicle.com/article/Why-Tuvel-s-Article-So/240029.

Zakaria, Rafia. 2021. *Against White Feminism: Notes on Disruption*. New York: W. W. Norton.

Candice Merritt

Lest We Forget Black Patriarchy;
or, Why I'm Over Calling Out White Women

I share with a Black female friend that I am in the throes of writing an article about white women as feminist theory's bad objects. She nods and says, "Of course! They are a problem. They are always fucking up." She proceeds to provide the latest example of a wealthy white woman committing a racial-gender faux pas. This time, an award-winning film director, Jane Campion, jokingly compares her sexist battles with men in the film industry to the struggles Serena and Venus Williams faced in the white-dominated tennis world. While accepting her speech, Campion expresses, "You're such marvels. However, you don't play against the guys, like I have to" (Ginsberg 2022). The op-eds hailed the moment as "peak white feminism" or yet another moment where white women center themselves at the expense of Black women and other women of color in the name of women's progress (Agarwal 2022). I retort that Campion cannot and should not stand for all white women, especially those committed to feminist struggle in all locales and times. After all, I did not recall Campion laying any claims to feminist movement. My friend didn't buy it.

In the age of Black Lives Matter, one can find any plethora of blogs, op-eds, long form articles,

The South Atlantic Quarterly 122:3, July 2023
DOI 10.1215/00382876-10643987 © 2023 Duke University Press

tweets, memes, etc., on the systemic and interpersonal instances of anti-Black racism dealt by white women, most likely in the form of their tears and calls to police. Likewise, sustained academic attention has been given to the issue of white women as a barrier to feminist progress and solidarity and a growing genre of how to be a better anti-racist ally has flourished.[1] The exchange with my friend reflected this cultural zeitgeist around white women—a moment that can be described as feeling like the following: if white women could just stop crying, calling the police, supporting Trump, taking up space and/or the lead in feminist movements, and simply embrace Black feminist works, then the problems plaguing Black women's lives would vanish.

While it may be pleasurable and necessary to draw attention to the political failings of individual white women, I, still, insist asking: what of Black women's anger at men, and at Black men, specifically?[2] I do not pose this question lightly, and answering it feels even more difficult. As a Black mother to a Black son in the United States, I am viscerally aware of the threats upon his life and those surrounding other Black men and boys for existing in their own flesh. Yet, I am equally worried of how the quest to secure Black masculinity and power risks deadly harm against the women, girls, queer, and trans folk who may or may not enter his life.[3] Thus, just as I hold the growing catalog of names of Black men and boys whose lives have been cut short by the US policing apparatus, I also feel my boiling madness at the less publicly uttered names of Black women, like Oluwatoyin Salau, Hayden Davis, Ashley Lockhart, Martasia Richmond—Black women (cis and trans) who have recently been killed by those they share home, neighborhood, and intimate spaces with. Put differently, their names are among the many known and unknown Black women killed by Black men.

As focus on correcting white women's racism rages on, I stand by the necessity to keep this line of inquiry as two preoccupations arise. I worry about the fervor overshadowing naming the everyday gendered and sexual violence and suffering Black women experience at the hands of Black men, especially when popular feminist texts like Mikki Kendall's *Hood Feminism* continue to claim that "solidarity is still for white women" (Kendall [2020] 2021: 1). In 2020 alone, an average of five Black women and girls were killed per day and a third of those numbers includes those killed by a partner or kinfolk (Beckett and Clayton 2022). This statistic is in addition to the unequal caretaking load Black women experience as communities continue to be wrought by the COVID-19 pandemic (Hayes and Mason 2021: 3–4; Lindsey 2020). I also fear the implication of hailing Black feminism, in the words of Kyla Schuller (2021: 5), as both a historical and contemporary fight "against white feminism," when there exists a long legacy and tradition of Black feminist writing and activism that names Black patriarchy as the problem to name, struggle against, and eradicate within the lives of Black women and their communities. Thus, I write from the presumption that even if in a world where the bad white woman object is successfully disciplined—she follows every recommended task put forth by Black women and other women of color (cede space; stand back; listen; uplift)—the abuse, molestation, rape, harassment, and unequal domestic partnerships Black women suffer would not subside. In short, Black women won't get free until Black patriarchy ends.

In effort to redirect attention to the sexual/gendered intramural struggles within Black social life, this article contends that the fervor for correcting white women and their brand of feminism overlooks the many moments when Black feminists did not center white women—their targets of address were Black men and Black women. While varied feminists have explored the political import of rage in general to feminist political mobilization, others like Jennifer Nash and Samantha Pinto (2021), have charted the varied genealogies of rage within Black feminist thought—in particular, Black feminist feelings of ambivalence and uncertainty at rage's capacity to resolve white women's racism. Thinking alongside Nash and Pinto, this article sits with the long tradition of Black feminist writing filled with rage, but in a different direction—at Black men and toward the end of diagnosing Black patriarchy. Doing so constitutes a commitment to transform existing conversations where white women are the presumptive enemy.

In a media landscape that primarily calls attention to the deaths of Black men and boys by state agents and individual white women's perpetuation of anti-Black racism, what happens when we recall moments when Black feminists took Black men to task, such as Audre Lorde and Nikki Giovanni's heated exchanges with James Baldwin for deprioritizing sexual politics and violence against women in Black communities, or more recent contentions between the Crunk Feminist Collective and rapper Talib Kweli for his lack of allyship to Black women? By closely reading selected texts by the Combahee River Collective, Ntozake Shange, Audre Lorde, and bell hooks from the 1970s–1980s, I contend that present-day focus on Black feminist anger at white women obscures the old and ongoing Black feminist struggle against Black patriarchy. Collectively, the compiled archive illustrates a Black feminist commitment and astute analysis that explicitly names Black male power and Black female complicity in perpetuating patriarchy. Returning to these works not only illustrates a more complex telling of Black feminist history, but also provides critical import to our contemporary moment.

Remembering Rage at Black Patriarchy

Let's be clear: "Black feminists speak as women because we are women," so wrote Audre Lorde (1979: 17) in 1979 in response to Robert Staples panning Black feminist writing as a "'collective appetite for black male blood'" (17). Today, one may be hard-pressed to think of Black feminists' investment in taking up gender (and by extension the category of woman)—absent its intersections with race and class—as a primary oppression impacting the lives of Black women.[4] Or in other words, Black feminism and white feminism share few commonalities; they are diametrically opposed. Nowhere is this more reflected in the bemoaning of white feminism's prioritization of the woman category. Rafia Zakaria (2021: 54) contends that white feminist theory—represented by the choice of canonical texts such as Simone de Beauvoir's *Second Sex* and Kate Millett's *Sexual Politics*—"lack epistemological room" to apprehend the lives of women who experience multiple oppressions. Such texts are marked by the "erasure of Black women" and "dismissal of Brown women" and reveal that the "general term 'woman' has, in the Western world, been intentionally deployed to mean 'white' women" (54). Shoniqua Roach (2021) concurs that white feminists have historically presumed the whiteness of woman and that Black feminists over the centuries have pointed to the insufficiencies of white feminist accounts of gender. Kyla Schuler (2021: 19) furthers that womanhood constitutes a racializing discourse to exclusively refer to white women. Ruby Hamad (2019: 22) concludes that Black women do not "experience sexism in the same way white women do . . . what is common about the experiences of women of colour is an unspoken assumption that we always lack a defining feature of womanhood that white women have by default."

Such criticism is accompanied by varied moments across time where Black feminists have called attention to individual white women's racial and class solipsism and have seemingly provided the necessary correction. Hamad (2019: 135) describes Lorde's book *Sister Outsider*, as offering "medicine" by advocating for white women "to drop their defensiveness and their imposition that gender is the master oppression" (134). Most concerning is the valuation of intersectionality as the correction. Hamad writes "Like Lorde, Crenshaw made a point to include economic disempowerment in her analysis; in fact, it is essential to it" (134). Zakaria (2021: 171) relays Leslie McCall's declaration of intersectionality as "the most important theoretical contribution that Women's Studies in conjunction with related fields has made so far."

Yet that contribution gets described as naming "structural inequality and systemic racism"—not patriarchy and misogyny—as "integral to understanding the experiences of women of color within a white-dominated world" (171). Thereby, "white feminists, in their own lives and careers" should no longer ignore the differential experiences (169). In these accounts rarely, if ever, does Black feminist struggle appear to name the insufficiencies of antiracist and anticapitalism analyses to account for the bloodshed of Black women suffered by Black men. No mention of Lorde's or Crenshaw's naming Black male sexism and patriarchy as problems plaguing Black communities nor the major intervention into showcasing the de-prioritization of sexual politics and violence against Black women in antiracist politics. Consequently, the popular hailing of Black feminist analyses engage in a selective remembering, and that reduces Black feminism to a preoccupation with white women's lack. As such, it obscures the *long durée* struggle of Black feminists contending with and naming the sexual antagonism with Black men.

Following Clare Hemmings (2011), the stories we tell about Black feminist histories and what gets highlighted as the invaluable contribution to feminist theory and praxis matter. Who Black feminists fought alongside, with, and against and who Black feminists named as enemies and potential allies varied and were contingent. It was not so clear that white women were *the* enemy to be overcome, nor were Black men and Black women presumed to be given allies. Solidarity and political alliances were not natural occurrences; they were relationships that required constant struggle and labor to maintain. As such, Black feminists expressed what Patricia Hill Collins (1998) has called, "fighting words" to Black men and other Black women. Yet, what happens when accounts of Black feminist intervention fail to name these essential intramural struggles?

When not positioned as a sole address to white feminism, Black feminist critique broadens to an explicit accounting of patriarchy as male dominance and paternalism and the systematic sexual oppression of women. The Combahee River Collective (CRC) has been heralded as the revolutionary call for white feminism to move beyond analyses that premised patriarchy. Yet, the CRC developed primarily as an urgent need and deep commitment to the survival of Black women's lives, community, and culture. The Combahee River Collective's 1977 statement has been canonized as an essential document of radical Black feminism—celebrated for its call to center an interlocking analysis of oppression under capitalism and its attention to the significance of identity politics. Less discussed, yet no less significant, is the collective's highly circulated 1979 pamphlet, *Six Black Women: Why Did They Die?* The pamphlet showcased an analysis of sexual violence as a primary oppression in the lives of Black women and called for women to "join together to demand our rights as human beings to be free of physical abuse, to be free of fear" (CRC 1979: 45).

Six Black Women served as the collective's primary tool in their organizing around violence against women in the Roxbury neighborhood in Boston, when in 1979 the brutal murders of twelve Black women were not given sufficient media and police attention. The pamphlet underwent various reprints as the murders of Black women accrued, and roughly 30,000 copies were distributed. Remarking upon what prompted the creation of the pamphlet, Barbara Smith reflected:

> One of the things that made the murders so visible is that things were happening quickly; a great number in such a short period of time. This was not a serial killer; there were several people identified as having perpetrated the murders. Some of the murders were never solved and have never been solved. It was such a concentration of violence against Black women in particular; the fact that the murders were originally defined by members of the Black community as being racial murders only, yet all the people who were murdered were women and were sexually assaulted. . . . This is the wonderful combination that patriarchy gives us: the rape-murder. . . . The pamphlet that we created—originally titled *Six Black Women: Why Did They Die?* (1979)— was written in response to going to rallies [about the] murders and having them be described solely as racial crimes. No mention of violence against women, gendered violence, or anything like that. And then, having men suggest, as a way that we could protect ourselves and avoid being hurt or killed, was to be dependent upon male protection. We were not having that as young Black feminists. (Hassan 2022)

Terrion Williamson (2017: 331) has read the pamphlet's analysis of the Black women's deaths as reflecting the collective's critique of the "socially and politically constructed outcome of the various intersecting modalities of oppression endured by Black women—including sexism, heterosexism, classism, and racism." Yet, what I find most profound in Smith's reflection on the murders and the pamphlet is her focus on Black women's structural vulnerability as women under patriarchy and not their compounded status as Black and poor.

The pamphlet expressed the shared sentiment and struggle across feminist communities—"Black, white Hispanic, Asian, Native American, old, young, rich, poor and in between" (CRC 1979: 45)—to name and eradicate the force of patriarchy. The perspective places tension on the presumption that Black, and other women of color, experience sexism differently from white women and thereby cannot have a shared analysis. More importantly, it shows a Black feminist investment in naming sexual oppression via violence and male paternalism in the larger culture as well as in local Black communities. The pamphlet reflected a Black feminist necessity to "identify *all* of its causes, including sexual oppression" (46). Wedging against dominant communal framings of racism, the CRC emphasized the gendered/sexual difference of the crimes. The pamphlet contended: "It's true that the victims were all Black and that Black people have always been targets of racist violence in this society, but they were also *all women*. Our sisters died *because* they were women just as surely as they died because they were Black. If the murders were only racial, young teen-age boys and older Black men might also have been the unfortunate victim. They might now be petrified to walk the streets as women have always been" (44).

What followed the reframing of the Black women's deaths as primarily gendered/sexual cause was not a litany of statistics that emphasize racial and class disparities between women, but "statistics [that] apply to all women" (45). The pamphlet detailed countrywide trends:

> 1 out of 3 women will be raped in their lifetimes or 1/3 of *all* the women in this country; at least 1 woman is beaten by her husband or boyfriend every 18 seconds; 1 out of every 4 women experiences some form of sexual abuse *before* she reaches the age of 18 (child molesting, rape, incest) 75% of the time by someone they know and 38% of the time by a family member; 9 out of 10 women in a recent survey had received unwanted sexual advances and harassment at their jobs. Another way to think about these figures is that while you have been reading this pamphlet a woman somewhere in this city, in this state, in this country has been beaten, raped and even murdered. (44)

The account illustrates Black feminists articulating gender and sexual oppression absent its emphasis on its intersections with race and class. They invoke the collective pronoun *us* under the category of woman—the "attacks on women are so widespread . . . to keep us down, to keep us oppressed . . . to be made afraid . . . feel powerless and also like we're second best" (45). The collectivity showcases an understanding of violence against Black women endemic to American culture and follows patterns of the cultural milieu of misogyny. It makes explicit that "society also constantly encourages the violence through the media: movies, pornography, *Playboy, Players, Hustler, JET*, record covers, advertisements and disco songs. . . .

What has happened in Boston's Black community is a thread in the fabric of violence against women" (45).

As such, the CRC's "outrage" in the pamphlet called for not the restructuring of society or the ending of the capitalism (46). It ended with a call for women to learn to protect themselves with a separate page of bulleted points of concrete actions under the title of "Self-Protection" (47). These steps were also accompanied by a demand to take up an analysis of sexual oppression for "ending this particular crisis and violence against women in our community" and direct instructions for men (46). The collective redeployed the discourse of male protection by calling for men to labor and organize alongside other men. Men who actively perpetuated harm against women had "to check out the ways in which they put down and intimidate women in the streets at home, to stop being verbally and physically abusive to us and to tell men they know who mistreat women to stop it and stop it quick" (46). For men who had stated and/or felt commitments to ending violence against women, the CRC demanded immediacy and desired ongoing praxis to living out such political commitments. "Men who are committed to stopping violence against women," the pamphlet detailed, "should start *seriously* discussing this issue with other men and organizing in supportive ways" (46).

Turning to Black feminists' deployment of poetry further illustrates their rage and labor to name patriarchy as a primary force that compels Black women's death. Ntozake Shange's "with no immediate cause" poem, first published in 1972 in her collection *Nappy Edges,* accompanied the pamphlet after subsequent deaths beginning with the third reprint. It stands as a lyric poem that follows the obscene acts of violence against women in the space of the mundane. Told from the first person point of view, the individual accounting offers a window into Black feminist feelings of fear and anger at the public disregard of systematic and routine violence against women and children by men. The poem repeats the refrain, "every 3 minutes a woman is beaten/every five minutes a woman is raped/every ten minutes a lil girl is molested" (48). The repetition occurs as the speaker recounts everyday living such as taking the subway and siting alongside an old man, witnessing young boys on the train, and buying a periodical from the newsstand man. At each encounter with a male figure, the speaker queries about the real possibility of each committing horrendous harm against women and girls (the speaker included) as reported in the news media. The speaker states "i rode the subway today/i sat next to an old man who/may have beaten his old wife" (48). Another iteration occurs:

> i rode the subway today
> & bought a paper from a
> man who might
> have held his old lady onto
> a hot pressing iron/i don't know
> maybe he catches lil girls in the
> park & rips open their behinds
> with steel rods/i can't decide
> what he might have done i only
> know every 3 minutes
> every 5 minutes every 10 minutes/so (48)

The poem concludes with a critique of the public disregard of violence against women and the illegibility of women's murderous rage against men. The speaker cites a newspaper account fragment:

> there is some concern
> that alleged battered women
> might start to murder their
> husbands & lovers with no
> immediate cause. (49)

The speaker reacts viscerally at the incredulity:

> i spit up i vomit i am screaming
> we all have immediate cause
> every 3 minutes
> every 5 minutes
> every 10 minutes
> every day
> women's bodies are found
> in alleys & bedrooms/ at the top of the stairs

Given the structural disregard of violence from newspaper accounts to state agents, Shange's narrator engages in direct confrontation through crude querying. The speaker contextualizes what may seem inappropriate and unreasonable—"i have to ask these obscene questions/the authorities require me to/establish/ immediate cause" (49)—in the everyday social encounters with men. The speaker asks:

> before i ride the subway/buy a paper/drink
> coffee/i must know/

> have you hurt a woman today
> did you beat a woman today
> throw a child across a room
> are the lil girl's panties
> in yr pocket
>
> did you hurt a woman today
> [. . .] cause
> every three minutes
> every five minutes
> every ten minutes
> every day. (49)

Audre Lorde further elaborated and provided critical analysis of the phenomenon and connected violence against Black women across history and geography. Her poem "Need: A Chorale for Black Woman Voices" reflects her
long commitment to name the force and effect of patriarchy in Black wom-
en's lives. Originally written in 1979 and published in her 1982 collection
Chosen Poems: Old and New, Lorde also revised and republished the poem
with Kitchen Table Press in 1990, reflecting her commitment to continuing
"dialogue between and among Black women and Black men on the subject
of violence against women within our communities" (Lorde 1990: 3). Its
republication also signaled an ongoing necessity to keep naming and analyzing violence against Black women by Black men as one primarily perpetuated by patriarchy as male domination—not because of Black men's experience of racial and/or class exploitation. In her prefacing remarks to the latter
edition, Lorde detailed her felt life prior to crafting her poem:

> I wrote *Need: A Chorale for Black Woman Voices* because I felt I had to use the
> intensity of fury, frustration and fear I was feeling to create something that
> could help alter the reasons for what I felt. Someone had to speak, beyond
> these events and this time, yet out of their terrible immediacy, to the
> repeated fact of the blood of Black women flowing through the streets of our
> communities—so often shed by our brothers, and so often without com-
> ment or note. Or worse, having that blood justified or explained away by
> those horrific effects of racism which we share as Black people. (3)

Lorde raises the dead by giving voice to Patricia Cowan and Bobbie Jean Graham, two Black women separated by time and place but joined in death in
the space of Lorde's chorale poem. Both women suffered violent deaths by

Black men—Cowan, twenty, was bludgeoned to death in Detroit in 1978 by a Black playwright during a play audition, and Graham, thirty-four, was found beaten to death in Boston in 1979 and was one of the twelve murdered Black women that fueled the advocacy of the Combahee River Collective. The choice of form is important. The chorale poem spans centuries from antiquity onward. Lorde begins with a dedication to Cowan and Graham and prefaces the poem with a play on the children's nursery rhyme "Tell Tale Tit." Both the form and chosen nursery rhyme connote Black women's death by men as something old and ongoing, something that happens again and again and starts anew. The nursery rhyme signifies violence against women as something mundane, common, and lighthearted—something that mothers will sing to children, and the boys will internalize and learn to cannibalize women, especially those who tattle.

Regardless of risk, the women and nameless poet tell on. Embedded in the poem is a collective, intimate, and direct address to you—the male perpetrator of the women's death. Through posed queries, Lorde offers the reason why Black women die violently at the hands of men. The speaker, Pat, queries:

> *I need you.* For what?
> Was there no better place
> to dig for your manhood
> except in my woman's bone? . . .
> When you opened my head with your hammer
> . . . did your manhood lay in my skull
> like a netted fish
> or impotent fury off the tips of your fingers
> as your sledgehammer clove my bone
> to let the light out
> did you touch it as it flew away? (11–12)

The central questions reflect the critique of masculine need of woman to confirm and elevate male existence. It explicitly exposes the price of Black masculine need which requires repeated sacrifices of Black female flesh and blood. The second speaker, Bobbie, repeats the essential query: "And what do you need me for, brother,/ to move for you feel for you die for you" (11)? Lorde names the need as pathological and tenuous as Pat describes it as "impotent" and fleeting. As such, the poet narrator catalogs the varied violences upon Black female flesh by Black masculine need:

Dead Black women haunt the black maled streets
paying our cities' secret and familiar tithe of blood
burn blood beat blood cut blood
seven-year-old-child rape-victim blood
of a sodomized grandmother blood
on the hands of my brother
as women we were meant to bleed
but not this useless blood (9)

Recalling her 1985 conversation with James Baldwin at Hampshire College about the twelve murders of Black women in Boston, Lorde remarked, "Not enough has changed since then" and that "Jimmy and one of the older Black men were in agreement that under the tremendous pressures of racism, Black men could not be held responsible for their violence against Black women, since it was a response to an unjust system, and Black women were only incidental victims" (5). Another Black man retorted, "The Black male is not attacking a Black female; it would be a sheep if that's what was there" (5). The collective framings show the undervaluing of Black women's lives and the interchangeability of Black women with non-human objects. "To this I replied, and still reply," Lorde writes, "'Yes, but I'm not a sheep, I'm your sister . . . who is learning to use a gun. If we wind up having to kill each other instead of our enemies, what a terrible waste for us all'" (5). Like Shange's narrator, who enumerates the "immediate causes," or the varied reasons for women's self-defense and/or retribution against men, Lorde insists on fighting within the most intimate realms of Black women's living even against those who bear the mark of kinship—either fictive or blood. Her invocation of the gun suggests that Black women—living under conditions of systematic disregard by the state and among their own—may respond to the violence meted out by men through any means necessary.

Black feminism—positioned as a correction to white feminism—loses analytic power to name Black men as perpetuators of patriarchal violence. Yet, Black feminists have deployed a separate analysis of patriarchy and identified the major roadblocks to its full embrace in left politics. In "Notes Toward Another Paper on Black Feminism; or Will the Real Enemy Please Stand Up," Barbara Smith (1979) cautioned against neglecting a development of an analysis of patriarchy into revolutionary politics. Smith emphasizes the concrete and points to the limits of abstract concepts of power such as that of the ruling class. What stands so prominently is Smith's provocations, which bear sentiments that today can be described as those of white feminism. Smith contends that "by naming sexual oppression as a problem it would appear that we would have to identify as threatening a group we have heretofore assumed to be our allies—Black men" (124). Naming men as the enemy cannot be written off. Smith furthers,

> The phrase "men are not the enemy" dismisses some major realities. If we cannot entertain the idea that some men *are* the enemy, especially white men and in a different sense Black men too, then we will never be able to figure out all the reasons why, for example, we are being beaten up every day, why we are sterilized against our wills, why we are being raped by our neighbors, why we are pregnant at age twelve and why we are at home on welfare with more children than we can support or care for. (124)

Smith goes to the heart of what gets in the way of Black women to engage in an analysis of sexual oppression and politics within their lives because it would strike to the most intimate spheres of their living and dying. To do so would require direct confrontation with the Black men and boys who are closest to them—family, friends, partners, etc.

Importantly, remembering the CRC, Smith's, Shange's, and Lorde's rage at Black patriarchy illustrates Black feminists' commitment to diagnosing sexual oppression and fighting Black men. It also illuminates Black feminist critique of the limits of antiracist and anticapitalist analyses. Curing capitalism and achieving socialism would not preclude Black men's violence against Black women. If Black men were to be successful in securing manhood by securing the head of household and breadwinner status in families and no longer policed, the issue of masculine need of feminine submission and confirmation would remain. Black male desire to achieve and exercise the "borrowed hymns" (Lorde 1990: 12), or norms, of white patriarchs in and outside the home will not be resolved. Or as Smith (1979: 125) noted, even if "capitalism is destroyed" a "poor Black woman probably would no longer be a welfare mother. She would still, however, be a mother, suffering the sole responsibility for the care of her children, the isolation and overwork inherent in the role under patriarchy. She also might very well still be raped, beaten, sterilized, or pregnant against her will since these kinds of oppression are not solely motivated by economic causes."

What I find most profound (and disturbing) in my return is the echo of the struggle to prioritize intramural violence Black women experience in the present day. Audre Lorde's words reverberate loudly and still feel all too relevant:

> I do not even know all their names.
> Black women's deaths are not noteworthy
> not threatening or glamourous enough
> to decorate the evening news
> not important enough to be fossilized
> between right-to-life pickets
> and a march against gun-control
> we are refuse in this city's war
> with no medals no exchange of prisoners
> no packages from home no time off
> for good behavior
> no victories. No victors. (10)

The Say Her Name campaign has done profound work in bringing attention to the deaths of Black women perpetuated by police and other state agents, but their deaths instigated by familiars, by men, still fail to meet the urgency of the Movement for Black Lives (BLM). In a political moment that focuses on the deaths of Black men and boys by police and upon individual white women's calls to the police on Black bystanders engaging in mundane activities like barbecuing or birdwatching (see Jennifer "Barbecue Becky" Schulte and Amy Cooper), thinking of Black men as perpetuators or aggressors seems antithetical, even politically incorrect, to advancing the necessary work of liberation movements. Yet, public analysis and accountability must occur. Consider the rhetoric of the late Kevin Samuels, Black relationship advice guru, who told his 1.4 million social media followers that "submission is a trait of femininity just like leadership and protection is a trait of masculinity" (Samuels 2022). The modern Black woman—ruined by feminism—will only end up alone. Even when attempts are made to name Black men's systematic participation in misogyny and patriarchal violence, Black men have actively thwarted this in public discourse. So happened with Damon Young's (2017) op-ed for *The Root* headlined "Straight Black Men Are the White People of Black People." Young's exploration of Black men's "collective danger" to Black women as they walk home, wait for buses, and via domestic abuse was met with censure by Black men (and some women). Comments ensued from labeling the piece divisive propaganda, separatist, to others calling for giving Black men a break since they carry the burden of racism (as if Black women do not), to not all Black men. These recent examples show that work remains—not simply on the part of white women to get it together—but for Black men and boys to become conscious, collectivize, and organize against patriarchal ideology, power, and violence.

And What of the Black Woman?

Where would Black patriarchy be without Black female participation and complicity? The hyper focus upon the bad white woman object also obscures the long legacy of Black feminist writing that names the "enemy within" or the self-work that Black women must engage to come to feminist consciousness. Brittney Cooper offers a recent assessment regarding white women and their "perennial threat" to forging and sustaining cross-racial feminist solidarity. Cooper (2021) proclaims,

> One of the biggest challenges I have faced as a Black feminist teacher and writer has been convincing Black women that feminism is relevant to their lives. Black women's resistance to feminist politics and ideas has never been about a resistance to gender equality. We live with the intimate and structural consequences of patriarchy every day. The biggest stumbling block in Black women's journey to fly the flag of feminism has been white women. Somewhere a white woman is talking about how we all need to be united "as women," regardless of race or creed. And somewhere a black woman is giving that white woman a side eye. (ix)

The rhetorical moves are both powerful and seductive. The use of the declarative and hyperbole—"has never been"—so clearly outlines who and what is a problem that needs to be resolved in order for feminist politics to unleash its transformative project across racial groups. As formulated, since time in memoriam, the white woman object has been *the* mountain to overcome for Black women to proudly proclaim the proverbial f-word.

After initial reading, I chuckled at this hypothetical involving these abstract characters—a Black woman side-eyeing and a white woman desiring feminist unity. How many times have I given a side eye—a complex, Black female embodied gesture often communicative of unspoken disproval—to someone or something to which I verbally wanted to say, "Please, take a seat and be quiet?" Upon further scrutiny of popular renderings of white women as *the* barrier to feminist solidarity, critical questions and concerns remain. Living with the daily consequences of patriarchy does not a feminist make. The formulation conflates experience with consciousness and consciousness with politics. The Black woman subject lives in systems of power and inequity, but does it mean that category of persons will be radical in political thinking and praxis? Cooper's Black woman is already somehow politicized and privy to the ideas and practices of gender equality.

Despite popular discourse that hails the Black woman as already radical, Black feminists have not always rendered the Black woman category as such. While censure has been doled to white women's racism and Black male sexism, Black feminists have also invested in sustained commitments "to a continual examination of Black feminist politics" via "self-criticism" (Combahee River Collective 1977: 27). The turn toward self, to inward gazing and assessment, troubles the good/bad object dichotomy that plays out in white woman versus Black woman discourses. The orientation toward self, toward the inside, illustrates a larger Black feminist commitment to a kind of humanist universalism that sees the self in the other, the other in the self. That understands that each body with a self encompasses multiple capacities to harm and heal and to hate and love.[5] The shift also marks a different paradigm of understanding power and the concrete efforts that must be taken to accomplish the vision of a better world. Rather than rely upon static abstractions of power and critiques of institutional power, Black feminists have also theorized power and the Black woman category in more fraught and messy ways—as shifting. The robust conception of power and its structures in the intimate realms of day-to-day living enables the possibility to think of self as agent, self as embedded in a larger social world, that one moves and is moved, that one can be harmed and can harm.

Such conceptions are essential to remembering Black feminist struggle to account for the intricate and intimate knots that hold patriarchal ideology and arrangements intact. bell hooks (1989: 20), in *Talking Back: Thinking Feminist, Thinking Black,* contends that male power and authority over women "should not obscure the reality that women can and do participate in politics of domination, as perpetrators as well as victims—that we dominate, that we are dominated." Because sexism manifests primarily through power relationships in the most intimate arenas of daily living—home and family—"whether it be domination over parent over child, or male over female" (21), Black feminists have treated Black women as capacious agents who can (and continues to) participate in patriarchy that can be seen across varied Black feminist texts detailing the problematics of Black female competition for male approval and anti-lesbian sentiment.[6] Those moments reflect the unfinished struggle to embrace sisterhood and solidarity even among one another.

Since I began to craft this article, news of white women's political misdeeds and shootings of Black men by police have railed on. So too have accounts of Black women's deaths in what have been considered "domestic disputes." Yet, outrage over violence against Black women by men has not been (and maybe never will be) comparable to the number of academic books, articles, op-eds, think pieces, and expressed social unrest over the anti-Black climate and culture of the United States. The present will do well to remember Black feminism not as a callout to white women's racism but to the necessity to keep struggling to name and directly confront male power writ large and Black male violence against Black women, in particular. The return to the long tradition of Black feminist activism and analyses of the sexual and gendered oppression of Black women through the works by the Combahee River Collective, Barbara Smith, Ntozake Shange, Audre Lorde, and bell hooks revalues Black feminist contribution and struggle to explicitly confront Black men. This return cautions us: lest we forget, Black women won't get free.

Notes

1　See Robin DiAngelo, *White Fragility: Why It's So Hard for White People to Talk about Racism* (Boston: Beacon Press, 2018); Hamad 2019; Ibrahim Kendi, *How to Be an Antiracist* (New York: One World, 2019); Koa Beck, *White Feminism: From the Suffragettes to Influencers and Who They Leave Behind* (New York: Atria Books, 2021); Jessie Daniels, *Nice White Ladies: The Truth about White Supremacy, Our Role in It, and How We can Help Dismantle It* (New York: Seal Press, 2021); Ilsa Govan and Tilman Smith, *What's Up with White Women? Unpacking Sexism and White Privilege in Pursuit of Racial Justice* (Gabriola, British Columbia, Canada: New Society Publishers, 2021); Kendall (2020) 2021; Zakaria 2021; Schuller 2021.

2　See Patricia Williams's (2021) commentary on Black women's rage at white women and the popular usage of the term *Karen* in a *Signs* "Ask a Feminist" forum. Williams states, "I understand what is meant by the term Karen or Miss Anne. I also think it's risky to resort . . . to those plurifications. It's easy, and it sometimes can be funny, and we can roll our eyes . . . but I think it serves us better to talk about the specific instances, the specific people . . . to label that person a Karen is a gesture that I think is comforting on the one level, but it's a riposte."

3　I am also thinking of how pursuing masculinity can also be harmful to men and boys in unique ways such as the inability to show vulnerability and experience intimate relationships with themselves, other men, and with women and the turn to violence to resolve disputes.

4　See growing Black feminist conversations extending Hortense Spillers's concept of ungendering, as expressed in "Mama's Baby, Papa's Maybe: An American Grammar Book," *Diacritics* 17, no. 2 (1987): 65–81, such as Patrice Douglass, "Black Feminist Theory for the Dead and Dying," *Theory & Event* 21, no. 1 (2018): 106–23; Selamawit D. Terrefe, "The Pornotrope of Decolonial Feminism," *Critical Philosophy of Race* 8, nos. 1–2 (2020): 134–64; and Alexis Pauline Gumbs, "Forget Hallmark: Why Mother's Day Is a Queer Black Left Feminist Thing," in *Revolutionary Mothering: Love on the Front Lines*, ed. Alexis Pauline Gumbs, China Martens, and Mai'a Williams (Oakland, CA: PM Press, 2016), 117–22. These works stress the expulsion of Blackness from the category of gender and thereby excludes Black women from "woman" and its normative protocols. For extended discussion on the resurgence of Spillers's formulations in the fields of Black studies, Black feminist historiography, and sexuality studies, see Samantha Pinto's "Black Feminist Literacies: Ungendering, Flesh, and Post-Spillers Epistemologies of Embodied and Emotional Justice," *Journal of Black Sexuality and Relationships* 4, no. 1 (2017): 22–45.

5   One can see this in the works of Frances Watkins Harper when she remarks that "we
     are all bound up together in one great bundle of humanity," quoted in Schuller (2021:
     24). See also Jennifer Nash's "Practicing Love: Black Feminism, Love-Politics, and
     Post-Intersectionality," *Meridians* 11, no. 2 (2011): 1–24.
6   See works such as Toni Cade Bambara's "The Pill: Genocide or Liberation?," in *The Black
     Woman: An Anthology*, ed. Toni Cade Bambara (New York: Washington Square Press,
     1970), 203–12; Audre Lorde's "Eye to Eye: Black Women, Hatred, and Anger" and
     "Scratching the Surface: Some Notes on Barriers to Women and Loving," in *Sister Out-
     sider* (Crossing Press, 1984); "Black Women and Feminism," in hooks 1989: 177–182; and
     Cheryl Clarke's "Lesbianism: An Act of Resistance," in *Still Brave: The Evolution of Black
     Women's Studies*, ed. Stanlie M. James, Frances Smith Foster, and Beverly Guy-Sheftal
     (New York: The Feminist Press at the City University of New York, 2009), 12–21.

References

Agarwal, Pragya. 2022. "Jane Campion's Quip about the Williams Sisters Is Peak White Fem-
     inism." *Independent*, March 15. https://www.independent.co.uk/voices/jane-campion
     -venus-serena-williams-white-feminism-b2035989.html.
Beckett, Lois, and Abené Clayton. 2022. "'An unspoken epidemic': Homicide Rate Increase
     for Black Women Rivals That of Black Men." *The Guardian*, June 25. https://www.the
     guardian.com/world/2022/jun/25/homicide-violence-against-black-women-us.
Collins, Patricia Hill. 1998. *Fighting Words: Black Women and the Search for Justice*. Minneapo-
     lis: University of Minnesota Press.
Combahee River Collective. 1977. "The Combahee River Collective Statement." In *How We Get
     Free: Black Feminism and the Combahee River Collective*, edited by Keeanga-Yamahtta
     Taylor, 15–27. Chicago: Haymarket Books.
Combahee River Collective. 1979. "Six Black Women: Why Did They Die?" *Radical America* 13,
     no. 6: 41–49.
Cooper, Britney. 2021. Preface to *The Trouble with White Women: A Counterhistory of Feminism*,
     by Kyla Schuller, ix–xi. New York: Bold Type Books.
Ginsberg, Merle. 2022. "Insiders Say Jane Campion Will Win Oscar Despite Williams Sisters
     Comment." *New York Post*, March 24. https://nypost.com/2022/03/24/jane-campion-
     will-win-oscar-despite-williams-sisters-joke-insiders/.
Hamad, Ruby. 2019. *White Tears/Brown Scars*. Melbourne: University of Melbourne Press.
Hassan, Huda. 2022. "Eleven Black Women: Why Did They Die? An Interview with Black
     Feminist Socialist Barbara Smith." *Mother, Loosen My Tongue*, March 8. https://huda
     hassan.substack.com/p/eleven-black-women-why-did-they-die.
Hayes, Jeff, and C. Nicole Mason. 2021. *All Work and Little Play: IWPR Survey Shows Worrying
     Challenges for Working Mothers*. Washington, DC: Institute for Women's Policy Research.
     https://iwpr.org/wp-content/uploads/2021/05/All-Work-and-Little-Pay-Mothers-Day.pdf.
Hemmings, Clare. 2011. *Why Stories Matter: The Political Grammar of Feminist Theory*.
     Durham, NC: Duke University Press.
hooks, bell. 1989. *Talking Back: Thinking Feminist Thinking Black*. Boston: South End Press.
Kendall, Mikki. (2020) 2021. *Hood Feminism: Notes from the Women That a Movement Forgot*.
     New York: Penguin.

Lindsey, Treva. 2020. "Why Covid-19 Is Hitting Black Women So Hard." *Women's Media Center*, April 17. https://womensmediacenter.com/news-features/why-covid-19–is-hitting-black-women-so-hard.

Lorde, Audre. 1979. "The Great American Disease." *The Black Scholar* 10, nos. 8–9: 17–20.

Lorde, Audre. 1990. *Need: A Chorale for Black Woman Voices*. Latham, NY: Kitchen Table: Women of Color Press.

Nash, Jennifer, and Samantha Pinto. 2021. "A New Genealogy of 'Intelligent Rage,'; or Other Ways to Think about White Women in Feminism." *Signs: Journal of Women in Culture and Society* 46, no. 4: 883–910.

Roach, Shoniqua. 2021. "Becoming Women of Color." In "Short Takes: Rafia Zakaria's *Against White Feminism*." *Signs*. http://signsjournal.org/zakaria/.

Samuels, Kevin. 2022. "Modern Women Charge for Submission: How Much Does It Cost." YouTube, April 27. https://www.youtube.com/watch?v=P1MnZrxhJ1s.

Schuller, Kyla. 2021. *The Trouble with White Women: A Counter History of Feminism*. New York: Bold Type Books.

Smith, Barbara. 1979. "Notes for Yet Another Paper on Black Feminism, Or Will the Real Enemy Please Stand Up." *Conditions: Five* 2, no. 2: 123–27.

Williams, Patricia J., Carla Kaplan, and Durba Mitra. 2021. "Ask a Feminist: Patricia Williams Discusses Rage and Humor as an Act of Disobedience with Carla Kaplan and Durba Mitra." *Signs: Journal of Women in Culture and Society* 46, no. 4: 1073–88.

Williamson, Terrion L. 2017. "Why Did They Die? On Combahee and the Serialization of Black Death." *Souls* 19, no. 3: 328–41.

Young, Damon. 2017. "Straight Black Men Are the White People of Black People." *The Root*, September 19. https://www.theroot.com/straight-black-men-are-the-white-people-of-black-people-1814157214.

Zakaria, Rafia. 2021. *Against White Feminism: Notes on Disruption*. New York: W. W. Norton & Company.

Heather Berg

Free Sex

> Among the populace of plentiful johns,
> getting paid was my most political act.
> —Charlotte Shane, interview by author (2020)

A poet, a sex worker, and an anti-capitalist, Charlotte Shane thinks a lot about money and politics. What makes getting paid a political act, especially for someone who knows that waged work fuels capitalism rather than threatens it? Shane's (2020) answer is also a story about feminist genealogy: "I'm still hopelessly influenced by older feminisms that focused on how this world wants all of us as women to be used sexually without actually benefitting from that use. It doesn't want us to say, 'here's how much it costs, and here's exactly what you're gonna get when you pay.'" Saying the thing that should not be said is a way of doing politics. Charging for sex is not the most crucial form of resistance we have, Shane adds, nor is it a tidy one—commodification feels bad for many people, and it sometimes feels bad for her too. And still, "I do think that sex work is the—or a—key to totally blowing open the whole heterosexual dynamic."

"Of course, not all sex workers are women. Not all clients are men," she adds. Thinkers on the sex worker left echo the same caveat while also

The South Atlantic Quarterly 122:3, July 2023
DOI 10.1215/00382876-10644001 © 2023 Duke University Press

pushing back against allies' interest in exceptional counterexamples to this gendered dynamic. A focus away from sex work as a space where struggles over heterosexuality are waged contests anti–sex worker narratives by relocating the terms of debate, but many sex worker radicals want to dwell in that terrain. Most clients *are* cis, straight men, they reminded, and most hire people they believe are women (i.e., cis and trans women and genderqueer people and trans men who advertise as women for work). Left sex worker thinkers are, by and large, more interested than their contemporary allies in retaining "older feminisms'" sense that the exchange has something to say about heterosexual life. Their conclusions about what this something is take us places those feminisms were unable to go.

This essay explores left sex worker theorizing about sex work as a confrontation with unpaid heterosexuality, and it sits with the uneasy affinity with "older feminisms" Shane marks. Here, as for Shane, "older feminisms" evoke the radical feminism of the long 1970s. They carry that tradition's expansive political horizon and also the whiteness, gender essentialism, and whorephobia that violently foreshortened it. The feminists Shane gestures to never saw sex workers' struggles as bound up with theirs, and their politics around race, class, and transness make it risky for a community that is disproportionately non-white, poor, and gender nonconforming to share conceptual space. But thinkers in this archive insist on risking that close contact, finding moments of recognition in a framework that was not built for them. To radical feminist claims that the expectation of free hetero sex is one engine of patriarchal capitalism, they theorize demands for pay as one mode of confrontation. They also grapple with the limits of that confrontation: commodification is the norm for life lived under this system, how could it be its undoing? The money flows across the usual hierarchies of race and nation, and it is never enough to make the right people go broke. And still, the force of the confrontation can be measured by the extent to which demands for pay are violently policed, and by how the demand changes things for those who make it.

Methodology of a Bad Object

This essay is grounded in interviews with fifty-nine left-identified sex workers. For some, sexual labor was a radicalizing encounter with white supremacy, wealth inequality, state violence, and masculinities at turns violent and pitiable. Others came to sex work after they came to their politics, finding there a job where one might be free of bosses without having to become one, downwardly redistribute wealth, and refuse sex that takes more than it gives. Interviewees echoed Sonya Aragon's (2021: 111) invitation to think about "whore [as] an orientation. Not a sexual one; a political one." This essay considers unpaid hetero sex from the perspective of that orientation. In so doing, it engages two bad feminist objects: the critique of unpaid hetero sex alongside the "older feminisms" associated with its most explicit critique.

Negativity about free hetero sex is a "bad object" for sex workers who speak publicly. They know that spectators are eager for confirmation that sex workers have broken relationships to men and sex either because of the work or as an explanation for having done it. Q (2020) described conservative (and here included sex worker exclusionary radical feminist, or "SWERF") readers as always "waiting" for evidence. "I imagine hungry dogs watching you cut up a steak." Sex workers confront the threat that negativity about sex with clients, or even men as such, will be taken out of the context that police (also frequent agents of sexual violence) earn more negativity still—none of these critiques posed protection from a violent state as the solution. Sex worker sex positivity emerges as an attempt to intervene in these overdetermined debates (Swift 2021). But our conversations came at a moment in sex worker politics when sex worker thinkers are increasingly fatigued with trying to frame their stories to guard against anti–sex workers' appropriation.

I am running up against my own sense, as someone disciplined in feminist studies, that the language I am using here is "out of time" with the field. To talk about "men" as such and about hetero sex through the lens of negativity summons radical feminist anachronisms, ones that "'fail' to recognize sexual subjectivity" (Hemmings 2011: 49). They also trade in essentialism (Wiegman 2001: 359; Weeks 2015: 735) that gives way to trans exclusion and overestimates both solidarities among women (across race, class, and nation) and the homogeneity of male dominance. Left feminists have always had good reason to be wary of what Claudia Jones (1949: 13) called the "the rotten bourgeois notion about a 'battle of the sexes.'"

Workers in this archive—all leftists and most sharply critical of self-defined *radical* feminists—shared these concerns. And yet many did talk about masculinity (as such) as a problem, and one concentrated in the relations of unpaid hetero sex. Sex worker radicals articulate a critique of free sex with cis men, but one that is rigorously attentive both to questions of sexual subjectivity and to the inadequacy of gender as a coherent analytic. Most of the workers included in the archive are part of the working class and poor, Black and brown, disabled, and queer and gender nonconforming communities who have historically found little relief in solidarities among "women." They come knowing exactly how much harm sex workers have experienced at the hands of elite women "helpers" (Agustín 2007). Sex worker critiques of straight masculinity do not come from the usual place of assuming sisterhood on the other side.

While radical feminists have largely abandoned straightforward critiques of free sex with men in favor of paid sexual labor as *the* site of patriarchal domination, many of the sex workers in this archive pushed to keep some version of those critiques in our sights. In an invitation for a radical feminism that commits to its own politics, they frame unpaid heterosexuality as a site of exploitation and romance as a bad deal. Before we get there, I want to pause to recall the radical feminisms with which the thinkers in this archive find some common cause, and think about what it means that the critiques they advanced are now self-consciously "out of time" even for the political tradition that once claimed them.

Those Older Feminisms

Nineteen seventies radical feminists engaged paid sex first and foremost through its proximity to the unpaid hetero sex that sustains the nuclear family. For Ti-Grace Atkinson, "The suppression of women is synonymous with being forced into prostitution, but if that's the way it is, I say, let's not go for free, let's up the charge" (Fosburgh 1970). "Prostitutes are the only honest women, because they charge for their services, rather than submitting to a marriage contract which forces them to work for life without pay." Atkinson's invitation to "up the charge" is particular in making explicit the idea that paid sex might pose a challenge to its alternatives, but a critique of unpaid hetero sex and the mystifying affects that prop it up was standard among radical feminists of her time (see Jackson 1995: 113). Most famously, Shulamith Firestone took aim at romance as a tool for reinforcing the failing institution of heterosexual monogamy. It was "a cultural tool of male power to keep women from knowing their conditions" (1970: 131), and one that undermined solidarity through the "privatization" of women (133). That privatization was most pronounced in the marriage contract. Romantic love was the bait and free sex outside marriage a kind of training.

While Firestone is never able to articulate anything like solidarity with sex workers—this is one place in which her dialectical commitments break down and shared struggle disappears—her account makes clear that anything the reader finds troubling about prostitution is also true of unpaid hetero sex—sex that is not actually for free but to "gain other ends" (Firestone 1970:

126). Likewise, for Kate Millett (1970: 62), a true sexual revolution would destroy heterosexual monogamy, unremunerated exploitation as it was, together with prostitution. Neither had a place in the futures early radical feminists were dreaming up. During the same period, Wages for Housework feminists were plotting a parallel critique that explicitly named the housewife as performing a kind of unwaged prostitution (New York Wages for Housework 1976).

But sex work appears for self-defined radical feminist thinkers as an adjunct to the exploitation of the marriage contract rather than as a confrontation with it. This is strange given how central the *unpaid* work of hetero sex is to these critiques. "The conventions of romantic love are drenched in appeals to the 'natural . . . [they] evoke this aura of a little world immune from the vulgar cash-nexus of modern society,'" wrote Michèle Barrett and Mary McIntosh (1982: 27). But marriage is, at its core, "a form that conflates the sexual with the economic" (56). For Monique Wittig ([1982] 1992: 54), "unpaid work" is one of the chief stipulations of the marriage contract that structures heterosexual life, and unpaid sex—the "obligation of coitus"—is key to the job description.

If early radical feminists made a case for how "the ethic of service to men" (Jackson 1995: 23) was fundamental to the status quo, they under theorized the extent to which pay matters. What could be less romantic than the exchange of pre-negotiated sexual services for cold, hard cash? These critiques were unable to imagine paid sex as the sexual form that most obviously laid bare "the vulgar cash-nexus." Instead, sex work appears as support for radical feminists' racist fantasies about Black women's misplaced "envy" for white women's economic security (Firestone 1970: 112); a symbolic "warning" (Wittig [1982] 1992: 53) to non–sex working women; or exceptional evidence of male entitlement (Barrett and McIntosh 1982: 73). These thinkers are not able to ask, what becomes of the obligation Wittig names when we charge, screen, negotiate, and sometimes decline? Nor are they able to imagine that anxieties about sex work and (interpersonal and state) violence against sex workers might have something to do with the threat it poses to the bourgeois family form. Nonetheless, and without knowing it, they help lay the theoretical groundwork for that conclusion. As Firestone (1970: 113) herself writes, "The panic felt at any threat to love is a good clue to its political significance." How else to read whorephobia?

For all their missed opportunities at sex worker solidarity, early radical feminists are refreshing in their targeting romance and unpaid hetero sex for critique. This is remarkable especially because it feels so distant from contemporary radical feminist thinking. Today, what we can expect from dominant voices who place themselves in the tradition is a laser focus on paid sex as *the* evidence of patriarchy's harms. In her postmortem for 1960s and 1970s radical feminism, Alice Echols (2002: 108) writes that "as feminism found harbor inside the academy, theoretical moves too often became career moves"; theoretical risk taking "was the casualty." This does not map on to contemporary feminist thought writ large, where there is a rich archive of risky critiques of white supremacist, bourgeois sexual forms (see Rodríguez 2014; Horton-Stallings 2015; Willey 2016; TallBear 2018). But I do think it helps explain how a self-defined radical feminist tradition moved from trenchant critiques of romantic—that is, unpaid—heterosexual love and the family to ones that implicitly seek to shore them up.

If early radical feminists framed unpaid sex as a problem because it looked like prostitution, those who claim the title today mark prostitution as a problem because it does not look like free sex. This mirrors a conservative trend in radical feminist theorizing about the reproductive family more generally. If, per Sophie Lewis's (2019: 45) analysis of the surrogacy question, these feminists are "too busy, worrying about what surrogacy being pregnancy makes surrogacy, to think about what that very same realization makes pregnancy," the same is true of what anxieties about paid sex obscure about sex for free. All that separates the two, after all "is the possibility of a wage" (2019: 44). With Lewis, sex worker radicals find themselves looking backward to a feminism radical enough to dream up the abolition of both. Sex worker radicals look backward (but at a slant) because contemporary alternatives leave their questions unanswered. Today's vanguard in queer sexuality studies shares sex workers' critique of hetero sex but does not take aim at unpaidness as one of its primary faults. Where it posits nonnormative—but still routinely nonpaid—sex as *the* alternative, it falls short of answering sex worker radicals' desires to put questions of economy front and center. And where queer thought freely assigns radical potential to nonnormative sex, it departs from sex worker radicals' interest (one for which some find recognition in feminist anachronisms) in the ambivalences of sex that is within as much as it is against the systems that structure it.

If I am flirting here with a kind of "loss narrative" (Hemmings 2011) it is because I cannot find another explanation for how a tradition that once illuminated its harms came to so violently defend unpaid sex. It is true, as Kathi Weeks outlines in her meditation on Firestone's work, that "feminist theorists seem today more reticent to level their critical gaze at 'private' life and institutions like marriage and motherhood for fear that some will 'take it personally'" (Weeks 2015: 742). Those someones might be other feminists who bristle at the suggestion of false consciousness. They are as likely to be the moneyed, conservative power brokers with whom radical feminists increasingly find "easy agreement," not least around questions of family values (Bernstein 2018: 36). For robust critiques of unpaid hetero sex, then, one would have to turn to the very sex workers that radical feminists have long since disavowed any kind of kinship with. This might be because radical sex workers have less to lose in taking aim at "these shibboleths of bourgeois propriety" (Weeks 2015: 741).

Commodification as Confrontation

"Within heterosexuality, women really get a bad deal," said Jessie Sage (2020). She wondered if this sounded silly coming from a twice married mother of three, but joked that this was perhaps why she was qualified to say it. This bad deal is not something we can simply opt out of, she said, and it is not made better by having a partner who does more of the work. And so, "it makes a lot of sense to me to say, 'why not use sexuality to your own economic advantage?' You have more control in sex work than you do in monogamous heterosexual relationships." For Sage as for early radical feminist thinkers, this bad deal was epitomized in the marriage contract but also extended beyond to free hetero sex more broadly.

Where early radical feminists placed prostitution alongside unpaid romantic hetero sex, sex worker radicals articulate the distance between the two. Money brings freedom to maneuver, not least to leave homes (and couplings) that harm. It can also bring boundedness (see Bernstein 2007) and space to negotiate. Where romantic couplings tend to entrench raced and classed hierarchy for those who enter into it—most people make horizontal moves—sex worker radicals talk about the redistributive power of pay, directing cash to people and communities who are not supposed to have it. And, demands for pay reveal all the work we do for free.

Again and again, the thinkers in this archive name an alienated affinity with radical feminist critiques of unpaid feminized labor. Cybèle Lespérance (2020) describes a draw to early radical feminist theorizing, especially writing from lesbian feminists who argued that, having refused the performance attached to womanhood, they were "not women" at all. "I like that idea," she said, having found it in her search for "radical feminists that don't make me hate radical feminists." This search came from a desire for mutual understanding:

I want to see their point. I want to see what the tipping point is where I could maybe make them lean in my direction. I don't think we're collaborating with patriarchy more than other classes of women. Not less than married women, to start with. It's very similar to the relationship to capitalism. We live in that system right now, we're trying to at least make our way into it without crashing. And at some point we want to even live, maybe thrive! It's even more obvious with sex work being subversive—we're trying to change the usual rules by expliciting [*sic*] sex as a transaction.

Her critique offers something that readers so often found missing in early radical feminist writing on free sex—a set of clues about what it might look like to live (maybe thrive!) under systems as they are, but one that also offers the hope of changing the rules as we go. Crucially, Lespérance's is a frame that does not assume the theorist is herself capable of opting out of those systems through force of will. There is a deep humility, and solidaristic impulse, in her "we're trying." It is this combination of an incisive critique of free hetero sex and estrangement with the theoretical tradition that once named it most explicitly that makes sex worker radicalism such a rich place to turn.

In reappropriating rules in hopes of undermining them, sex worker radicals find kinship with other queer and feminist thinkers who play with the politics of confrontation. This is part of a world of tactics that include what José Muñoz (1999) calls "disidentification" and what Verónica Gago describes as "flight at the same moment as recognition," "contempt at the same time as counting" (Gago 2020: 35). Such confrontations are a way of doing politics for those who, unable to access what Sarah Sharma (2020: 121) calls the "patriarchal penchant and inclination towards exit," cannot afford to simply take their leave. When Nick Mitchell (Ben-Moshe et al. 2015: 271) invites us to "inhabit normativity in ways that are corrosive to it," I see sex worker radicals acting in the spirit of this call.

Sex worker critiques of free sex articulate a contempt/counting dialectic in a particularly sharp way. And sex work's uneasy proximity to sex that is unpaid but, as Marxist feminists have long insisted (see New York Wages for Housework [1975] 2018), nonetheless work, reveals questions here that are more submerged in other forms of labor: can paid sex be work and a refusal of work at the same time? Is sex work a space in which reproductive labor has been, per the demand, waged? If it is true that counting is, under capitalism, the best way to make work visible as *work* (Gallant 2019: 187), does it follow that visibility paves the way for refusal?

Maya Andrea Gonzalez and Cassandra Troyan (2016) answer this way: "When love and care are exploited under the conditions of erasure, to continue to labor is to continue to struggle." To do care is to do work; to charge is to make that visible. Later, they figure paid sex as a kind of "human strike," one that lays bare the work of heterosexuality. This kind of making visible does answer Wages for Housework feminists' calls to make gendered labor *count* (Nayar 2017: 10). "Only though a clear identification of sex work will women then have the power to refuse it," writes Morgane Merteuil (2015), situating this within the broader Wages for Housework tradition.

But sex workers have more theoretical work to do here, because Wages for Housework under-theorized the precise connection between counting and strike. It is a tradition that forgets that Black and brown women have long been paid for housework and in ways that reproduce rather than transform capitalist social relations (Davis 1983: 237). It is also a tradition that might suggest too tidy a connection between housewives and sex workers (see Federici 2012; Fortunati 1981), over-reading the extent to which these workers do social reproduction in similar ways (Kotiswaran 2011: 60). And so, sex worker radicals are drawn to the potential of charging-as-strike, but they also caution against celebratory readings (including those from other sex workers) that overestimate the transformative potential of charging.

The sex worker writer Irene Silt (2020: 18) brings us exactly here, recalling these lines from Wages for Housework's classic document: "More smiles? More money." She writes about the brief satisfaction that comes from the demand, but also the "solitude that we face on the other side of refusal." The demand is only a provocation. Its unanswered question, "How do we take our refusal so seriously that we do not return to business as usual—ever?" Sex worker radicals grapple with just this—how to escalate the provocation that is sex for pay, a form of refusal and also a service people with money get to buy.

These positions only sometimes represent two poles within the sex worker left. Deep ambivalence marks most of the analyses around this theme, and the same thinkers articulate counting's confrontational potential and the ways it can preserve the status quo. Lucia Rey (2020) talked about how, for some sex workers, charging is "like seeing the matrix," revealing all the ways that sex is transactional in civilian life. Just a few minutes later, they said, **"I** don't think there's anything inherently radical about sex work, and it goes back to sex work being work, but I think that sex work can oftentimes radicalize people." Rey situated the work alongside other service labors dominated by working-class women and queers of color like them—for some clients, paying for sex is like paying for dry cleaning. Taking men's money can feel empowering, "but there's no politics to that." My inclination as an ethnographer informed by queer and autonomist thought is to say that there are politics to everything. Some workers are not so sure. They are not sure, at least, that those politics are radical ones.

Many thinkers in this archive qualified statements about sex work's transformative potential with the caveat that this operates on an individual, rather than a structural level. Fatigued by empowerment narratives in sex work discourse, they wanted to be clear that the sense of power the work can confer is often brittle, and fleeting. At stake is whether counting is itself a confrontation with the status quo of hetero sex. When I asked Allie (2020) whether making men pay works this way, they responded, flatly, "It doesn't at all. [Clients] revel in their purchasing power." White, monied men like Allie's clients "have set up a society where they have the money. . . . All we have is our labor to sell." Sex worker radicals caution against a tendency to pretend this is not true.

Having only our labor to sell is the status quo for working-class and poor women and queers, especially (trans and cis) women of color and those struggling against colonial domination. In her critique of Wages for House-work, Angela Davis (1983: 337) reminds: if counting were radical on its own terms, it would not have such a long history of easy assimilation into the daily life of racial capitalism. Paid sex is also the norm, rather than the exception, in trans women's encounters with waged work and sexual life (Gabriel 2020). And the way the counting happens reinscribes capitalist logics in a particularly bald way; raced, cissexist, and classed differentials in pay, working conditions, and exposure to client and state violence unsettle any conclusion that counting will, on its own, bring us closer to justice.

And still, sex workers' critics and their clients (sometimes the same people) see a connection between the charge and the threat of refusal. Why else would individual men, together with state agents and concerned outsiders, react so hatefully? For Chanelle Gallant (2020), the answer is that sex work "forces the conversation about sex as a form of labor." This is why, when I asked Kiarra Thomas (2020) whether she thought charging was disruptive or just another way that men with money get to buy the services they want, she reminded that this is not true: "They get what I give them." Charging is "a power grab, because men all think that we should just be free to them." "Bad johns are like incels," she said, both share a sharp hatred for sex workers who grab power in this way. She confronted such hatred routinely. And still, "grabbing that power feels good."

In our conversations, cis, white sex worker leftists often articulated a similar sense that the charge is a power grab for them, but offered the caveat that this is only true for those with race privilege and for whom sex work's pay was not necessary to immediate survival. I asked Thomas, a Black trans woman who runs a safe house for other trans sex workers, about this, and she talked about how frustrating it was for "ivory tower girls, sitting up in the condos away from the real concerns that street-based sex workers have . . . to say that they have some sort of kinship with us, or understanding." They did not know her concerns, but they were not in a position to diminish her power grabs, either. Counterclaims about the impossibility of taking power through counting should be very careful not to assume that the capacity for grabbing power is limited to those who already have more of it. "Pleasure is a regulatory regime," writes Angela Jones (2020: 24), and one of unequal access, and yet people struggle against its hierarchies all the time. Sometimes the pleasure they find is sexual, and sometimes it comes from taking power, or money. Jones (38) argues that sex work prohibitions emerge precisely to control pleasure's insurgent potential.

Even when the work is shaped by violent hierarchy, and even when the pay is sorely needed, the question remains, if paid sex really does simply re-inscribe the status quo, why is it so violently policed? For Sybil Fury (2020), if it were true that sex work is "just another service that was provided, and if it did effectively reproduce the worker, then it should be fine. It should be, in fact, welcomed." It is not, nor has it reliably been in the history of global capitalism. Alongside individuals' anxiety about what it means to make sexual labor count, elites have long understood that sex work can be politically explosive (even when the people who do it are already marked as available for work and for sexual access). In the transition to capitalism, paid sex posed the threat of visible—and messy—interclass relations (Chitty 2020: 71), and in the colonial context it embodied "the perils of deracinating modernity . . . [creating] dissonant spaces of possibility, zones of instability where hierarchies were unsettled" (Macharia 2019: 99). The history of US anti–sex worker law is bound up in attempts to control sex work's capacity to destabilize racial apartheid and women's mobility (Pliley 2014; Lee 2021). Contemporary panics around sexual labor bear the traces of these histories, and the contemporary social relations of sex work carry this destabilizing promise.

Closer to home, the charge also threatens to do something to the couple form. L. H. Stallings (2015: 122) makes explicit the connection between "funk"—tethered in the public imagination to "sexual barter" in all sorts of ways—and trouble for the couple form. "What does funk do to love?" she asks. "The marriage industrial complex remains a sex industry regulated by sexual morals and work ethics that center monogamy, coupling, and heterosexuality as less illicit than other trade activities" (123). Here writing against the project to "save" marriage in Black communities, she takes on its own terms the fear that "funky love"—"undomesticated female sexuality"—is dangerous to the couple form (123). For Stallings, and for many sex worker radicals too, this is a good thing.

Counting as Refusal

The stakes shift when the question turns inward. The charge that feels potentially incendiary from the distance of history or abstraction can feel less so when it pays the bills in the here and now. And so even thinkers who theorize counting as a kind of political confrontation talk about how, in everyday life, charging can feel just like working a job, and paid hetero sex can feel like a variation on the rule rather than an inversion of it. For others (and, again, sometimes for the same people at different times) charging does make a difference, operating as a regular practice of refusing compulsory free sex and its gendered attachments. That refusal can shift subjectivity, making one queerer over time. Sex worker radicals grapple with the question of whether that counts as political.

"It's a nice idea, but I do not claim to be bringing down the pillars of Western society one marriage at a time," writes Celeste (2015:116). "Frankly, I don't think straight people need my help destroying the institution of marriage or the nuclear family." She echoes others quoted here who find in the charge a provocative kind of counting, but also refuses to take on the burdens of making a living and toppling the hetero family at the same time: "I don't trick as a tactic to start some kind of sexual/social revolt or to change my johns in any intentional way. I don't trick out of pity, desperation, or joy. At the end of the day, I trick for the alms. I do it for money and autonomy." Previously in my writing I have focused on the alms piece of sex work—the money—and the autonomy it confers. Like many thinkers in this archive, this came from a place of fatigue with civilians' inordinate interest in the sexual subjectivity of a community of working-class people who overwhelmingly trick for the alms. But the autonomy Celeste gestures to can bleed into sexual life. Whether or not sex work's counting gives way to structural transformation, it does often change how individual sex workers understand the labor of sex. Following Gago's (2020: 11) theorizing of the strike's capacity to serve both immediate ends and generate analytical perspectives that have a broader horizon, I do want to argue that there is a "politics to that" (Rey 2020).

After theorizing civilian reactivity to commodification, Zila (2020) talked about how seismically sex working shifted her own thinking about gendered labor. This is not the cliché—"the jaded, bitter sex worker who sees everybody as a walking wallet," she said. Instead, "I see power dynamics, I see exchange, I see transactions all the time." She said that sex work had queering potential even for cis, straight sex workers, joking, "Are there even any? I guess!" Sex working teaches how much gender is a performance we do for other people. Having learned this, Zila said, it is easier to choose when we do it, and for what returns. Sometimes, though, the reverse is also true: "Work follows me home," writes the poet Kay Kassirer (2019: 76),

> what I mean is
> most nights
> I don't know the difference between sex and acting

The distance between charging and more durable refusal can feel like a chasm. And still, for others or for the same people at different times, the work does help us learn the difference between sex and acting. Juliet (2020) framed sex working as a healing encounter with past selves that "couldn't say 'no' in the right way . . . couldn't defend ourselves. . . . In this job, I can really put my own limits." Charging makes the difference, and even when clients are callous or cruel, she thinks, "At least I'm gonna take their money." Against the anti–sex work narrative that such cruelty is unique to paid sexual labor, Juliet added, "Inside us [there is] that girl or woman that was suffering because a man was abusive. Probably that part of me feels like, 'Okay, now give me your money.'" This sense of taking power is, again, not limited to sex workers who have particularly great working conditions or who do not need the cash. Undocumented and a recent migrant, Juliet works by the hour at a massage parlor. It is possible to work at healing and hustle for rent at the same time.

It is to risk engaging a bad, appropriable object from the perspective of sex worker activism to acknowledge that the work can tap into trauma, or even deep rage. Mistress X (2020) talked about their work as a dominatrix as an avenue for doing something with that rage. "People like me"—Black women and gender-nonconforming femmes—are "always expected to settle for less, to deprive ourselves, to do without. That transitioned me into becoming a dom." Domming helped X heal their relationship to sex, one of many places in which others expected them to settle for less, and it changed how they navigated the rest of their life: "It informed my politics, it has made me increasingly radical and a lot less tolerant of other people's intolerance." X is also a scientist, and brought this shifted perspective to interactions in that job as well as in their dominatrix work. Refusing to repeat the party line that domming is about care, not the desire to harm, they added, "I used to try to sit and listen to people who would say something racist or homophobic, and I'd be like, oh, 'it's my job to change their mind.' And at this point, I'm like, 'no, it's my job to make you hurt and then maybe we'll figure it out." X's clients, mostly white men, are people "directly benefiting from the fact that [I] have less." It felt good to make them pay.

White women, socialized in a different way to politely accept too little, also talked about how the work "completely changed my relationship with sex" (Fury 2020). "I think that it's done this for most people that I know," Sybil Fury added. This is because sex work pushes you to confront trauma, "not because sex workers have more than anyone else, but because doing the work that we do forces you, at some point, to confront the sexual trauma that you inevitably have." The "inevitably" is doing a lot of work here. It gestures again to sex worker radicalism's uneasy affinity with radical feminists who theorized trauma as constitutive of living in a feminized body. Where the affinity breaks down is, again, at the moment where sex workers say that counting can be harm reduction under this system. Negotiating with clients, and sometimes telling them "no," has made it easier to negotiate with other partners in her unpaid sexual life, Fury said. Now, rather than watch the clock and wait for bad Tinder sex to be over, she tells people to leave. "That has made an enormous difference in my sense of self," she said.

Sex worker radicals talk about how charging can teach them to refuse sex that takes more than it gives, but also how it moves them to pursue the opposite. Many said that sex work made them queerer. "It's not that I want all my relationships to be sex work relationships," Q (2020) said. Getting paid to have sex with men, and to perform womanhood during sessions, helped Q refine their relationship to both. Over time, Q moved toward genderqueer identification and a preference for unpaid relationships with other women and genderqueer people. This was not because sex with clients or other men was particularly traumatic—Q talked about dynamics of friendship and care—sex working just helped reveal how much of this sex, whether or not it was paid, was labored. Others echoed this, though some articulated something closer to fatigued pity at confronting the deep, sometimes clumsy, need clients bring to what is for many the only space they allow themselves vulnerability. For Q, over time, "when I did start sleeping with a cis guy and I realized that I wasn't getting anything out of it, I just realized in my head, 'he should just be a client.'" And clients could reciprocate for sexual labor in material ways that made the exchange feel worthwhile. Q and their partner were expecting their first child when we spoke, and money from sex working would fund this queer family. Sex work can enable queerness in this more direct way, too.

Again and again, thinkers in this archive talked about how the charge helped them refine their own desires, and often in ways that led toward queerness. "Because I have so many interactions with cis men," Yaz (2020) said, "'if you want me, you're gonna have to pay.' If you're a woman, though, 'what's good?'" Again, this spoke to the asymmetrical tedium of straight sex rather than (as anti–sex worker feminist frames would suggest) exceptional trauma within it. "If I don't cum, it's like, 'well, I have 200 euros, so good for me.' It's not that big of a deal. . . . If I'm getting money for it. I don't mind doing the emotional labor." "Money makes me cum," say sex workers in earnest and in jest. Sometimes this is literal—the money itself has an erotic charge—and sometimes the money makes other pleasures possible (see Glover 2021; McClanahan and Settell 2021; Walters 2016). The charge's capacity here follows Jennifer Nash's (2012: 514) call for ways of thinking pleasure that is "experienced in a multiplicity of ways, including those that were not sexual." Charging can be pleasureful and so too can the things that follow it.

I asked Vanessa Carlisle (2020) about the phrase "money makes me cum," and she talked about it as a referendum on heterosexual relations. Under current conditions "getting paid makes sense. And it definitely revealed to me what parts of heteronorms I was willing to play out for free and which ones I wasn't. And it turns out I'm not interested in most of them, I'm not straight." When they do have sex with men for free, "I'm not interested in playing out hetero norms with them." Others echoed this—those who pursue unpaid sex with men come with a shifted sense of what those dynamics can or should look like. In taking the performance of hetero norms to their logical limit, sex working reveals their constructedness, and this opens up some options as much as it fatigues us of others. "It shows you the falsity of the fixed meaning, but also the beautiful possibility of a constructed reality," Lorelei Lee (2020) told me. That constructed reality is, for Lee, "essential to my understanding of my own gender and my understanding of my own queerness. Early on, I found huge value in artifice as a space for understanding, possibility . . . and the more I did sex work the less I had sex with men for free." Artifice, and together with it explicit exchange, can have its own pleasures.

Sex worker radicals' analyses of desire-as-process and play are somewhat "out of time" for sexuality studies, too, discordant with the field's preference for viewing sex through the "domesticating lenses of identity" (Dean 2015: 623). Visiting one kind of sexuality can refine wants for alternatives.

Sex working is "like being a tourist to heterosexuality," said Eloise M (2021), who echoed others in the sense that sex working made her less interested in free hetero sex over time. Now, she said, she had "fine" experiences with straight men clients and "then I go home, and I get to be an out dyke having great sex and living my life." "I'm so glad that this is my work and not the life that I live," she said. "I get to try it on, and remember that this is the life I fought so hard not to have. This sex is not what I want." This is not the political lesbianism of "those older feminists." But it is, to be sure, lesbianism that is political.

Conclusion

Yearning for a hard break with the status quo and at once hopeful and restrained about the possibility that charging might make that break come sooner, sex worker radicals refuse easy answers about the meaning of the charge. After talking about the radical difference sex working made in her "sense of self," Sybil Fury (2020) added, "in terms of fighting the patriarchy, this I'm less convinced of." This might be a place where sex work is just another service labor, and one that requires us to go to great lengths "to help our clients forget about the fact that they're paying us." The force of the confrontation is limited when the charge itself has to be so laboriously obscured. And it is not obvious that anything disruptive happens for clients when they pay. Then, we return to the question of prohibitions against paid sex, and to Fury's own words: if sex work did preserve the status quo, it would be welcomed rather than harshly punished. And still, sex worker radicals are not convinced that prohibitions against the work reflect its insurgent potential.

Sex workers' ambivalence here brings us back into uneasy affinity with "those older feminists." Thinking together—and at odds—these traditions grapple a shared set of questions: Does a change to one's "sense of self" do much to fight the patriarchy? How do the social and the state work together to preserve the status quo? If people in power hate what we are doing, is that evidence that we are doing the right thing? Sex worker radicals refuse to leave these questions in the past. Theorizing and also trying to survive (maybe even thrive!) in real time, they sap resources from the same system they hope to one day see crumble. Experimenting at the intersection of hopes for a radical otherwise and everyday labors that can feel very much stuck in the now, thinkers on the sex worker left are not so sure that that sapping—charging—will make that crumbling come sooner. But maybe, sometimes, it provokes.

References

Agustín, Laura María. 2007. *Sex at the Margins: Migration, Labour Markets, and the Rescue Industry.* London: Zed Books.

Allie. 2020. Interview by author. Video call.

Aragon, Sonya. 2021. "Whores at the End of the World." In *We Too: Essays on Sex Work and Survival,* edited by Natalie West and Tina Horn, 104–15. New York: The Feminist Press.

Barrett, Michèle, and Mary McIntosh. 1982. *The Anti-Social Family.* Brooklyn, NY: Verso.

Ben-Moshe, Liat, Che Gossett, Nick Mitchell, and Eric Stanley. 2015. "Critical Theory, Queer Resistance, and the Ends of Capture." In *Death and Other Penalties,* edited by Geoffrey Adelsberg, Lisa Guenther, and Scott Zeman, 266–96. New York: Fordham University Press.

Bernstein, Elizabeth. 2007. *Temporarily Yours: Intimacy, Authenticity, and the Commerce of Sex.* Chicago: University of Chicago Press.

Bernstein, Elizabeth. 2018. *Brokered Subjects: Sex, Trafficking, and The Politics of Freedom.* Chicago: The University of Chicago Press.

Carlisle, Vanessa. 2020. Interview by author. Video call.

Celeste, Angustina. 2015. "Prorate Confidant: Beyond Despoiled Innocence and Empowerment." *Rolling Thunder,* no. 12: 114–19.

Chitty, Christopher. 2020. *Sexual Hegemony: Statecraft, Sodomy, and Capital in The Rise of The World System.* Theory Q. Durham, NC: Duke University Press.

Davis, Angela. 1983. *Women, Race, and Class.* New York: Vintage Books.

Dean, Tim. 2015. "No Sex Please, We're American." *American Literary History* 27, no. 3: 614–24.

Echols, Alice. 2002. *Shaky Ground: The '60s and Its Aftershocks.* New York: Columbia University Press.

Federici, Silvia. 2012. *Revolution at Point Zero: Housework, Reproduction, and Feminist Struggle.* Oakland, CA: PM Press.

Firestone, Shulamith. 1970. *The Dialectic of Sex: The Case for Feminist Revolution.* New York: Farrar, Straus and Giroux.

Fortunati, Leopoldina. 1981. *The Arcane of Reproduction: Housework, Prostitution, Labor, and Capital.* Translated by Hilary Creek. Brooklyn, NY: Autonomedia.

Fosburgh, Lacey. 1970. "Women's Liberationist Hails the Prostitute." *New York Times,* May 29. https://www.nytimes.com/1970/05/29/archives/womens-liberationist-hails-the-prostitute.html.

Fury, Sybil. 2020. Interview by author. Video call.

Gabriel, Kay. 2020. "Gender as Accumulation Strategy." *Invert Journal,* no. 1. https://invert journal.org.uk/posts?view=articles&post=7106265#gender-as-accumulation-strategy.

Gago, Verónica. 2020. *Feminist International: How to Change Everything.* London: Verso.

Gallant, Chanelle. 2019. "Fuck You, Pay Me: The Pleasures of Sex Work." In *Pleasure Activism: The Politics of Feeling Good,* edited by Adrienne Maree Brown, 177–88. Chico, CA: AK Press.

Gallant, Chanelle. 2020. Interview by author. Video call.

Glover, Julian. 2021. "Customer Service Representatives: Sex Work among Black Transgender Women in Chicago's Ballroom Scene." *South Atlantic Quarterly* 120, no. 3: 553–71.

Gonzalez, Maya Andrea, and Cassandra Troyan. 2016. "Heart of a Heartless World." *Blindfield Journal.* https://blindfieldjournal.com/2016/05/26/3-of-a-heartless-world/ (accessed January 15, 2020).

Hemmings, Clare. 2011. *Why Stories Matter: The Political Grammar of Feminist Theory*. Durham, NC: Duke University Press.

Horton-Stallings, LaMonda. 2015. *Funk the Erotic: Transaesthetics and Black Sexual Cultures*. Urbana: University of Illinois Press.

Jackson, Stevi. 1995. "Women and Heterosexual Love." In *Romance Revisited*, edited by Lynne Pearce and Jackie Stacey, 49–62. New York: New York University Press.

Jones, Angela. 2020. *Camming: Money, Power, and Pleasure in the Sex Work Industry*. New York: New York University Press.

Jones, Claudia. 1949. "An End to the Neglect of the Problems of the Negro Woman!" *Political Affairs*, June.

Juliet. 2020. Interview by author. Video call.

Kassirer, Kay. 2019. "Work Follows Me Home." In *Whore's Manifesto: An Anthology of Writing and Artwork by Sex Workers*, edited by Kay Kassirer, 76. Portland, OR: Thorntree Press.

Kotiswaran, Prabha. 2011. *Dangerous Sex, Invisible Labor: Sex Work and the Law in India*. Princeton, NJ: Princeton University Press.

Lee, Lorelei. 2020. Interview by author. Video call.

Lee, Lorelei. 2021. "The Roots of 'Modern Day Slavery': The Page Act and the Mann Act." *Columbia Human Rights Law Review* 52, no. 3: 1119–1239.

Lespérance, Cybèle. 2020. Interview by author. Video call.

Lewis, Sophie. 2019. *Full Surrogacy Now: Feminism against Family*. London: Verso.

M, Eloise. 2021. Interview by author. Video call.

Macharia, Keguro. 2019. *Frottage: Frictions of Intimacy Across the Black Diaspora*. New York: New York University Press.

McClanahan, Annie, and Jon-David Settell. 2021. "Service Work, Sex Work, and the 'Prostitute Imaginary.'" *South Atlantic Quarterly* 120, no. 3: 493–514.

Merteuil, Morgane. 2015. "Sex Work against Work." *Viewpoint Magazine*, October. https://viewpointmag.com/2015/10/31/sex-work-against-work/.

Millett, Kate. 1970. *Sexual Politics*. New York: Columbia University Press.

Muñoz, José Esteban. 1999. *Disidentifications: Queers of Color and the Performance of Politics*. Minneapolis: University of Minnesota Press.

Nash, Jennifer. 2012. "Theorizing Pleasure: New Directions in Black Feminist Studies." *Feminist Studies* 38, no. 2: 507–15.

Nayar, Kavita Ilona. 2017. "Sweetening the Deal: Dating for Compensation in the Digital Age." *Journal of Gender Studies* 26, no. 3: 335–46.

New York Wages for Housework. 2018. "On Sexuality as Work." In *The New York Wages for Housework Committee 1972–1977: History, Theory and Documents*, edited by Silvia Federici and Arlen Austin, 88–94. New York: Autonomedia.

Pliley, Jessica. 2014. *Policing Sexuality: The Mann Act and the Making of the FBI*. Cambridge, MA: Harvard University Press.

Q. 2020. Interview by author. Video call.

Rey, Lucia. 2020. Interview by author. Video call.

Rodríguez, Juana María. 2014. *Sexual Futures, Queer Gestures, and Other Latina Longings*. New York: NYU Press.

Sage, Jessie. 2020. Interview by author. Video call.

Shane, Charlotte. 2020. Interview by author. Video call.

Sharma, Sarah. 2020. "Exit and the Extensions of Man." In *Come Closer: The Biennale Reader*, edited by Vít Havránek and Tereza Stejskalová, 119–32. London: Sternberg Press.

Silt, Irene. 2020. "The Tricking Hour." *Tripwire* 7.

Swift, Jayne. 2021. "Toxic Positivity? Rethinking Respectability, Revaluing Pleasure." *South Atlantic Quarterly* 120, no. 2: 591–608.

TallBear, Kim. 2018. "Making Love and Relations Beyond Settler Sex and Family." In *Making Kin Not Population*, edited by Adele Clarke and Donna Haraway, 145–66. Chicago: Prickly Paradigm.

Thomas, Kiarra. 2020. Interview by author. Video call.

Walters, Kimberly. 2016. "The Stickiness of Sex Work: Pleasure, Habit, and Intersubstantiality in South India." *Signs: Journal of Women in Culture and Society* 42, no. 1: 99–121.

Weeks, Kathi. 2015. "The Vanishing Dialectic: Shulamith Firestone and the Future of the Feminist 1970s." *South Atlantic Quarterly* 114, no. 4: 735–54.

Wiegman, Robyn. 2001. "Object Lessons: Men, Masculinity, and the Sign Women." *Signs: Journal of Women in Culture and Society* 26, no. 2: 355–88.

Willey, Angela. 2016. *Undoing Monogamy: The Politics of Science and The Possibilities of Biology*. Durham, NC: Duke University Press.

Wittig, Monique. (1982) 1992. *The Straight Mind and Other Essays*. Boston: Beacon Press.

X, Mistress. 2020. Interview by author. Video call.

Yaz. 2020. Interview by author. Video call.

Zila. 2020. Interview by author. Video call.

Leticia Alvarado

To Have and to Hoard:
Xandra Ibarra's Object Lessons

In the geometric graphic *Lumpy Lumpen* (2018), artist Xandra Ibarra offers a thoroughly opaque interpretation of language as a sign system to render laborers arrayed in proximity yet isolation (fig. 1). Part of an invited response to Michelle Handelman's video and performance *Hustlers and Empires* (2018), the graphic is paired with *It's a Thing* (2018), a narrative account of a staged hustle presented as a public dialogue between two characters—"White Thing with Power" (WTwP) and "Brown Thing" (BT)—through which we glimpse an artist's negotiation of institutional expectations for minoritized artists and the accompanying incitement to discourse bolstered by art institutions, their funders, and experts.[1] Legible as a one of the culture industry's adjudicators, WTwP activates the staged dialogue with the mimed swipe of a credit card between BT's "butt cheeks," introducing her as "another mediocre artist of color." Having purchased her time, WTwP keeps BT on their lap, their sticky stroking hands busy, as they endeavor to expose BT's interiority.

Instead of the sought-after exposure of vulnerability, BT is quick to render legible the hustle going down. Recognizing her "game" in not where

The South Atlantic Quarterly 122:3, July 2023
DOI 10.1215/00382876-10644015 © 2023 Duke University Press

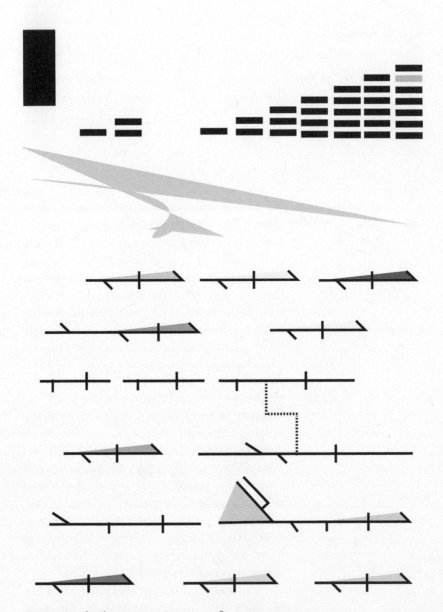

Figure 1. Xandra Ibarra, *Lumpy Lumpen*, 2018.

it should be for the artworld's rules of inclusion, she enumerates the understood expectation she be "an upstanding citizen making work about displacement, immigration, HIV/AIDS, police violence, war, prisons; [her] race, gender, sexuality, class and/or disability" and to do so in a "neat and digestible" fashion. More to the point she shares that she "recognize[s] game," telling her interviewer: "If we are going to hustle, let's hustle . . . If I am surplus, if I am out here because you're gonna check a box on your report. Then I wanna take this money, be dirty, offensive, obscene, wasteful, messy, delinquent, criminal. I wanna hustle YOU con estilo." BT both names the identitarian rubrics through which, as a "brown thing," she is in the service of routine nods to diversity as ultimately disposable surplus but also claims the hustle for herself, mobilizing negative affects as aesthetic directives. From lumpen to surplus, BT's articulation of her position as a racialized laborer renders dense the power dynamic on display in the exchange, and, one can speculate, the modes by which the artist, Xandra Ibarra, interfaces with art presenters and art audiences as she enfolds them—us—into the scene with the apostrophic declaration, "I wanna hustle YOU." This, too, is augmented by Ibarra's decision to render the exchange as one between clearly identified *things* (Brown *Thing* and White *Thing* with Power), identifying the players within the hustle as objects.

Across her body of work Ibarra gathers, hoards, and circulates objects thick with discursive and material resonance. She gathers objects of "spictacular" racial limitation—compulsory Latina femme performance as well as those of haunting unachievable whiteness—architecting them into a practice that explores, in her words, "abjection and joy and the borders between proper and improper racialized, gendered, and queer subjects."[2] Largely decorative and in deep relation to her body, across her archive wigs, heels, costume jewelry, and synthetic breasts are some of the few objects that draw our attention to the artist's use and engagement with the vibrancy of matter.[3] Oriented by the above work, this essay considers Ibarra's object play and the object lessons illuminated through it, considering both her practice of amassment and insistence on the things she gathers as in a relational matrix with individuals slotted into the liminal and mutable status of object. I am interested, as well, in the way this aesthetic strategy intervenes in scholarly conversations on nonhuman matter to also illuminate something of minoritarian relationality and the animation of negative affects toward oppositional orientation to the successes of incorporation as we consider "things" and the relations and affects activated when we ponder the routes through which art "things" circulate.

In an interview with Andy Campbell (2019) for *Artforum*, Ibarra elaborates on both "thing" status and the thingification process. "A thing," she tells us, "[describes] works, art and non, that are purposefully created or come to be used as market-friendly racial content. It's a well-funded, sanitized, feel-good, nonprofit-y product . . . Oftentimes this product functions as a form of social management because it's paired with 'community engagement.'" For Ibarra, then, "things" bear a specific relationship to the market, as do objects in her practice and that of others without thing-status though always under its threat, which requires we think with the legacies of racial capitalism and its ability to incorporate and instrumentalize difference, specifically within and through institutions that collect and display art. In *It's a Thing* (2018), Ibarra gives us the minoritarian artist, a brown thing, as resistive, a bad object within these circuits. BT is both an uneasy and willful token, too much in the know for proper performance of the role she is permitted and a too willing participant who has monetized artistic engagement with herself as an eroticized object of consumption for those that would paint her as victim. Considered in the context highlighted by BT and Ibarra herself requires, then, that we take into account the artist and the performing body as an important site to help us think through the complexities of these relationships in curation and circulation both in art spaces and, as we will see below, closely linked academic ones.

Performers whose work centers race as an exhibitionary optic have long played with and explored these dynamics, whether taking up the vulgarities of the auction block, the exhibition of indigenous peoples, or the display of the supposed sexual excess of Black and brown peoples often blurring the distinction, as art historian Jennifer Gonzalez (2008) has told us, between object and subject of display. Ibarra also entreats us to consider the circulation of women of color, materially and epistemologically, as a mode of exhausting affective extraction. In what follows, I dwell with Ibarra's object lessons to consider complex encounters with things and the possibilities posed by bad objects among them, especially in networks of negative affect wrought by duress within a hegemonic order where proper objects buttress white subjecthood. Ultimately, these object lessons further an understanding of hustlers and empires—that prompt with which Ibarra, and therein we, began above—within the specificity of art work, its many players and their relationship to projects of empire with their uneven distribution of goods.[4] I am, then, also thinking of collection, of amassment, of hoarding across different sites of and relations to power as organized in the realm of art under the influence of aesthetic epistemes. With the word "hoard" I seek, too, to entangle my analysis with the disabling medical gaze with which Ibarra tarries.

In her essay "Powers of the Hoard," Jane Bennett (2012: 247, 246) urges us to "consider the possibility that the person who hoards and the artist who creates share something of perceptual comportment, one unusually aware of or susceptible to the enchantment-powers of things" with their "exquisite sensitivity to the somatic effectivity of objects." In short, she argues artists as and like hoarders are particularly attuned to "thing power," the call from objects beyond "a figure of speech" and "a projection of voice," which, she underscores, we should take seriously for an amplified understanding of the affect of materiality and an enriched sense of how to coinhabit the world (240). Further, thinking with theorizations of hysteria as "the prototypical psychopathology of Victorian England," Bennett understands "hoarding [as] the madness appropriate to a political economy devoted to over-consumption, planned obsolescence, relentless extraction of natural resources [. . .] and vast mountains of disavowed waste" (248). If we follow this contention, what might hoarding mean for minoritarian subjects for whom certain object relations reify social positions of subjection within majoritarian orders, social positions within an unfriendly medical regime within which pathology is mobilized as excuse for population control?[5] Ibarra's work provides an answer that also draws our attention to the social/medical categories Bennett identifies as a perhaps particularly apt contemporary relation to our objects, adding minoritarian relation to our object status. In other words, while "hoarding" enjoys wide quotidian use to signal hyperbolic accumulation, thinking with Ibarra I am distinctly conscientious of the discursive force of the medical category, particularly as it adheres to women of color.[6]

Grappling with a broader medical regime and its imbrication with other social structures, Ibarra's work entreats us to follow the lead of disability studies scholars who elaborate a social model of disability (as opposed to a pathologizing medical model) to understand the kinds of diagnoses that attach an act (hoarding) to an identity (hoarder) creating, as La Marr Jurelle Bruce (2021) argues, "a set of social exclusions, obstructions, and derogations imposed on persons who diverge from a dominant, 'abled' norm" (13). Activating this model, for example, Scott Herring (2014: 17, 7) maintains that *there is no natural relation to our objects* and approaches "hoarding as a unique moral panic over material goods, or an object panic whereby forms of social deviance attach not only to interpersonal behaviors but also to material ones." This then frames my own understanding of the ways Ibarra hoards as a minoritarian aesthetic gesture from a social position of deviance, to navigate the management of both minoritized communities and objects of and in relation to these communities. While mindful and methodical, in other words, Ibarra's gathering of objects is filtered through her racialized position in a social web of relations that dictates the chain of signification that itself accumulates to render irrelevant the distinction between hoarding and collection for certain subjects even, as I argue, Ibarra wields the first to comment on the second mode of amassment.[7] To be clear, I am not claiming she lives under the medical discursive, and therefore material, sign. Nor is it my intent to think metaphorically about disability. Rather I grapple with its presence as a social force in the aesthetic interplay of Ibarra's work through this rubric as part of the material she circulates.

There is, too, the "madness" that envelops the "hoard." These proximal pathological designations are readily attached to women, queers, and femmes of color—hordes, or even, those who have whored, as Ibarra's take on art world hustlers leads us to imagine. I turn to recent work in mad studies to understand this dynamic, first taking cues from what Anna Mollow (2013) calls "mad feminism," that entreats us to center "subject positions at the margins of madness: of those people who might not bear any psychiatric diagnosis label but are nonetheless regarded by the dominant culture as crazy [including] people of color seen as emotionally erratic," among others. Similarly and more specifically, Therí Pickens (2019: 4, 13) entreats us to bear in mind the intertwined nature of race and ability through which we might understand "raced and gendered madness at the seam of the Enlightenment project" and its formulation of the human, which so heavily informs cultures of reception and exhibition, bearing in mind Bruce's (2021) reminder that medicalized madness is a "politicized process, epistemological operation, and sociohistorical construction" that require ethical critical engagement (7).[8] To this madness, Larry La Fountain-Stokes (2021) adds the adjacent category *locura*. In his work on translocas, in which he parses out the relationship between the literal meaning of *loca*—madwoman—and its queer invocation, La Fountain-Stokes (2021: 20) explains that *loca* "suggest a form of hysterical identity, pathologized at the clinical level, scandalous at the popular one, constitutive of the individual lacking sanity, composure, or ascription to dominant norms: effeminate homosexuals, madwomen, rebels for any cause"—a category forged in and through social structures that readily attach to Ibarra. As we will see, Ibarra places her object play in relation to the medicalized emergency of affective excess read as madness or *locura* that happens in tandem with a designation of less-than-human against the propriety of white womanhood. Invoking the aesthetic enactment of hoarding, Ibarra's amassing of objects of gendered and racial signification and their exhibition seeds a sense of malady, of *locura* at the juncture of medical and arts ideologies, that forces a reflection on circulation of "woman of color" as object.

The Thing Is . . .

Moved by a trash heap comprised of organic and nonorganic debris (a work glove, matted pollen, a dead rat, a bottle cap, and a stick), Bennett (2012: 239) is propelled by the transformation of "sullen objects" into "expressive 'actants.'" The resulting book, *Vibrant Matter: A Political Ecology of Things*, has become representative intervention of new materialism, a scholarly grouping born of feminist debates about postmodern neglect of the biological, the real, and material in favor of the linguistic and discursive, signaling a majoritarian scholarly interest in nonhuman matter.[9] Minoritarian theorists whom I follow in my work, however, have long hewn together theory and matter. From the women of color feminist theorizing of theory in flesh to queer of color critique's engagement with Marxism to understand normativity's capitalist requirements of nonnormativity, these bodies of scholarship have long, as Sarah Ahmed (2008) argues, explored the "sedimentation" of the discursive in the material.[10] Further, Native and Indigenous studies scholars alongside critical race scholars have shown us Indigenous and First Nations peoples have long nourished ontologies and epistemologies of relation with the nonhuman world.[11]

In her essay on the limits of new materialist philosophy, Kyla W. Thompkins (2016) argues that new materialism, and especially a strand known as Object Oriented Ontology in particular (OOO), sees their work as a corrective to identity-driven projects and their narratives of representation. Instead, OOO, "seeks to theorize object life in its most radically non-relational forms [. . .] beyond," Tompkins tells us "representational systems such as language [. . . coming] into legibility only as form." Important, then, that from a deeply relational vantage, Ibarra will direct us, below, to think specifically about the form of her work, the form of the exhibition of her work, and forms of circulation even while leveraging her own critiques of representational politics. New materialism's majoritarian interest in matter, which I engage here in a disidentificatory capacity, joins in my writing minoritarian epistemologies from women of color feminist and queer of color scholarship and that which emerges from Ibarra's oeuvre when thinking the social life of objects and the sociality of lives lived in conscious relation, even as Ibarra's work leads us, too, to reflect on the limitations of liberatory epistemologies and related accompanying calls for social justice that emerge from these same bodies of scholarship. With Ibarra, I turn now to the objects to which she directs our attention, the social work these perform, their transformation in collection—in adjacent vibrancy—channeled in exhibition and distribution as commodities.

Doing Things with Things

In conversation with scholar art critic Dorothy Santos on her prints made with menstrual blood, Xandra Ibarra shares, "I am a hoarder of weird things so I just stored them. After a year or so I began to see them as Rorschach inkblots and as an opportunity for staging a performance where I could 'read' or pathologize the general public" (Leon, 284). In a recent visit of her storage spaces, when I asked how she made decisions about what items to keep and which to discard, Ibarra repeatedly shared that she simply couldn't get rid of some things (bags of fishnet stockings, G-strings, and gloves, a mound of stripper shoes, synthetic monster hands and masks among them). She had spent too much time making a costume, or had invested too much labor finding the object, or, simply, that she loved looking at them. "It would be real hard for me to throw these things away," she explained, "that's just crazy" (pers. comm., September 3, 2021).

In her description of object accumulation it is clear that, for Ibarra, her objects present an opportunity to enter in, create, and share social relations forged in and reflecting societal constructs of race, gender, and ability. She is also aware and purposeful with strategies for circulation as leveraging relations within the form of art commodity. Famously, Karl Marx's concept of commodity fetishism diagnoses the obfuscation of social relations as an object becomes a commodity. Labor power is abstracted and alienated in capitalism's elevation of the commodity to its exchange value, in its transformation to magical fetish (Chin, 2016: 24). But as Elizabeth Chin alerts us in her *My Life with Things: The Consumer Diaries*, Marx's conceptualization of the fetish relied on racist misreading of African fetishes and pivoted on insult via simile "stating directly that those who bought commodities were as primitive and backward as Africans" for his condemnation of capitalism to resonate (27).[12] In other words, the term also captures problematic race ideologies informing Marx's diagnoses of relations to capital and within capitalism, particularly as we think about the life of commodities, even while we can acknowledge the utility of the concept for identifying the trauma inherent to capitalism. I note this, as central to my thinking with Ibarra's object

Figure 2. Xandra Ibarra, installation view of *Inventory of Exhaustion*, 2016.

play is the relationship between her material accumulation and the racial specters that haunt the introduction of what she methodically gathers and distributes via circuits of exchange in exhibition spaces and markets.

Carefully attuned to her oeuvre and its objects and prepared with exhibition in mind, Ibarra's *Inventory of Exhaustion* (2016) indexes exhaustion with racializing tropes, with being read through them, with reverse discourse's effort to complicate their signification in performance—overall with cultural production's unanticipated interpretation within the successes of inclusion (fig. 2). The work consists of "vacuum-sealed costumes" photographed to capture the sheen of the clear plastic rectangular encasing holding them, each a "Spic Skin" of performance labeled by the artist: "Cucaracha," "Mambo," "Tortillera," "Cortez," and "Virgin" (figs. 3 and 4). Carefully preserved, their collection as much on display as Ibarra's performance history, these are the "sloughed off material and shed skin," of the performance persona Ibarra assumed and then performatively "killed-off" (Wilkinson, 2019). In this amassing work, I recognize wardrobe selections from various La Chica Boom "spictacle" performances including the masturbating Guadalupe of *Vigensota Jota*, the recently censored Tapatio ejaculating *Tortillera*, and the Hernán Cortez of *Skull Fucking* alongside those featured in another photography series, *Spic in Ecdysis*, including: *Molting Showgirl* with her ruffles

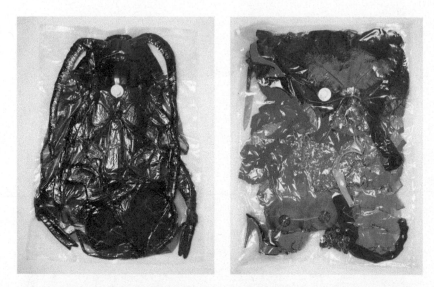

Figure 3. Xandra Ibarra, (a) *Spic Skin (Cucaracha)*; (b) *Spic Skin (Mambo)*, from *Inventory of Exhaustion* (2016).

Figure 4. (a) Xandra Ibarra, (a) *Spic Skin (Tortillera)*; (b) *Spic Skin (Cortez)*; (c) *Spic Skin (Virgin)*, from *Inventory of Exhaustion* (2016).

and feathers on sun-burned grass, *Carcass* with its complementary red and green against a border scene of sand and sun, and the shimmering cucarachica roach carcass floating next to Ibarra's black-pastied recumbent body in *Molting in Pool* (Ibarra, 2015: 354–56).

Printed with archival pigment, architected in proxy museum tactics, in *Inventory of Exhaustion* Ibarra thoroughly mediates our exchange knowing, as Susan Stewart (1992: 161) argues that it is "the museum . . . which must

serve as the central metaphor for collection." She shares only the documentation of the stylized objects, the photographs—objects themselves—that carry
not only the aura of the artist but also that of the objects Ibarra still hoards,
the stuff she can't part with, with which she would be "crazy" to part, in her
own account of material engagement. What Ibarra is looking to circulate in
this work, however, is not the vibrancy of direct object encounter, the liveness
of the exchange, but instead, lingering on relations of exchange, deploys accumulated affect as medium. Sarah Ahmed (2014: 45) has theorized "emotions
work as a form of capital" and that cumulative affect is "produced as an effect
of its circulation . . . distributed across a social as well as psychic field." She
offers further, "Affect does not reside in an object or sign, but is an effect of
the circulation between objects and signs. . . . Signs increase in affective value
as an effect of the movement between signs: the more signs circulate, the
more affective they become" (45). While Ahmed's claim that affect does not
reside in an object may seem at odds with what I am working through here, I
read her as underscoring the relational rubric of exchange to operationalize
affect, with that circulation occurring across realms—social and psychic—in
a broadening of the economic. Following Ahmed, Ibarra's photographs allow
her to present the combined affective force of previously circulated performance skins, their histories, and her exhaustion, all the while creating
another object to accumulate affect in relation to the mechanisms of control
the work puts on display: archiving and exhibition.

A project about managing exhaustion, the photograph also proactively
documents Ibarra's career transition filtered through her feelings of being
hustled, of "the affective dimensions of being fatigued, fucked raw, emptied
of matter, never reaching completion"(Wilkinson, 2019)—that status of full
subjecthood denied to minoritized individuals. Attending to, hoarding, her
performance objects (her matter) privately, Ibarra lingers in frustration,
mining what Christina León (2017: 372) has described as stuckness to reorient her practice—a stuckness that through opacity embraces an impasse
"wherein the future is uncertain but the mere persistence of aesthetics
implies the potential for dwelling in that very impasse." Ibarra moved from
performance via her avatar, La Chica Boom, to largely sculptural, film, and
video work, after what she describes as failure to anticipate audience
responses to her "explicit, abject, and humorous forms of Mexicanidad (spictacles)"—a misrecognition that occurred "not just in performance but in
[her] life in dealing with institutions, people, the state" (Wilkinson, 2019).
Ibarra reorients to center on reflection of the consumption of her work, of a
process she says renders her surplus. If, as Ahmed (2014: 45) summarizes,
for Marx the circulation—"the movement of commodities and money in the

formula (M-C-M: money to commodity to money)"—is what creates surplus value, the circulation and accumulation of abject racialized excess, its affect, is what Ibarra is managing, what she is carefully negotiating as she recognizes *herself* as surplus in the capitalist scene of biopolitical control that is the gallery, museum, and exhibition hall. Highlighting affective management through the institutional mechanism of the museum Ibarra evinces negotiation of the ideological space of both art circulation and the circulation of ideas of proper Latinidad in curation of type, in the use of taxonomy, that has led to Ibarra's misrecognition and censorship.[13]

In contrast to the exhibition of objects thick with sticky Mexicanity her spictacles exhausted, what of those objects that repel instead of adhere, whose proximity hurls the artist into violent spasms confoundingly triggered by mad laughter? Thinking very explicitly about scenes of exchange she enters when displaying her work, in describing her performance (fig. 5) *Nude Laughing*, Ibarra notes her art-historically minded response to John Currin's painting *Laughing Nude* (1998) to "[examine] the vexed relation racialized subjects have to not only one's own skin, but also one's own entanglements and knots (skeins) with whiteness and white womanhood."[14] She responds to this vexed relationship, inclusive of the whiteness of the medium, of the form of Currin's work and its sites of exhibition, with performance alongside a series of objects in relation.

In *Nude Laughing* Ibarra meets her audience dragging a trailing translucent sack behind her. Ibarra is nude, wearing an amplifying breastplate. As she walks, down hallways, around the white cube of the gallery, up stairways, she teeters on yellow heels. She emits sultry, nervous, bubbly, loud, desperate laughs that resonate with discomforting vibration. Moving close to audience members, the performance taunts engagement. Her performance of this work at Brown University on November 14, 2016, climaxed in an empty studio arrived at after ascending several narrow flights of stairs. After circling the perimeter, Ibarra crawled into the flaccid sheath that had trailed behind her, full of what she tells us are "paradigmatic 'white lady accouterments'" (fig. 6).[15] Her shoes had fallen off her feet as she struggled, arching, kneeling, to negotiate her proximity to objects that don't/won't adhere to her brown body, laughing still after moments of writhing. As she came out of the cocoon, long dark tresses matted to her face from the sweat of exertion, its contents spilled. Silent, she left the room, having pushed herself, struggling for breath, to the limits of her capacity. The objects she had gathered remain on the floor with us, her audience.

If *Inventory of Exhaustion* reflected an invocation to circulate as object, as a brown thing, in performance resplendent in racial signifiers, *Nude*

Figure 5. Live performance documentation of *Nude Laughing*, by John Tain at The Broad Museum, 2016.

Laughing serves as a response to other white things with power. We might think of Ibarra's hoarding in her translucent sack and her laughter as designating, after Larry La Fountain-Stokes (2021), a *loca*'s response specifically to the violence of white womanhood across its organic and nonorganic sites, its different capacities for accumulation of wealth and worth (La Fountain-Stokes 2021). Ibarra's might be, as Bennet surmises of hoarding in the contemporary moment, the "appropriate madness"—accompanied by different modes of haunted and haunting laughter—to the perpetual violence of white womanhood on different registers as well as those racial logics that suffuse relations of exchange: Ibarra's relationship to the gathered objects, her practice of gathering them and their signification, presenting this signification in social exchange simultaneous to its delivery as commodity in

Figure 6. Xandra Ibarra, *White Lady Accoutrements* (2016).

Figure 7. Xandra Ibarra, installation view of *Ashes of Women of Color Texts* (2020).

the museum, gallery, academy—all art market vectors. After this scene of exchange, of course, Ibarra returns to where her performance ended, to gather her objects to continue to hold them not only, and not necessarily principally, for future performances, but because she would be "crazy" to discard them. Burdened by hegemonic signification of gendered ideals that cannot adhere to Ibarra's brown body, in sharing her hoarding she shares her tarrying with white ghosts—the hysteric position it creates—but also creates the scene for revelation of these relations as well as those of shared ambivalent experience to matter and the racialized hierarchy in which it exists.

Things Fall Apart; or, To Have and to Hold, Till Death Do Us Part . . .

From exhaustion in extractive performance and the madness of limited object relations, Ibarra turns to actants that have been influential to her as an activist, educator, and artist, in her recent *Ashes of Five Feminist of Color Texts* Ibarra fulfills a long-desired urge to burn books that have, in the artist's lexicon described above, been made into "a thing," into "market friendly racial content" (fig. 7). She does this to "reconsider," she tells us, "the larger conditions around their circulation" noting the way "these frames inform and undergird supposedly inclusive sections of the art-market and museum

Figure 8. Xandra Ibarra, *This Bridge, Aflame* (2020), from *Ashes of Women of Color Texts* installation (2020).

world, as well as the way liberal nonprofit funding structures function" (Campbell, 2019). In planning this work, Ibarra identifies insidious effects of evaluative institutions (museums, universities, nonprofits) that create exchange value for artwork but also liberatory utopic epistemologies like those represented by feminists of color specifically at the site of increased symbolic deployment, the university, as the project served as capstone to her second advanced degree.

For *Ashes of Five Feminist of Color Texts* Ibarra uses citation frequency to determine the texts to accumulate in her premeditated act of bibliocide. The ultimate selection included "Mapping the Margins: Intersectionality, Identity Politics and Violence against Women of Color," by Kimberlé Crenshaw (1994); *Black Feminist Thought,* by Patricia Hill Collins (1990); *This Bridge Called My Back,* edited by Cherrie Moraga and Gloria Anzaldúa (1983); *Sister Outsider: Essays and Speeches,* by Audre Lorde (1984); and *Borderlands/La Frontera: The New Mestiza,* by Gloria Anzaldúa (1987). Ibarra then burns these works and gathers their ashes into book jackets (fig. 8). The jackets she has made are not slick glossy marketing tools but rather matte-black textured casket/urns recalling communal library editions (fig. 9). These are displayed open flat with their corresponding Dewey decimal call numbers stamped on their spine indicating alternate spatial logics as well as

Figure 9. Xandra Ibarra, detail of *Ashes of Women of Color Texts* (2020).

their continued lives in public collection. In yet another way to think of ways to have and hold these materials, Ibarra erects these as in a mausoleum, so in keeping with gallery hanging conventions if not for the crassness of the red funerary carpet and *rasquache* artificial flowers in brass vases aside the entombed ashes (fig. 10).

Ibarra trains her attention on the object form that holds feminist epistemologies, bringing her into material relation with them as "things," art market commodities, even while she puts on display her own disenchantment, her own exhaustion and depression with art markets and the cooptation of the ideas in texts that she "deeply respects" and "reveres" but with which she has become "frustrated" in the face of their simplification and depoliticization (Campbell 2019). Transposing a work about the institutional life of the concept of intersectionality and Black feminism more broadly, Ibarra tells us, "Jennifer Nash's *Black Feminism Reimagined: After Intersectionality*, helped me realize how these writings came to be flattened in my intellectual and political life. Sure, we can expose well-meaning students to these authors, but doing so often means simplifying and depoliticizing their work. In other words, women of color feminisms are made into 'a thing,' even though they were never intended to be that and have meant so much to me beyond that condition" (Campbell 2019). Nash's (2019) book, indeed,

Figure 10. Xandra Ibarra, installation detail of *Ashes of Women of Color Texts* (2020).

reflects on the incorporation of Black feminism into the academy and its circulation as a privileged symbol of reform within women's studies departments that nonetheless continue practices that harm black women, going on to say "the field retains little interest in the materiality of black women's bodies, the complexity of black women's experiences, or the heterogeneity of black women's intellectual and creative production" (3–4). This tendency, Nash argues, has produced what she describes as "defensiveness" in response to the crass popularization of intersectionality, a position in which Black women labor to recover the true and proper meaning and origins of the concept as entwined with Black feminism and "intimacy with black women" ultimately curtailing epistemological possibility (136–37). I am struck by Nash's description of the affective consequences of defensiveness. "I understand defensiveness," she explains, "to be a space marked by feelings of ownership and territoriality, and by loss and grief. The book, then, theorizes defensiveness as the feeling that emerges when intersectionality is thought to be a lost object or, worse, a stolen object" (32).

Thinking with epistemological proximity and, indeed, entanglement (as a work like *This Bridge Called My Back* evidences), Ibarra tarries with women of color feminisms as epistemological objects, but also with the object form these can take for circulation. It is her engagement with the latter that results in a different though related affective possibility than the one outlined by Nash, even if they share a "holding on." Ibarra's engagement with these texts as objects provides a site to perform her own affective irresolution and to invite the same from viewers likely to be shocked by book burning, an act that might initially be read as echoing conservative censorship of the kind to which Ibarra has been subjected. She offers, then, object lessons on transformation of these epistemologies for the art market, for purchase and display, and of herself as a continued bad object for Latina representation. As these texts become enshrined as commodities, they also mark the transformation from what we have, to what we hold in mourning. There is no effort to recover here, to restore, or return. There are only the ashes that are the result of her own confrontation. The burning of such cherished texts, of both genuine political visioning and of hollow diversity and inclusion projects delivers an unavoidable caution about self-congratulatory efforts to increase the prevalence of minoritized artists and epistemologies in majoritarian institutions and its consequences.

My turn to Ibarra's object lessons responds to important art advocacy-focused demands for representation and inclusion. Often the call for a shift in numbers is treated as the only kind of work that can make a change, overlooking what the aesthetic gesture of the objects interjected into spaces of exhibition can offer us. In her most recent book, Arlene Dávila (2020: 2), for example, identifies Latinx art as a "productive category . . . revealing of how matters of class, race, and nationality are operationalized in contemporary art worlds." Her focus on "structural change" toward "an equitable presence in communities, in collections, in museums, and in the world" (21, 175) is productively thought alongside the way minoritized artists are themselves navigating what Dávila calls "the entire ecosystem of museums, critics, collectors . . . involved in the process of evaluation" even while Dávila declares that "on their own representations themselves," the work that hangs in art spaces, "can do little to challenge racism" and further, that "art alone is not going to save us" (21). While I agree with Dávila about racism as structurally instituted, I want to direct our attention to the work of objects, which we know from the above also includes the work of "brown things" like Ibarra. Minoritized artists are often intimately aware of the potential for their work to be transformed into, as Ibarra might say, "a thing" in the process of commodity fetishism, but her object play within relations of exchange thickens our understanding of the fraught and important work of art presentation. As so elegantly captured by Jennifer Ponce de León (2021: 4), aesthetic gestures and the force of ideology they impart, powerfully structure our worldview, and can be "produced, reproduced, and transformed" at these sites.

As described by Jodi Melamed (2015: 78), following Ruth Wilson Gilmore, racial capitalism functions as "a technology of antirelationality (a technology for reducing collective life to the relations that sustain neoliberal democratic capitalism)." Ibarra shows us how this technology structures exhibition spaces. She also, however, offers us a counter technology, an object lesson that instigates and queries relational exchange building by hoarding, by holding on, as minoritarian disruption that dwells with the reality of exhaustion, depression, and *locura* as response to being made "a thing," a craziness that echoes what Jose Esteban Muñoz (2020: 23) saw in the contributors of *This Bridge Called My Back* who showed "that this craziness was a powerful way of being in the world, a mode of being that those in power needed to call crazy because it challenged the very tenets of their existence," themselves now made into things, held in mourning.

Notes

Written with gratitude for the generosity displayed by her editors and for support from The Andy Warhol Foundation Arts Writers Grant.

1   Handelman was exhibited in *Limited Edition*. Per the Museum's website, "An Open Space partnership with CounterPulse, The Lab, ODC Theater, Performance at SFMOMA, and Z Space, *Limited Edition* explores questions of legacy and lineage through performances, discussions, and gatherings at various locations throughout the city from January to March 2018, with commissioned texts appearing regularly here." https://openspace.sfmoma.org/series/limited_edition/. To view Ibarra's response, visit https://openspace.sfmoma.org/2018/04/its-a-thing/.

2   See Ibarra's website: https://www.xandraibarra.com/about/.

3   I mean, here, to invoke the famous title of Jane Bennet's book (2010) that takes up and inaugurates for many a renewed interest in nonhuman matter.

4   As might be evident to the reader, I am not engaged here, in a study of psychoanalytic object relations. Though not what I am after here, Chin 2016 carefully elaborates the value of this model for understanding the socialization of the individual as the ideal consuming capitalist subject and indeed of the individual as organizing episteme for capitalism. Instead, like for Gordon Hall (2013), my use of "object lessons" refers to "a methodology in which we might understand our lived experiences of sculptural [and performance] works as capable of teaching us conceptual frameworks through which to recognize new or different genders in one another and in ourselves," and for me, how we experience and deploy racialized gender as object.

5   On this history see, for example, Briggs 2003 and Stern 2017.

6   Hoarding is included in the DSM-5 as a compulsive spectrum disorder and distinguished from collecting by the American Psychiatric Association. See American Psychiatric Association (2021).

7   In her *On Longing: Narratives of the Miniature, the Gigantic, the Souvenir, the Collection*, Susan Stewart (1993) differentiates between collection and accumulation, noting objects in the latter are "without seriality, without relation to one another or to a context of acquisition" (153). She notes additionally that "accumulation is obviously not connected to the culture and the economy in the same way that the collection proper is connected to such structures" (156). These definitions help us understand how Ibarra exploits, as a minoritized artist, her ability to complicate the distinction particularly to place into focus the cultural and economic structures into which she herself enters as collected object.

8   I elaborate on the perseverance of this Enlightenment tradition in my book *Abject Performances* (Alvarado 2018).

9   See Alaimo and Hekman 2008 for what they describe and seek to foment in their edited collection as the "material turn" in feminist theory against the "linguistic turn. For a rebuttal of feminist materialism see Ahmed 2008.

10 See Anzaldúa and Moraga 1981, Ferguson 2003, Muñoz 1999 to start.

11 See Tompkins 2016, Tallbear 2017: 97; Harvey 2017: 490; and Gomez-Barris 2018.

12 Chin (2016: 26) explains, "Similarly, race is at the very foundation of the notion of the fetish. The word 'fetish' comes from the Portuguese and was used to describe the mistake animist Africans supposedly made in believing that tree stumps and the like were in habited by spirits. In fact, it was Portuguese who were confused when they witnessed African religions rituals. While animists might well believe that a particular rock or tree or whatever has a spirit residing in it, it is the spirit that is important, not the object that houses it; once the spirit leaves, the object is worthless. The veneration of the object is most certainly not the point of animism. So, from the very start, the history of the idea of the fetish is one of confusion and poor translations."

13 For more on the well-covered 2020 censorship of Ibarra's contribution to the exhibit *XicanaX: New Visions*, see Durón 2020; Lefebvre 2020; *Hyperallergic* 2020; and *Artforum* 2020)

14 See Ibarra's website: https://www.xandraibarra.com/nude-laughing/.

15 See Ibarra's website: https://www.xandraibarra.com/nude-laughing/.

References

Ahmed, Sarah. 2008. "Open Forum Imaginary Prohibitions: Some Preliminary Remarks on the Founding Gestures of the 'New Materialism." *European Journal of Women's Studies* 15, no. 1: 23–39.

Ahmed, Sarah. 2014. *Cultural Politics of Emotion*. London: Routledge.

Alaimo, Stacy, and Susan Hekman. 2008. Introduction: Emerging Models of Materiality in Feminist Theory. In *Material Feminisms*, edited by Stacy Alaimo and Susan Hekman, 1–19. Bloomington: Indiana University Press.

Alvarado, Leticia. 2018. *Abject Performances: Aesthetic Strategies in Latino Cultural Production*. Durham, NC: Duke University Press.

American Psychiatric Association. 2021. "Expert Q&A: Hoarding Disorder." December 2. https://www.psychiatry.org/patients-families/hoarding-disorder

Artforum 2020. "City of San Antonio Pulls Xandra Ibarra Work from Exhibition Over Its 'Obscene' Content." February. https://www.artforum.com/news/city-of-san-antonio-pulls-xandra-ibarra-work-from-exhibition-over-its-obscene-content-82253

Bennet, Jane. 2010. *Vibrant Matter: A Political Ecology of Things.* Durham, NC: Duke University Press.

Bennet, Jane. 2012. "Powers of the Hoard: Further Notes on Material Agency." In *Animal, Vegetable, Mineral: Ethics and Objects,* edited by Jeffrey Jerome Cohen, 237–69. Washington, DC: Oliphaunt Books.

Alvarado, Leticia. 2018. *Abject Performances: Aesthetic Strategies in Latino Cultural Production.* Durham, NC: Duke University Press.

Briggs, Laura. 2003. *Reproducing Empire: Race, Sex, Science, and U.S. Imperialism in Puerto Rico.* Oakland: University of California Press.

Bruce, La Marr Jurelle. 2021. *How to Go Mad without Losing Your Mind: Madness and Black Radical Creativity.* Durham, NC: Duke University Press.

Campbell, Andy. 2019. "Xandra Ibarra: Xandra Ibarra on Sidelines, Bibliocide, and Her Life/Work Lexicon." *Artforum.* https://www.artforum.com/interviews/xandra-ibarra-80626

Chin, Elizabeth. 2016. *My Life with Things: The Consumer Diaries.* Durham, NC: Duke University Press.

Dávila, Arlene. 2020. *Latinx Art: Artists, Markets, and Politics.* Durham, NC: Duke University Press.

Durón, Maximilíano. 2020. "San Antonio City Attorney Removed Video Work by Queer Chicana Artist, Calling It 'Obscene.'" *ARTnews,* February 21. https://www.artnews.com/art-news/news/xandra-ibarra-work-removed-san-antonio-1202678675/

Ferguson, Roderick A. 2003. *Aberrations in Black: Toward a Queer of Color Critique.* Minneapolis: University of Minnesota Press.

Gomez-Barris, Macarena. 2018. *Beyond the Pink Tide: Art and Political Undercurrents in the Americas.* Oakland: University of California Press.

Gonzalez, Jennifer. 2008. *Subject to Display: Reframing Race in Contemporary Installation Art.* Cambridge, MA: The MIT Press.

Hall, Gordon. 2013. "Object Lessons: Thinking Gender Variance through Minimalist Sculpture." *Art Journal* 72, no. 4: 47–56.

Harvey, Graham. 2017. "If Not All Stones Are Alive . . . : Radical Relationality in Animism Studies." *Journal for the Study of Religion, Nature and Culture* 11, no. 4: 481–97.

Herring, Scott. 2014. *The Hoarders: Material Deviance in Modern American Culture.* Chicago: The University of Chicago Press.

Hyperallergic. 2020. "Censored Video by Xandra Ibarra Might Go Back on View." February 26. https://hyperallergic.com/544827/censored-video-by-xandra-ibarra-might-go-back-on-view/

Ibarra, Xandra. 2015. "Ecdysis: The Molting of a Cucarachica." *Women and Performance: A Journal of Feminist Theory* 25, no. 3: 354–56.

Ibarra, Xandra. 2018. "It's a Thing." Open Space, *Limited Edition.* April 19. https://openspace.sfmoma.org/2018/04/its-a-thing/

Lefebvre, Sam. 2020. "Texas City Censors Oakland Artist Xandra Ibarra's 'Obscene' Feminist Video." KQED Arts. February 25. https://www.kqed.org/arts/13875472/texas-city-censors-oakland-artist-xandra-ibarras-obscene-feminist-video

León, Christina A. 2017. "Forms of Opacity: Roaches, Blood, and Being Stuck in Xandra Ibarra's Corpus." *ASAP/Journal* 2, no. 2: 369–94.

Melamed, Jodi. 2015. "Racial Capitalism." *Critical Ethnic Studies,* 1, no. 1: 76–85.

Mollow, Anna. 2013. "Mad Feminism." *Social Text Periscope.* https://socialtextjournal.org /periscope_article/mad-feminism/

Muñoz, José Esteban. 2020. *The Sense of Brown.* Durham, NC: Duke University Press.

Nash, Jennifer. 2019. *Black Feminism Reimagined: After Intersectionality.* Durham, NC: Duke University Press.

Ponce de León, Jennifer. 2021. *Another Aesthetic Is Possible: Arts of Rebellion in the Fourth World War.* Durham, NC: Duke University Press.

Stern, Alexandra Minna. 2017. "Sterilization." In *Keywords for Latina/o Studies,* edited by Deborah R. Vargas, Nancy Raquel Mirabal, and Lawrence La Fountain-Stokes, 217–20. New York: New York University Press.

Stewart, Susan. 1992. *On Longing: Narratives of the Miniature, the Gigantic, the Souvenir, and the Collection.* Durham, NC: Duke University Press.

TallBear, Kim. 2017. "Beyond the Life/Not-Life Binary: A Feminist-Indigenous Reading of Cryopreservation, Interspecies Thinking, and the New Materialisms." In *Cryptopolitics: Frozen Life in a Melting World,* edited by Joanna Radiin and Emma Kowal, 179–202. Cambridge, MA: The MIT Press.

Tompkins, Kyla Wazana. 2016. "On the Limits and Promise of New Materialist Philosophy." *Lateral: Journal of the Cultural Studies Association* 5, no. 1. https://csalateral.org /issue/5-1/forum-alt-humanities-new-materialist-philosophy-tompkins/

Wilkinson, Alexis. 2019. "Xandra Ibarra: Endurance and Excess." *Art Papers.* https://www.art papers.org/xandra-ibarra-endurance-and-excess/

Emily Owens

Doing Laundry with the TERF

"So, what's a lesbian?" I asked.

The question, asked in my course on lesbian studies, reiterates the provocation with which Mairead Sullivan opens *Lesbian Death* (2022) and signals a dense set of cultural, political, and theoretical debates that have swirled around the category "lesbian" at least since 1970. The tension that immediately gripped the room was familiar because "lesbian" has been a problem for as long as she has shared a bed with "feminist." And while this tension may express the location of lesbian as a sister, outside, it is also a nod to dramas of identity, political purity, and definitional policing *within* lesbian feminist cultures and to the central presence of the lesbian in feminism's various "wars."

The classroom brainstorm gained steam when one student spelled out "T-E-R-F," for "transexclusionary radical feminist," as a term that could affiliate with "lesbian." The announcement of TERF crystallized their discussion to that point, which had, as Sullivan might have predicted, suggested that "lesbian" "no longer carries political weight . . . [is] too readily aligned with gender essentialism . . . [and has been] superseded by queer, now trans" (Sullivan 2022: 1). Together my students proceeded to compile a definition of

The South Atlantic Quarterly 122:3, July 2023
DOI 10.1215/00382876-10644029 © 2023 Duke University Press

TERF from their immersion in the zeitgeist of young(er) feminist culture: they had learned the term online, on YouTube, in movement spaces or in the dining hall. Though they couldn't quite specify the ideological contours of TERFness, or point to any particular scholar and/or feminist and/or lesbian as a TERF, they could pinpoint her as a *figure* for whom they reserved some bad feelings, and they knew her when they saw her (or, they went looking for her among their classmates, and especially among their teachers, administrators, and parents). She was easier to describe visually and by association— she was white and old(er), and maybe she wore a pussy hat—and she could easily attach to other bad feminisms: she was probably a white feminist, a liberal feminist, a carceral feminist, which is to say, she was out of step with the cutting edge of today's feminist politics. The main thing about her, students agreed, is that "she" isn't down for transpeople. Which is also to say, TERFs, in their telling, are *bad*.

I begin in the classroom because generation is an inescapable frame of what scholars have variously coined as the "continually reiterated conflict," "*the* debate," and "the familiar and field-forming complaint" (Awkward-Rich 2017; Garber 2001, my emphasis; Wiegman 2011) that arrives alongside the term "lesbian." Generational difference is not, in fact, the decisive quality of definitional conflict around the category lesbian, but I am interested in how useful generation can seem to be as an explanatory device. It would be a familiar gesture, as I will explore in this essay, for me to emphasize my surprise, horror, or disbelief at my students' easy association of lesbians and trans-exclusion; it would be quaint to situate myself as an old lesbian among young queers. But what interests me in this essay is less the presumed difference between myself and my students, and more how paying attention to that always available difference makes other kinds of problems, questions, curiosities, and rhetorical habits around both TERF and lesbian more difficult to see. Thus the generational conflict through which I am staging this inquiry highlights the frame of the extant discourse as, itself, the object of study at issue here, rather than the taken-for-granted baseline of this investigation of the term lesbian.

That my students connected lesbian to TERF is not incidental, but neither is it obvious. Their connection pointed to an affective intensity around TERF that far exceeds what Finn Mackay defines as "a label put onto *anyone* who voices transphobic views, standpoints against trans inclusion in any spaces, but particularly women-only spaces" (2021: 10, emphasis in original). Mackay notes the capaciousness of the label TERF, which is flexible enough to describe "anyone" who espouses anti-trans viewpoints, including people who are not feminists. What interests me here is the affective intensity that

TERF accrues *within* feminist spaces and more to the point, the habits through which feminists *resist* association with the label. In this essay, I excavate ways that TERF circulates among academic feminists in text as well as among feminists in the academy, as in the space of my classroom. That my students did not simply attach "trans-exclusion" to "feminist" but intuited the connection of both to "lesbian," and did so after a long period of tense silence, presents a dense tangle of bad objects (or bad feelings attached to feminist objects) that I take as a point of entry.

The shape of this tangle of bad objects—TERF, feminist, and lesbian—is thus the subject of this essay. I want to understand TERF as bigger than a single person, or even a group of people; as I will discuss below, the term TERF has yet to become a name of self-identification, but rather is a term of *other*-identification, a mode through which some feminists name, describe, and, importantly, disavow, others (who may or may not be feminists). Where "*a* TERF" may offer a way of naming a specific and/or paradigmatic feminist theorist, I am in general inclined to situate such a feminist by her name and work, not because I am interested in rescuing particular feminist ideas or scholars from the netherworld of disavowal but because this essay concerns itself with the life of the *category* TERF: I take TERF as the object of study rather than as an object that simply exists.

I will therefore use the term in this essay usually to signal the tangle of meanings associated with a figure *and* to signal a "debate" that I am arguing is not really a debate. When I write "TERF walks into the room," I am signaling the moment when a person names the presence of an ideology and/or person and/or caricature. These moments, like the one I experienced with my students, tend to be vague, dismissive, and/or distancing—rarely do they site trans-exclusion with specific reference to texts or events, and they may also flag temporal or geographic distance between the TERF and the now (perhaps noting that trans-exclusion is a problem of British feminists, not US feminists, or a problem of feminists in the past, not the present). Such invocations stand in contrast to the parsing of the material impact of specific feminist ideas exemplified in Cameron Awkward-Rich's careful analysis of Janice Raymond's *Transsexual Empire*, which he notes provided the academic justification for "decades-long legal exclusion of trans health care from public insurance" (2017: 827) or Finn Mackay's (2021) careful and multidimensional historicization of debates that gripped the Michigan Womyn's Music Festival and led to the establishment of Camp Trans in the early 1990s.

It is not the arrival of an anti-trans feminist that interests me so much as the ways that the spectral figure of the TERF gets invited into conversation, when, and by whom. My hunch is that the moment I experienced with my students will be familiar to readers immersed in the vernacular habits of what Jen Jack Geiseking broadly construes as "lesbian-queer spaces" (Geiseking 2020: xvi), at conferences, in women's and gender studies departments, or with our familiars over a drink after a member of our community adopts new pronouns. These moments accumulate into discursive routines that present as *anti*-anti-trans, but (and) primarily function to preserve a sense of the threatened status of lesbians. My inquiry proceeds from the experientially rooted, if optimistic, presumption that we *do* live among one another, and we belong to and with one another, through a set of partially shared ephemeral cultural referents, even as long-term political solidarities and theoretical convergences remain fleeting, intractable, or, to use Tey Meadow's affectively precise description, "disappointing" (Cohen 2005; Herring and Wallace 2021; Schulman 2022; Meadow 2022).

In the following pages I explore what happens when TERF walks into the room. I am interested in how lesbians make the invitation and in how they (we) also announce the disavowal that purports to show TERF the door. I argue that this discursive cycle—that is, doing laundry with the TERF—has a cleansing effect, in which the invitation is disavowal's condition of possibility, which in turn makes space for the recuperation of the speaker. The incessant return to TERF as a central drama of lesbian and/or feminist studies is a clue to its function: If the loud disavowals seem to banish the TERF herself, this cycle nonetheless sustains the relevance of trans-exclusion as a discourse within (lesbian) feminism. I argue that TERF (searching her out, monitoring her presence, and distancing ourselves from her) is doing purifying work *for* lesbians and lesbian feminisms, while seeming to do work for trans survival (which it is not doing).

In the first section, I probe the association of TERF with lesbian, asking how we (or, my students) know that TERFs are lesbians, or that lesbians are TERFs. In these stories, TERF arrives as bad *prima facie*, and the heat in the stories ignites when TERF makes contact with the other categories, lesbian and feminist. This section is primarily concerned with the slippage between TERF, lesbian, and feminist. In the second section, I explore the ways that feminists interact with and respond to those TERF stories. I rehearse a few modes of response to TERF stories, each of which differently distances the speaker from TERF. In the final section, I consider the work these modes of disavowal do, and for whom. The "TERF wars" are staged, I want to suggest, as a debate between lesbians (feminists) and transpeople (queers), or lesbian studies (women's studies) and trans studies (gender studies). But, I argue, these rhetorical habits actually index a set of debates between and among lesbians, and the work that they do is recuperative *of lesbians, for lesbians.*

TERF Stories

My students' association of "lesbian" and "TERF" relied on what Cameron Awkward-Rich calls "the often-told story about the persistent conflict between trans and lesbian feminist theory, activism, and communities" (Awkward-Rich 2017: 819). This story—often mis-framed as debate, which I will return to in the final section—takes a number of adjacent forms. But really, it is a few stories that hover around lesbian, queer, and trans communities, cultures, and theoretical formations that form a prismatic bad object that glints differently, depending on the light.

As Finn Mackay explains, the term TERF is a fairly recent innovation, hailing from an Australian-based feminist blog in 2008. Mackay writes that "feminist activist Viv Smythe is widely credited with having first coined the term" as a way to distinguish the comments of some blog posters from others. Smythe invented TERF to differentiate commentary that she understood as trans-exclusionary from commentary that she understood to be otherwise, all under the aegis of a group self-described as "radical feminists." Thus the label "TERF" operated, in Mackay's telling, as a mode of "discerning . . . because not all Radical Feminists agree on trans inclusion or exclusion" (2021: 10).

Smythe's "TERF" thus fashioned a sector within radical feminism, constituting trans-inclusion and trans-exclusion as camps, distinguishing them from one another, and maintaining the presence and credibility of trans-exclusion within the overall project of radical feminism. As Mackay explains, "If all Radical Feminist theories were exclusively anti-trans and all Radical Feminist activism anti-trans-inclusion, then there would have been no need for any specific term to distinguish activists who supported trans inclusion from those who did not" (2021: 47). The visual scope of the blog illustrates the original work of the concept: by marking some comments as "TERF" but not denying such commenters the ability to post, Smythe's innovation essentially staged a debate within a group of feminists, making some hyper-visible, but nonetheless allowing and even inviting those comments.

The recent coinage of "TERF" belatedly encapsulated a set of cultural and institutional flashpoints of 1970s and 1980s feminist history. A series of conflicts at the Michigan Womyn's Music Festival are perhaps the most well-known, and serve as a metonym for contests around inclusion, authenticity, and identity staged on "women's land." Mackay historicizes these conflicts and concludes that Michigan became "shorthand for feminist trans-exclusion" because of "a long-running, though loose, largely undefined, and . . . unacted trans-exclusionary womyn-only policy" that exploded into public debate after the expulsion of festival-goer Nancy Burkholder in 1991 (2021: 76, 72). The series of protests and debates at and around Michigan pockmarked the 1990s but also points to a longer history of conflict around the premise of "women's land." Keridwen Luis suggests that "women's lands . . . sprang from the passionate experimentalism of feminism, lesbian feminism, and women of color(s) feminism" and that "one of the best-known conflicts among women's-space enthusiasts is over the admittance of trans women" (Luis 2018: 3, 186). Thus the series of conflicts at Michigan, significant in their own right, also serve to symbolize, in feminist storytelling, a fraught history of subtle and explicit surveillance borne of spatial projects that in practice have been "utopian for some . . . dystopian for others" (2018: 21).

The settings of the TERF story extend beyond cultural spaces like Michigan and Olivia Records, because the institutional spaces of Women's Lib—including conferences and nascent women's studies programs—also sited some notorious instances of trans-exclusion. Mackay's institutional history cites Robin Morgan's vitriolic comments about Beth Elliot at the 1973 West Coast Lesbian Conference, where Morgan referenced Elliot as "an infiltrator . . . as a man in drag, a transvestite, a male-bodied transsexual and a man . . . not a sister" (2021: 48). Morgan's commentary was aimed at a transwoman and spoke the language of cultural feminism, whose hallmark gender essentialism provided the foundation for Morgan's suspicion of transgender authenticity. But the gender essentialism that underwrote Morgan's premise provided the foundation for wide-ranging policing of everything from gender expression to sexual practice and that also, Mackay continues, "singled out butch lesbians" (2021: 55) as dupes of internalized misogyny and that took on its fullest published expression in Janice Raymond's *The Transsexual Empire* and Mary Daly's *Gyn/Ecology*, which, Awkward-Rich points out, "repeated and extended Raymond's anti-trans talking points" (Awkward-Rich 2022).

Even as the full-throated gender essentialism of self-identified political lesbians like Morgan falls within the vernacular category of "out of date, politically incorrect and prissy feminism which will not be mourned when it dies out" (Mackay 2021: 46), its underwriting logic has not, in fact, died out. As Cameron Awkward-Rich writes of Sheila Jeffreys's 2014 *Gender Hurts*, Jeffreys is "flooded with bad feelings" about transmasculine people, "is horrified by what the patriarchy dupes us into doing to our bodies" and understands "the FTM as the product of mismanaged pain of the lesbian" (Awkward-Rich 2017: 831). If the intensity of Jeffreys's critique makes her somewhat of an outlier among contemporary feminists, the logic of her claim nonetheless resonates with the old and enduring histories of lesbians and/in feminism, including those that Jack Halberstam named the "Butch/FTM border wars" in which "some lesbians seem to see FTMs as traitors to a women's movement who cross over and become the enemy" (Halberstam 1998: 287).

There are also stories that do not explicitly implicate TERF, but that nonetheless facilitate the association of TERF with lesbian. The first of these is the story of the lesbian-queer divide, wherein lesbian studies is understood to have an antagonistic relationship to queer studies/theory. This is the story around which Linda Garber organizes her dissent in *Identity Poetics*, in which her central concern is "The debate between lesbian feminism and queer theory "which she argues is a red herring that cements "the marginalization of working class/lesbians of color" (Garber 2001: 5). Garber describes the terms of the debate thus: "Queer theory labels lesbian feminism essentialist (an academic code word for unsophisticated if not stupid)" (1). Robyn Wiegman charts the same debate in slightly different terms, wherein her "postmodern" vs. "identity" are cognates for Garber's "queer theory" vs. "essentialist," and in which Wiegman describes "lesbian scholars . . . [who are] tired of the lesbian's subordination to the sexy thrills of queer theory" (Wiegman 2011: 204). If Garber laments the ways that lesbian has been imagined as overly attached to identity, Wiegman laments lesbian studies' preoccupation with refuting that claim.

This debate also shows up in narratives about time, in which lesbians and lesbian feminism may not be explicitly named, but are coded into language about feminism, feminist theory, and a bygone era of women's studies, because, Clare Hemmings argues, "'radical feminism' and 'lesbian feminism' often come to stand in for one another in Western feminist progress narratives" (Hemmings 2011: 53). Suzanna Danuta Walters's concern that "feminism . . . is *no longer* the young upstart" exemplifies this narrative, which focuses "on the displacements of radical and lesbian feminism by a queer theory that often posits itself as the antidote to a 'retrograde' feminist theorizing" (Walters 1996: 832, my emphasis). Other accounts celebrate the contributions of feminist theory but nonetheless situate those contributions as previous (if not fully past), as in Treva Ellison, Kai M. Green, Matt Richardson, and C. Riley Snorton's homage to Black feminism as "perhaps [the] most important" entry point for Black trans studies (Ellison et al. 2017: 165).

The homage form does not foreclose the present tense of Black (lesbian) feminist theory, but is nonetheless available for the interpretation that Black feminism's most important contributions have already happened (Nash 2016, 2019), and in which feminist studies is imagined to have preceded queer and trans studies, if not to have also been eclipsed by the same. For those who articulate what Robyn Wiegman calls the "field-forming complaint" of lesbian studies, that situatedness in the past—even when celebratory—represents the endangerment of an ongoing, present, or future lesbian studies project.

TERF does not appear in the lesbian studies/queer theory debate—or, as Garber argues, the debate "which is not one"—but is adjacent to it; this discourse underwrites and fortifies an association of lesbian and TERF (Garber 2001: 1). Such narratives tell time, and they also rely heavily on slippages, including parallel loose associations of "feminist" with "lesbian," and "queer" with "trans." Mairead Sullivan's critique of this narrative (including their critique of its many lamentations) makes this explicit, where they ventriloquize this narrative as "lesbian has been superseded by queer, now trans" (Sullivan 2022: 1). By the same token, Ellison et al. chart that "what is *new* about Black queer studies . . . is 'trans'" (163, my emphasis). In this frame, trans (studies) becomes imagined as the new-new vanguard, which leaves the always already "anachronistic" (Hemmings 2011: 8) lesbian even further behind. If the lesbian-as-precursor-to-queer narrative triggers anxiety about the loss of the lesbian, then that fits unflatteringly beside—but beside nonetheless—the project of cultural feminists who understood trans-ing gender as a threat to feminist political power and thus women's and/or lesbian existence.

By the same token, while TERF has no articulated relation to the label "white feminism" that Jennifer Nash and Samantha Pinto assess, their description of white feminism's capaciousness is suggestive. Nash and Pinto explain that "the 'white' in the term 'white feminism' is amorphous—referring at once to forms of disavowed feminisms, including neoliberal feminism, carceral feminism, governance feminism, nonintersectional feminism, and essentialist feminism" (Nash and Pinto 2021: 887). It is meaningful that the most iconic TERFs—Raymond, Jeffreys, the presumably "old and grey . . . women" of Michigan (Mackay 2021: 77)—are white women, "in a moment when," Nash and Pinto continue, the disavowed form "white feminism" and "white women [are] always collapsed into each other" (2021: 888). More to the point, the visual imaginary that my students signaled when they described a TERF as probably adorning a pussyhat conflated what they understood as an ideology of trans-exclusion with the symbol par excellence of "white women's tears" in the wake of the 2016 election. Nash and Pinto explain that "white women's political action in the wake of Trump's election"—especially in the form of the Women's Marches that inaugurated the style of the pussy hat—is imagined as "a quintessential form of 'white lady tears'" in which "crying over Trump hides that white women effectively elected Trump" (891). The easy slippage of whiteness and TERF, or the presumed whiteness of the TERF, jives with narratives that understand Black feminism as a corrective (Nash 2019), while also forgetting instances of Black feminist trans-exclusion (Awkward-Rich 2022).

Finally, their age matters. The actual age of imagined "white feminists" as a conglomerate icon, and the age—as in *era*—to which they and their politics are imagined to belong, that is, the second wave, reinforce what Mackay denotes as "ageist anti-feminist stereotypes" (Mackay 2021: 46). "White feminist" as a caricature belongs to the same era that Clare Hemmings describes as "'the past'" in feminist storytelling, which "most often refers to the 1970s" (Hemmings 2011: 5). Both white feminist and TERF "index a set of problems imagined to have already been solved by feminisms" (Nash and Pinto 2021: 893), and so their presence can be represented as both out of time and unwelcome. If TERF and white feminism are not intentionally aligned, their close iconographic companionship works to shore up the extent to which, Mackay writes, "Second Wave has become a dirty word" (46).

A variety of stories tether TERF to lesbian. My students' association of TERF in an exercise about the category of the lesbian, then, is not incidental but rather expressed a series of feminist stories that make that association. The association of TERF and lesbian relies on specific instances of lesbian feminists making anti-trans claims, but also rests on a set of collapsed images of feminism—anti-trans, white, second wave, radical, lesbian, and cultural—all of which meet at the level of their unwelcome status in contemporary feminism.

TERF Walks into the Room (and Is Quickly Asked to Leave)

Within no serious feminist intellectual circle is Janice Raymond's *Transsexual Empire* a subject of debate, and the vitriolic anti-trans rhetoric of groups like the Women's Liberation Front (WoLF) finds them aligned with political conservatives like Governor Greg Abbott and Senator Ted Cruz of Texas and thus beyond the pale of most academic feminisms. No credible feminist position exists that would deny the reality of trans experiences or intentionally inhibit the ability of transpeople to live, to bear rights, to access medical care, and to grow up; the TERF "wars," within academic feminism, it would seem, are over. This consensus stands in profound contrast to both the political reality of existential threat for transpeople and what might be called trans-indifference within much of feminist scholarship.

Yet the presence of TERF, as illustrated above, haunts conversations that are very much alive within what I will call academic feminist *life*, in the conversations we have with our colleagues, as animating questions in conferences and in our classrooms. The TERF dialogue—by which I mean not the production and refutation of anti-trans rhetoric by feminists, but the discussion of the possibility of anti-trans presence within feminism—continues. The key is that the stories I discuss are not simply in circulation, but they are, again, "*often* told." Why are we talking about TERFs if we claim that they have been left behind to the dustbin of feminist history? And how do those conversations sound? In other words, why does TERF keep walking into the room? My contention is that she is actually a (quietly) invited guest, whose invitation is the necessary precondition of her ostentatious dismissal.

Responses to TERF stories take on a few forms. One mode of disavowal is *a story about time* that situates anti-trans rhetoric among feminists as a problem of the past that has already been solved, so that continuing to associate lesbians and/or feminists with TERFs can be construed as inaccurate. A version of this dismissal suggests simply that gender essentialism is a relic of the feminist past, as charted by Hemmings (2011). But subtle forms of this type of rescue are more intriguing: for example, Linda Garber draws attention to the ways that "early lesbian-feminist writers . . . were actively engaged in a version of the essentialism/constructionism debate itself" (Garber 2001: 17). Garber's story puts pressure on narratives that imagine lesbian feminism as past by revealing lesbian feminism of the 1970s as immersed in conversations that otherwise tend to be situated in later periods. Garber's thesis performs a kind of rescue, not by suggesting that contemporary lesbians have a theory of gender that is compatible with queer and/or trans theories of gender, but by performing what Jennifer Nash might call an "originalist" claim on the "essentialist/constructionism debate" (Nash 2019: 13; Garber 2001: 17).

Another time-oriented TERF disavowal suggests that contemporary communities think about gender in ways that are expansive, inclusive, and importantly that find *compatibility* between trans and lesbian lifeways and ways of knowing, thus situating the very question of gender essentialism as over. Jack Jen Geiseking's study of queer geographies in early 2000s New York City mobilizes the categories "lesbian-queer" and "lesbian and tgnc," wherein the hyphen and "and" lift up the *shared* nature of cultural idioms, intimate ties, and spaces of people under the sign of these categories (Geiseking 2020: xvi). Geiseking's argument for temporary-ness of lesbian-queer gathering spaces also lends itself to an emphasis on a present-day culture that permits a mobile relationship to identity categories. Matt Richardson similarly emphasizes "wonderfully creative" modes of belonging in queer of color communities in which "flexibility [of identification] allows for trans people to gather multiple communities around them" (Richardson 2013: 372). These articulations suture today's lesbian, queer, and queer of color communities—those of my own generation—as uninhibited by gender conflict.

Minimizing the history of trans-exclusion in lesbian and/or feminist communities by highlighting historical or otherwise empirical inaccuracies in TERF stories and suggesting that stories have exaggerated historical reality indexes yet another habit of TERF disavowal. Keridwen Luis performs this disavowal in her exploration of women's land, in which she explains that although "transphobia as an issue has heavily colored how women's land/ women's space is seen," in her fieldwork "few of my interviewees said transphobic things, at least to me" (Luis 2018: 188, 7, 21). This echoes the defensive posture that the Michigan Womyn's Music Festival articulated in "intermittently released public statements clarifying that women of many and varied gender identities had always attended . . . the festival" (Mackay 2021: 76). These claims acknowledge that transphobia is real and mark it as bad and wrong; they also admit that it is sometimes present within lesbian spaces and communities, but they minimize its presence and impact.

Yet another response argues for the *incompatibility* of trans-exclusion with feminism by emphasizing the collusion of some self-identified feminists with conservative political actors. Finn Mackay explains, "In 2019 WoLF also collaborated with the Heritage Foundation, the Family Policy Alliance and other groups to produce a parent resource guide, *Responding to the Transgender Issue*, published by the Minnesota Family Council, an affiliate of Alliance Defending Freedom and Focus on the Family, which was founded by the influential evangelical Christian, James Dobson. All these groups are against same-sex marriage and abortion" (Mackay 2021: 7). By pointing to the conservative political affiliations of a group like WoLF, Mackay discredits the group's self-identification as feminist; indeed, their affiliation with anti-abortion activists is particularly damning. Just as, Nash and Pinto write, "it is clear that the term 'white feminism' is an oxymoron: white feminism is decidedly *not* feminism" (Nash and Pinto 2021: 887), the incompatibility response suggests that the moniker TERF mis-attaches the word "feminism" (and its cousins, "radical feminism" and "lesbian feminism") to a specifically anti-feminist platform. Emphasizing the incompatibility of trans-exclusion with feminism suggests that real feminism (or radical feminism, or lesbian feminism) has nothing to with trans-exclusion, indeed that the two are mutually exclusive and at odds.

A promising mode of response to TERF stories emerges from scholars in trans studies who lean into complexity rather than disavowal. This mode may also attempt to complicate the TERF stories (and histories) by critiquing the erasure of transwomen in 1970s–1990s feminist spaces. Matt Richardson calls us to grapple with a complex history of transphobia within Black lesbian feminist communities, about which he recounts the oral history of a Black transwoman who was "kicked out" of African Ancestral Lesbians United for Society Change in the early 1990s. He explains, "Until she was outed, she had been . . . participating in dialogues and events and helping to sustain the organization" but nonetheless "members of the organization determined . . . that she was a 'male infiltrator' who had to be extracted" (Richardson 2013: 273).

Richardson asks us to consider from whence the fear and suspicion derive in a space like this one, but even as he asks the question he provides (yet) a(nother) piece of evidence of transwomen's presence in the political/ solidarity/community/friend/lover work that celebrated and sustained the sign "lesbian" in an earlier period. And, when Cameron Awkward-Rich draws attention to what might be called a trans-ambivalent or trans-indifferent theoretical position in the writing of Audre Lorde, who has become routinely attached to *good* feminist feelings, he similarly offers a path of feminist storytelling that neither denies histories of trans-exclusion in lesbian feminism nor imagines lesbian feminism as monolithically transphobic (Awkward-Rich 2022). These responses think vitriol, exclusion, tension, disagreement, insufficient or failed solidarities as part of a dynamic feminist account of feminist gender history.

Recounting the oft-told TERF stories makes plain that they are rife with oversimplifications and generalities. This recounting makes plain, too, that these stories are pretty easy to interrupt. The history of gender essentialism, non-essentialism, and anti-essentialism in lesbian feminist theory and practice is not simple, so telling reductive stories doesn't get us very far, even if those narratives are seductive. The premise of rehearsing these stories and their various rebuttals, then, is not to join the chorus that says that TERF stories are wrong, simplistic, or overblown. This is not an attempt to complicate the history of lesbian feminism—though that may be a worthy cause in its own right. This is not a rescue mission.

Instead, I rehearse these stories and their responses to highlight the peculiar frequency with which lesbian feminisms seem to attend to a set of questions we also seem to have answered. I write from a curiosity—perhaps even a suspicion—guided by Robyn Wiegman's caution that "we are always bound to that which we try to refuse" (Wiegman 2011: 204). I want to suggest that our habit of telling TERF stories and then undercutting their credibility is actually a legitimating practice that participates in what Wiegman calls "a collectivizing project invested in revamping the lesbian's critical reputation" (205). The TERF is an object of attention because she has the capacity to recuperate the bad object of the lesbian.

What is at issue, then, is not a tension between lesbian studies and trans studies, but the attachment of lesbian studies to TERF. The constant rebuttal of the charge of trans-exclusion requires a constant reanimation of the trans-exclusionary feminist; that she must be invoked in order to be disavowed is also a guarantee of her continued presence. When we turn toward the TERF—even or especially to then turn away from her—we have nonetheless provided her with some free publicity. The TERF has yet to wither in feminist obscurity because disavowal sustains interest and intrigue (where indifference is a surer path to forgetting). If the loud disavowals seem to banish the TERF herself, this cycle nonetheless sustains the relevance of trans-exclusion as a discourse within (lesbian) feminism.

Doing Laundry

That cycle may not be entirely terrible.

I will hurry to clarify that I am not suggesting that trans-exclusion has a rightful place in lesbian feminism. Instead, I am suggesting that the recursive turn to TERF should tell us that trans-exclusion *does* have a place in lesbian feminism, even if it is not right.

The discursive habit I've traced above attempts to sanitize the history and the present of lesbian feminism. It is lesbians who most loudly disavow TERF(s), and we do so *with one another*. As Linda Garber writes, the lesbian-queer divide is animated primarily by lesbians—"white lesbian academics—for let's be clear that that is primarily whom we are discussing" (Garber 2001: 3). Closer to home, when students who had self-selected into my lesbian studies course—which naturally has the word 'lesbian' in the title—they came to my office to quietly confess their identification as lesbians or to tell me that they *would* be lesbians *but for* their desire not to be labeled as TERFs. Their confession ritual alerted me to their (accurate) sense that TERFs and lesbians *are* related, and the extent to which their anxiety sounded a little like grievance—as in, it's a shame and unfair that identifying as lesbian is fraught—piqued my interest. Had my bombastic embrace of bad lesbian subjectivity made the space safe for their anxiety cum grievance? (I wondered: is this how white progressives find affiliation against "difficult" Black women when we're not around?) TERF disavowal is thus most interesting "even" or perhaps *especially* among "those who hold [TERFs] up as an example of what they resolutely are not" (Awkward-Rich 2017: 832). If feminists attach to Black feminism to accrue what Jen Nash calls "a woke credential" (Nash 2021: 5), then distancing from TERF has a similar effect.

Reifying the TERF as outrageous, minor, or extinct authorizes the extant unease within lesbian feminism, which Awkward-Rich encapsulates as *"what about women, what about lesbians"* (2017: 832). TERF is a helpful straw man among lesbian feminists, who can frame the concern as mild and appropriate in the face of that which is vitriolic and weird, so that the cycle of conjure, disavowal, and plea ultimately fortifies the lesbian-object as theoretically endangered while sidelining the material impact of some lesbian feminisms on trans life-chances. Lesbian/feminism emerges from this laundry cycle a bit cleaner; washed clean of the TERF, "lesbian" might be recuperated as "good."

But if doing laundry with TERFs attempts to expunge trans-exclusion from lesbian feminism, the process is nonetheless ineffective at cleaning up the tensions that live among feminist and trans theories of gender. Following Cameron Awkward-Rich's brilliant theorizing "against resolution," I want to pause on the possibility that lesbian (feminist) and trans may have "competing theories of gender that seem aimed at each other's annihilation," and then to ask what would happen if that premise could be taken "as a given, not necessarily loaded with moral weight" (Awkward-Rich 2017: 819, 836; Awkward-Rich 2022). And what about those theories of gender? It might be more accurate to say that lesbian feminist theories and cultures and trans theories and cultures are at odds within themselves as much as either is with the other when it comes to gender essentialism and non-essentialism. Indeed lesbian feminist theory's hallmark might be the openness of the question, to the extent that the field (must) claim, at once, Robin Morgan, Audre Lorde, Monique Wittig, and Gayle Rubin as intellectual cornerstones. By the same token, if "*trans* names a project of undoing (gender, disciplines, selves)," then that sits uneasily beside the extent to which "trans . . . despite protests to the contrary, is quite attached to a version of m/f (why else the insistence that you use 'my' pronouns to address me?)" (Awkward-Rich 2017: 833, 838). What if turning toward the pressure points that exist among and between lesbian and trans—rather than disavowing them, minimizing them, or simply willing them away—was imagined as fruitful in their unfinishedness rather than dangerous?

That is also to say that laundering our feminism may obscure important sites of trouble. Indeed the "complaint" that Robyn Wiegman establishes as "field forming" in lesbian studies did not emerge from thin air. That whispered *what about the women, what about the lesbians* is an index of under-historicized misogyny in queer activist as well as academic spaces (Walters 1996: 844). There remains a need for revisionist histories of US twentieth-century lesbian, queer, and trans pasts that can recover the palliative-care practices and community survival networks that lesbians developed in the HIV/AIDS epidemic and its various wakes (Lim Rogers 2021; Polk, forthcoming); that can describe the bookstores and bars that have become larger than life in memoriam but were fleeting in their own time (Geiseking 2020; Hogan 2016); and that can evidence the ways unmarked whiteness has dominated study design and thus reified concerns that are specific to white lesbian-queer communities as universal across lesbian-queer communities (Moore 2011: 114).

Finally, the reality is that the cycle of TERF disavowal is also tiresome. Doing laundry with TERFs has proven to be neither theoretically invigorating nor particularly effective for improving the rep of lesbian feminists. I want to follow Samantha Pinto's call to render ourselves "vulnerable . . . to embrace a state of risk that refuses critique as (only) a mode of shoring up, of certainty" and to acknowledge the "mutual but *radically uneven* experiences, effects, and aesthetics of vulnerability" (Pinto 2020: 19; my emphasis) that constitute the places where lesbian and trans meet. I want to ask, also, what other metaphors for cultural and historical relation *with difference* might describe our communities and our fields, and how might a systematic turn toward Black studies—whose metaphors of signifying (Gates 1998), *décalage* (Edwards 2003: 14), and syncopation (Shange 2019: 44) signal modes of being *with* that reflect our actual ways of living? We have much to learn from staying in those places, both "good" and "messy" in Matt Richardson's frame, where our intimate and political lives abutt and unfold. The twin phenomena toward which Richardson directs our attention is an example of this kind of thinking, when he asks: "What would happen if, instead of being an object of fear and suspicion, there was recognition among lesbians that transwomen have helped shape lesbian politics and culture?" and "How do we talk about the phenomenon of lesbian desire for (trans)men in our rendering of lesbian history?" (Richardson 2013: 373, 374). Imagining the location where lesbian and trans make contact as *lively* requires turning toward TERF not to perform disavowal, but also to mourn the many ways we remain in relation to those aspects of our feminist past and present that have been unsavory, ugly, and deadly, and then beginning from there.

References

Awkward-Rich, Cameron. 2017. "Trans, Feminism: Or, Reading Like a Depressed Transsexual." *Signs: Journal of Women in Culture and Society* 42, no. 4.

Awkward-Rich, Cameron. 2022. "Against Resolution." Unpublished conference paper, "Feminism for the Future," Northeastern University. Boston, MA, March.

Cohen, Cathy. 2005. "Punks, Bulldaggers and Welfare Queens: The Radical Potential of Queer Politics?" in *Black Queer Studies*, edited by E. Patrick Johnson and Mae Henderson. Durham, NC: Duke University Press.

Edwards, Brent Hayes. 2003. *The Practice of Diaspora: Literature, Translation, and the Rise of Black Internationalism*. Cambridge, MA: Harvard University Press.

Ellison, Treva, Kai M. Green, Matt Richardson and C. Riley Snorton. 2017. "We Got Issues: Toward a Black Trans*/Studies." *TSQ: Transgender Studies Quarterly* 4, no. 2 (May).

Garber, Linda. 2001. *Identity Poetics: Race, Class and the Lesbian Roots of Queer Theory*. New York: Columbia University Press.

Geiseking, Jen Jack. 2020. *A Queer New York: Geographies of Lesbians, Dykes, and Queers*. New York: New York University Press.

Halberstam, Jack. 1998. "Transgender Butch: Butch/FTM Border Wars and the Masculine Continuum." *GLQ* 4, no. 2.

Hemmings, Clare. 2011. *Why Stories Matter: The Political Grammar of Feminist Theory*. Durham: Duke University Press.

Herring, Scott, and Lee Wallace, eds. 2021. *Long Term: Essays on Queer Commitment*. Durham, NC: Duke University Press.

Hogan, Kristin. 2016. *The Feminist Bookstore Movement: Lesbian Antiracism and Feminist Accountability*. Durham, NC: Duke University Press.

Luis, Keridwen N. 2018. *Herlands: Exploring the Women's Land Movement*. Minneapolis: University of Minnesota Press.

Mackay, Finn. 2021. *Female Masculinities and the Gender Wars: The Politics of Sex*. London: I. B. Taurus.

Meadow, Tey. 2022. "Remarks." Unpublished conference paper, "Feminism for the Future," Northeastern University, Boston, MA, March.

Moore, Mignon. 2011. *Invisible Families: Gay Identities, Relationships, and Motherhood among Black Women*. Berkeley: University of California Press.

Nash, Jennifer. 2016. "Feminist Originalism: Intersectionality and the Politics of Reading." *Feminist Theory* 17, no. 1.

Nash, Jennifer. 2019. *Black Feminism Reimagined: After Intersectionality*. Durham, NC: Duke University Press.

Nash, Jennifer. 2021. *Birthing Black Mothers*. Durham, NC: Duke University Press.

Nash, Jennifer, and Samantha Pinto. 2021. "A New Genealogy of 'Intelligent Rage,' or Other Ways to Think about White Women in Feminism." *Signs: Journal of Women in Culture and Society* 46, no. 4.

Pinto, Samantha. 2020. *Infamous Bodies: Early Black Women's Celebrity and the Afterlives of Rights*. Durham, NC: Duke University Press.

Polk, Olivia. Forthcoming. "We Can Dream the Dark: Black Lesbianism and the Ethic of Black Queerness," PhD. diss., Yale University.

Richardson, Matt. 2013. "Good and Messy: Lesbian and Transgender Identities." *Feminist Studies* 39, no. 2.

Rogers, Emily Lim. 2021. "Clinical Proximities: Chronic Fatigue Syndrome and Biomedicine's Binds in the US." PhD diss., New York University.

Schulman, Sarah. 2022. *Let the Record Show: A Political History of ACT UP New York, 1987–1993*. New York: Macmillan.

Shange, Savannah. 2019. "Play Aunties and Dyke Bitches: Gender, Generation, and the Ethics of Black Queer Kinship." *The Black Scholar* 49, no. 1.

Sullivan, Mairead. 2022. *Lesbian Death: Desire and Danger Between Feminist and Queer*. Minneapolis: University of Minnesota Press.

Walters, Suzanna Danuta. 1996. "From Here to Queer: Radical Feminism, Postmodernism, and the Lesbian Menace (Or, Why Can't a Woman Be More Like a Fag?)." *Signs: Journal of Women in Culture and Society* 21, no. 4.

Wiegman, Robyn. 2011. "Afterword: The Lesbian Premodern Meets the Lesbian Postmodern." In *The Lesbian Premodern*, edited Noreen Giffney, Michelle Sauer, and Dianne Watt. New York: Palgrave Macmillan.

Aren Aizura

Flailing at Feminized Labor: SOFFAs, 1990s Trans Care Networks, *Stone Butch Blues*, and the Devaluation of Social Reproduction

In 1999, a small circulation newsletter called *Your SOFFA Voice* began quarterly publication. *SOFFA* is an umbrella term for "significant others, friends, family, and allies." Rather than delimiting a sexual relation as *chaser* does, *SOFFA* delimits kinship and solidarity with trans people. In circulation from 1999 to 2002, *Your SOFFA Voice* published announcements and contact lists, as well as personal stories, poems, and letters. *Your SOFFA Voice* aimed to bring people identifying as SOFFAs together and to provide a space for self-expression, finding peers, and sometimes a place to vent. The editor, a cis femme and partner of a trans man, noted the need for partners of trans people to get support in the first issue: "Many SOs [significant others of trans people] feel that our issues and needs are pushed back, ignored, or forgotten when one of our guys is transitioning. Transitioning is a big deal, but being a partner and being supportive and having our needs met is important as well."

The first issue of *Your SOFFA Voice* contains an SO "Bill of Rights," written because "all of us who support someone going through transition forget that we too . . . are going through a tough time in our own life." Some of the rights listed include:

The South Atlantic Quarterly 122:3, July 2023
DOI 10.1215/00382876-10644043 © 2023 Duke University Press

I have the right to put myself first at times and to recognize that my needs are as important as the needs of others.

I have the right to make periodic mistakes, to "mess up," or not always live up to expectations of others.

I have the right to express my own opinions, preferences, and feelings; and feel they are as legitimate as the attitudes of others. (King 1998: 5)

The rights listed enumerate the messiness of doing what we might now call "emotional labor" in a marginalized community where adequate health care or social support is scarce, and where partners and family often bear the weight of supporting someone through transition and body modification while simultaneously educating themselves about transness.

The term SOFFA was coined by a white cis lesbian organizer and journalist based in Washington D.C., Loree Cook-Daniels. Becoming involved in trans organizing after her partner transitioned, Cook-Daniels herself saw the need for partners of trans men to have their own spaces in the trans community.[1] Cis partners of trans people have a long history of producing memoir, autobiography, or first-person accounts that appear in similar platforms as trans autobiographical narratives. For instance, crossdressers' wives published stories in *Transvestia* magazine in the 1960s. Minnie Bruce Pratt's memoir *S/He* (1995), about her relationship with Leslie Feinberg, and Helen Boyd's memoir *My Husband Betty* (2003) narrate witnessing their partners' gender trajectories, although in very different ways. The *Your SOFFA Voice* contributors and editors were, in Cait McKinney's term, information activists (2020: 2): people who generated information about queer and trans life themselves when they could not locate it elsewhere. Like other queer information activists, they doubtless drew upon experiences or knowledge of the lesbian and feminist print movement that peaked in the 1970s and 1980s. But what I call the SOFFA archive emerges later, from the late 1990s to the mid-2000s.

As the reference in the editor's letter to "guys" illustrates, SOFFA in *Your SOFFA Voice* often meant queer or lesbian-identifying cis women partners of trans men. Thus it is no coincidence that SOFFA cultural productions—whether ephemeral or widely published—mostly seem to be produced by women or feminized subjects (I include trans women in this awkward category). Indeed, the language of "guys" as partners appears to assume that the SOFFA is a feminized, caring subject in relation to a masculine trans partner. Jane Ward has written astutely about these dynamics in femme/transmasc relationships as gender labor, suggesting that femmes perform "emotional, physical, and sexual care-taking efforts aimed at . . .

helping others achieve the varied forms of gender recognition they long for" (2010: 236). Other scholarship on partners of trans men has argued that queer cis women often take on the emotional or social labors of caring for trans masculine subjects (Brown 2009; Pfeffer 2014). Yet this scholarship on partners of trans people often does not resolve a fundamental tension: how and why are intimate partnerships made to bear such utopian desires for community building and care, not to mention desire, while also clearly being a crucible for much of the mess, tension, and dysfunction of trans care?

The term *SOFFA* is rarely in use in queer/trans communities in the current decade. With the popularization of the principle "Nothing about us without us," many trans and queer people expect or demand trans organizations (both grassroots and more liberal rights-based orgs) to be led by trans people. The emergence of t4t as an erotics, a form of sociality or care, and an organizing principle has accompanied this expectation of trans autonomy (Awkward-Rich and Malatino 2022). Thus, previous models of trans sociality in which non-trans people were part of trans organizing as comrades can appear archaic, reminders of a time when trans subjects did not command autonomy or self-determination—although trans organizing is and has always involved many non-trans partners and comrades of trans people. Simultaneously, the gender identity lexicon has productively expanded to diminish the tensions trans poses to coherent conceptions of cis/trans and masculine/feminine. People who once might have understood themselves as SOFFAs, non-trans partners of trans people, now are just as likely to identify as nonbinary: "AFAB" (assigned female at birth) nonbinary femme is now a popular way of identifying (Amin 2022: 116). In a trans/queer subcultural context, nonbinary complicates the reductive calculus where gender nonconformity is understood as a marker of authenticity, and cisness is understood as a marker of privilege.[2]

Not surprisingly given all this, materials about SOFFAs seems to comprise a very small part of the trans archives now becoming more widely accessible with the digitization of archival materials. This absence is partly historiographic: current accounts of trans history produce a narrative of resistance to medicalization and discrimination, protest, and mutual aid that reflects the desires many of us have for a communal, public, radical trans politics (for instance, Susan Stryker's 2017 edition of *Transgender History* is subtitled "The Roots of Today's Revolution"). Beyond medicalization, the narratives that have congealed as trans history locate political and communal movements, rather than micropolitical or interpersonal relations, as key.[3] McKinney frames information activism at the intersections of queer and feminist marginalization as "affective labor that produces collectivity" (22). But rather than uncomplicatedly celebrating the resistance of information activists, we might also think carefully about the potential collectivities that were dispersed, subtended, or that never came into being partially because of the form and audience for which they were produced. *Your SOFFA Voice* is not a trans liberation guidebook: it does not offer a blueprint for a radical political imagination. Indeed, in their focus on interpersonal relations, it could be argued that SOFFA publications reproduced a status quo liberalism precisely through bracketing "the political." However, it is crucial for trans and feminist history to consider trans social forms that are not "radical": the messy, everyday efforts at making a livable life that characterize trans and queer life in late capitalism and which B. Aultman has called the "trans ordinary" (2019). These social forms have also shaped the contemporary emergence of what we understand as trans intimacy, care, and love. Tracking these forms allows us to see how capital and labor have contributed to the formation of trans life and vice versa. This is a crucial point, partially because the most visible trans organizing and political mobilization in the United States tends toward trans exceptionalism and liberalism, despite how the iconization of Black trans women can offer us token symbols of survival and mutual aid.

In this essay I'm interested in historicizing SOFFA cultural productions: locating them in relation to the economic, social, and financial shifts that can appear distant from articulations of transness as intimate and personal, or purely identity-based expression of "who we are." Documenting the history of trans liberalism and ordinariness gives trans studies and, more broadly, feminist and queer materialisms, the historical perspective we need to diagnose our own complicities and critiques. (The "we" here implicates intellectual and scholarly laborers, who reproduce a similar cultural economy of radicalism despite inhabiting institutional structures that preclude it.)

Inquiring into SOFFAs illuminates deeper questions about the social reproduction of trans movements: the kinds of informal, communal, affective, and political work that has gone under the name of support, community building, and sometimes mutual aid, what Hil Malatino calls trans care. Malatino points out that trans survival has demanded "extra" care, particularly when trans lives are lived in the interstices outside of conventional family structures and institutions (2020: 3). Drawing on a disability justice framing, Malatino understands these practices of trans care as care webs. As he points out, however, trans archival records are littered with the failure of trans care webs to prevent violence, suicide, bad feelings, or interpersonal and intracommunity conflict. Unsurprisingly, therefore, debating the politics of care—who does it, who is responsible for it, how can it be sustained—has long been a central part of trans life and community. The historical devaluation of care labor and the precarity of trans people's labor value makes this an urgent task, as the editors of *Transgender Marxism* show (Gleeson et al. 2021: 18). Necropolitical logics that frame whiteness, respectability, and normativity as traits worthy of protection, and Blackness and indigeneity, poverty, and resistance as active threats to the social order, or as "vulnerable" populations to be invoked representationally yet never fully reckoned with, complicate the ecology of trans care webs and trans organizing in general. Theories about the gendered nature of care need to be understood within this larger context, in which the slow racial violence of criminalization and carcerality, settler colonial dispossession, and state abandonment manifest especially in trans and nonbinary communities of color. Additionally, a twenty-first century version of trans is often opposed to disability in order to frame trans as exceptional, "galvanized through mobility, transformation, regeneration, flexibility, and the creative concocting of the body" (Puar 2017: 45). What Puar theorizes as the ideal "piecing" trans body is entrepreneurial, future focused, but also self-determining. As she points out, despite or perhaps because of trans's proximity to disability in its relationship to medicalization, trans exceptionalism often involves rejecting disability, and in the process, rejecting the lessons disability justice can teach us about interdependency. The capacity to self-invent also involves rejecting the material conditions of becoming, which are always interdependent. That is, whether we believe in care webs and others' contributions to our becoming or not, they happen anyhow. Critical disability studies, particularly what Jina Kim and Sami Schalk name a feminist-of-color disability studies (2020: 32) is thus crucial to appreciating how to think through how trans care webs have functioned, whether historically or in the present day.

This essay proceeds as follows: the first section reads selections from *Your SOFFA Voice,* many of which narrate an almost exclusive concern with romantic relationships, which seem to be firmly located within the domestic space of the home. The tensions that erupted for trans masculine subjects and their partners in the pages of *Your SOFFA Voice* were often articulated through recourse to the language of romance, coupledom, and loyalty. I read these narratives against the grain of accounts of earlier femme involvement in butch/trans life, such as working-class femmes (sex workers, clerical and factory workers, both cis and trans) who are in solidarity with each other during bar raids in Leslie Feinberg's autobiographical novel *Stone Butch Blues* ([1993] 2013). Reading these different narratives against each other helps trace the presence of late-twentieth-century crises of social reproduction and racial capital in queer and trans life-making. By making such a comparative reading, I argue that the social-economic transformations we often call neoliberalism also resulted in a strategic retreat for trans and trans-adjacent subjects who, rather than being able to invest in a narrative of trans liberation or social transformation, seemed to regard the defense of the family wage and domestic privacy as their only recourse.

The relative absence in *Your SOFFA Voice* of talk of queer and trans, or butch-femme solidarity through sex work, cross-community bar culture, domestic work, or low-paid jobs means that other questions need to be asked. To trace how feminized reproductive labor becomes naturalized as something that necessarily takes place inside the queer couple form and in the privacy of the home, rather than being understood as something collective and public, which sustained communities and queer visibility in more public spaces such as bars or the street, the second section turns to an examination of femme and SOFFA administrative and clerical labor. SOFFAs and trans men collaborated on organizing projects in which femmes' and SOFFAs' clerical and administrative capacities were central and sustaining. This clerical and administrative work represents what is effaced in trans men's demand for inclusion in an industrial or professional fantasy of manhood. It indicates the extent to which the devaluation of reproductive labor also means the stratification of care economies along racialized and gendered lines, even within trans communities.

These tensions both sustained and rested upon the devaluing and criminalization of social reproduction in the form of Black, indigenous, immigrant, and working-class feminized service labor through the end of the twentieth century and into the twenty-first. In addition to this, revitalization projects and increased criminalization in urban areas shrank the available places in which to do street-based sex work and shut down working-class bar areas. The cross-class and interracial mixing and solidarity spaces in which butches and femmes, drag and street queens, and sex workers could mingle and keep each other safe began to disappear. Newsletter and internet organizing emerged, with conventions that oriented readers toward respectability, even if their readers did not subscribe to a politics of homo or trans normativity. While respectability-oriented newsletters had existed since the 1960s for trans women and cross-dressers in particular (*Transvestia* is a good example), we can trace a line between the gradual loss of working-class bar culture and the emergence in the late 1980s of trans publications and nonprofits more concerned with fundraising via lobbying the corporate world or politicians and the emergence of trans consulting with businesses.[4] Jordy Rosenberg's meditation in *Transgender Marxism* has been deeply influential here, as Rosenberg offers a reading of *Stone Butch Blues* in relationship to deindustrialization and post-Fordism (2021: 261–63). My comments in the final section on labor are in the spirit of that inquiry. Finally, I ask what visions of trans capacity we lose when we hang on to a vision of trans selfhood and organizing as autonomous, or located in the couple-form or nuclear family, what Rosenberg calls "a narrative fixation that occludes its own historical context."

1990s US Trans Culture and the Emergence of the SOFFA

Trans community formations in the 1990s and early 2000s relied increasingly on online spaces as ways to bridge the gap between small local or city-based support groups and advocacy organizations. Hundreds of small support groups for many different trans populations existed across North America, while larger national advocacy organizations such as FTM International and GenderPAC were mainly based in large coastal cities. Print magazines and newsletters such as *Transgender Tapestry*, *Chrysalis*, and *FTM Newsletter* played a role, although information provision and community building were beginning to move online. Annual conferences or conventions filled the gaps between small support groups, larger advocacy organizations, and print publications, and provided an opportunity for in-person workshops and social events. Conventions organized for and by trans women or cross-dressers, such as the annual Fantasia Fair in Provincetown, had been in operation for decades. But in the 1990s a host of new conferences emerged, many of them focused on trans men or mixed trans spaces. The first FTM-dedicated conference, organized by FTM International, took place in San Francisco in 1995.

Information, support, and community building for partners of trans people was already common at the existing conventions and in trans literature dating back to the 1960s. However, the term *SOFFA* did not emerge until after 1995. Most early North American literature for partners of trans people was directed at cis women wives of heterosexual cross-dressers. *Transvestia* magazine, the publication Virginia Prince edited for "heterosexual cross-dressers and their wives" in 1960, regularly published letters from wives (Hill 2017: 233). Fantasia Fair held panels for spouses and friends as far back as 1982; the 1991 Fair scheduled a Partner's Orientation Program (Fantasia Fair 1990). As trans guys became more visible at conventions, partners of trans men began to meet each other, but organized workshops or conference tracks were rare. References to partners' concerns began to appear in *FTM Newsletter* in the early 1990s. However, partners were almost never the focus of *FTM Newsletter* and partner concerns were generally relegated to the letters section (entitled "Malebox"!) or to information and resource pages. In *FTM Newsletter* in July 1992, a letter from a partner of a trans man relates how she and her partner attended the 1992 IFGE "Coming Together" conference in Houston "in hope of meeting other partners to develop a support system for myself" (*FTM Newsletter* 1992: 7). She expresses disappointment at the lack of an IFGE conference track for partners of FTMs. In 1995 *FTM Newsletter* published a report by Marcy, the facilitator of multiple Friends, Family, and Partners workshops at the first FTM International conference in 1995; this report advertised a newsletter for partners of FTMs called PF3TM (1995: 13).⁵ In San Francisco, FTM International ran partner meetings concurrently with the regular meeting for trans guys. Most of these letters or reports appear to have been written by or for cis women.⁶ Letters relate concerns with rejection from the lesbian community after their trans masc partners transition; feelings of isolation when trans guys went "stealth"; and redefining identity terms after "lesbian" becomes untenable or contested by trans guy partners who identified as straight.

References to the term *SOFFA* didn't emerge until the late 1990s, when Loree Cook-Daniels, a DC-based journalist and LGBT advocate and cis partner of a trans guy, coined the term. Cook-Daniels's partner Marcelle had decided to transition in 1994. In a *Washington Blade* article from March 1995, Cook-Daniels explains how she "oppressed the one closest to me for over a decade because her sexual identity frightened and appalled me." Cook-Daniels goes on to reveal how her partner is "a transsexual." The article thinks through some of the complications of being a "very 'out', very political Lesbian feminist" with a trans partner: the silence about trans masculinity in the lesbian community, and the difficulty of resolving partner's fears and antipathy to trans masculinity (Cook-Daniels 1995). In a 2011 oral history, Cook-Daniels relates how publishing this article in the *Washington Blade* kickstarted her career as a "transgender activist" (Smith 2011). However, her existence as a much more "rabid" activist began the following year, when she and Marcelle attended the second FTM International conference. She attended a workshop for partners run by a therapist who had previously worked with female partners of trans women. In Cook-Daniels's account, the therapist "started to give us this lecture about how we had to support our husbands. And she was talking to a roomful of lesbian feminists. And I, I just, excuse me. . . . We did not want to hear somebody up in the front of the room tell us that we need to support our men." Cook-Daniels relates how shocked she was that the organizing committee had no SOFFAs on it, and how right after the conference she began sending complaint letters, which started what she calls the "SOFFA wars," a riff on the queer terminology of "sex wars" and "butch/FTM border wars" of the late 1990s (Halberstam 1998). Cook-Daniels relates how one trans guy in these debates agreed with her. According to Cook-Daniels, this person was planning an east coast regional FTM conference. Cook-Daniels convinced him to instead plan a national conference, and to design it as welcoming to anyone, not just trans people, and especially not as a conference for "men and their girlfriends" (Smith 2011). Cook-Daniels thus became a co-organizer and relied on Marcelle to support her while she dedicated work time to organizing the conference.

Around the same time, Cook-Daniels came up with the formulation of "significant others, friends, families, and allies" that would cohere into the SOFFA acronym. In *Trans Liberation: Beyond Pink or Blue*, Leslie Feinberg relates how Gary Bowen invited hir to speak at the first American Boyz conference in 1997. At this stage in the planning, the conference was called "F2M East Coast." Feinberg wrote back that given that she wasn't a trans guy, she would respect trans guys' need to organize together and wouldn't attend. Bowen replied that, rather than a trans guy specific conference, he had envisioned a convention that, as Feinberg describes, "brought together all the gender variance on what he called the F2M continuum, including our significant others, families, friends, allies, and loved ones" (Feinberg 1999: 45). Bowen also suggested a name change. "Gary drew on his Apache heritage," Feinberg writes, and offered the name True Spirit. Feinberg did speak at the conference, and the speech is published in *Trans Liberation*. From Feinberg's inclusion of the phrase "significant others, families, friends, allies" in this account, it would seem that Loree Cook-Daniels's bid for SOFFAs to be included did indeed inform Bowen's open vision of the conference. True Spirit became legendary, both for its popularity—a friend who attended recalls hotel rooms bursting with up to ten people to a room—and the sexual buzz of the trans guys, queers, bois, butches, femmes, and others in attendance. A short porn film, *True Spirit*, was made in the concrete stairwell of the convention hotel in 2001.

In the vision elaborated by Cook-Daniels, SOFFAs take on the responsibility of educating, passing on knowledge, training up allies, and through this, collaborating on the task of trans world building. At the time, Cook-Daniels also advocated for SOFFAs to be integrated into trans conferences, organizing, and social activities. A SOFFA flier published by Cook-Daniels much later asks that, among other things, trans people should "understand that SOFFAs face their own difficult issues, and be respectful and supportive as they work through them," as well as advising that trans orgs open leadership and public speaking positions to SOFFAs, and encourage SOFFAs to fill these roles.

Flailing at SOFFA Duties: Domestic Bliss in *Your SOFFA Voice*

Your SOFFA Voice emerged at the interstices of this combination of annual conferences, local support or social groups, and email listservs. The newsletter was produced and for both a metro and rural-based readership. Edited by Jodi Burchell, the femme partner of a trans guy based in middle Tennessee, *Your SOFFA Voice* began as a printed newsletter in 1998. Burchell treats American Boyz as the umbrella organization of *Your SOFFA Voice*: every issue contains a contact list for American Boyz SOFFA contacts. Loree Cook-Daniels was the National SOFFA Coordinator for American Boyz at the time, and Burchell credits her with the suggestion to start the newsletter. Burchell was also active in conference organizing: she facilitated a Partners Only caucus at True Spirit 1999 and enjoined True Spirit to schedule even more SOFFA content.

A series of poems and articles by a self-identified femme called Sonya Lorenzo offers a good example of how the domestic space of the home remains the central frame for these kinds of reflections. Over two years, Lorenzo narrates the shift in her relationship as her butch partner decides to get top surgery and start testosterone. The piece stands as a notable companion piece to *Stone Butch Blues*, partially because the partner Lorenzo writes about is around Feinberg's age, a veteran of the pre-1970s butch-femme bar scene and later a lesbian feminist. The first piece, a poem published early in 1999, is called "Domestic Bliss." It narrates how the author, doing dishes at home dressed in her "Donna Reed best, white apron over full skirted dress," sees her butch lover arrive home from work through the window, "your crew cut cruising by on the way to my front door" (1999a: 7). The lovers unite and start undressing each other, with references to the butch's white undershirt and "the mysterious shift of your breasts beneath the cloth." They engage in a little foreplay, but the femme character remembers the waiting dinner. Her lover reluctantly acquiesces: "Your shoulders slump; you sigh. / And in our respective states of disarray / we go about the rituals of the end of day." They eat, clean up, and retire to bed early, where "you lay your body on mine and push deep into me . . . /This is the way it was meant to be" (7). The poem is sexy but mundane. It lies in the butch-femme tradition of ironic nostalgia for 1950s "housewife" culture. But by its very softcore refusal to talk about binding, strap-ons, or anything more explicit, the poem also confirms the unironic domesticity of the encounter.

Another article by Lorenzo published six months later tells a different story. Narrated in short stream of consciousness episodes and again written in the second person, it opens with a similar idyllic romance plot as the poem. In the first scene Lorenzo makes love to her butch partner. In the second section, she agrees to marry them. "You will be my husband, for you are my butch, and I can call you no other way" (1999b: 3). But the following scenes narrate how Lorenzo's partner eventually admits he wants chest reconstruction surgery, and her reaction: "We read about procedures and options. We have an animated and revelatory conversation," she writes. "But inside me, a deep, overwhelming panic begins to build. I want to scream: I LOVE YOU . . . AS YOU ARE! . . . . In fear, I want you to agree with me: 'Perhaps if you had been recognized, accepted and validated as you are, maybe now you would not want to alter your body.' Please, my eyes beg. I want there to be an easier way." A strong implication here is that Lorenzo fears her partner will no longer need her post-transition, precisely because their bond is made through the private support she offers him when he encounters strangers' questions about his gender and the threat of attack. "I draw you into the circle of my arms and feel your tension ease. . . . You breathe, and I know you are quietly bringing yourself to me. . . . It is this I fear losing" (1999b: 10).

Queer culture has nursed a long tradition of cis women partners of trans men documenting their tears for the loss of their partner's breasts, or fears that a trans masculine partner might change irrevocably post-transition.[7] Working squarely within this tradition, Lorenzo's series narrates her working through grief, fear, rage, and rejection, until she arrives at an acceptance as her lover comes out of surgery. "You are woozy and weak but smile at me when you take my hand. I remember why I am willing to nurse you through this and anything." The poem-essay, however, is a three-part series. By the third part, published two issues later, Lorenzo is realizing that she, too, has undergone a transition. "[One] day, I make a word for myself: 'transensual.' And in naming myself, I feel substantial . . . connected. . . . My self has reached for these identifiers, found them and filled them out. Now I make them unique to me. Transensual Femme Lesbian." Arriving also at a new relational and sexual identity (and possibly coining the term "transensual femme"), Lorenzo arrives at a reconciliation with her partner's masculinity and with their new life. In the end scene, she writes about waking up next to her lover, "your chest softly rising and falling with each breath. I hardly notice the scars, you are so beautiful. Sleep well, my butch, my boy, my man. I will be here when you wake" (1999c: 3).

Lorenzo's themes and preoccupations are consistent with much of the content in *Your SOFFA Voice*. The theme of working through relationship conflict and ultimate reconciliation with a partner's transition is particularly relevant. The "happy ending" Lorenzo constructs in which she is reconciled to her partner being a man feels consistent with SOFFA attempts to stitch together the conflicts that erupt when a partner transitions, and also to act as a "good ally" by witnessing his body as manly. These attempts are flailing, in the sense Lauren Berlant uses the term, "a mode of crisis management that arises after an object, or object world, becomes disturbed in a way that intrudes on one's confidence about how to move in it" (2018: 157): it is striking that this narrative closure arrives when Lorenzo's partner is asleep, stripped of his power and agency and thus perhaps less threatening.

Nonetheless, let us stay with the spatial dimensions of Lorenzo's narrative. While the initial poem is unironically entitled "Domestic Bliss," the entire series of poems and articles takes place in their home, sometimes in a clinic, but overwhelmingly in the domestic domain featuring Lorenzo and her partner as the only characters. The writing explicitly invokes coupledom as the protected sphere to be maintained at all costs. While friends and support groups are mentioned, there does not appear to be a communal space happening here—and when it does happen, it is also attached to the couple-form: "We go to meetings and get to know other trans men and their lovers and wives" (Lorenzo 1999a: 8). Workplaces, colleagues, non-trans friends, and public or semi-public social spaces like bars appear to be inconsequential. The home and the couple are the crucibles in which, it is understood, transness and adjusting to transness matters most. Considering Cook-Daniels's earlier insistence that SOFFA as a term is about trans movements including non-trans people—partners, parents, friends, and "allies" all working together in the same spaces—it seems ironic that much of the content of the essay sustains a preoccupation with the couple-form as the crucible in which trans identity can be worked out and through which Lorenzo can make sense of becoming part of trans community.

We might also think about Lorenzo's preoccupation with the domestic in relation to contemporaneous and slightly earlier accounts of US butch/femme and trans masc sociality, in particular Leslie Feinberg's autobiographical novel *Stone Butch Blues*, which we can assume many of the *Your SOFFA Voice* readers would have eagerly devoured on its publication in 1993 and the years afterward. *Stone Butch Blues* was originally read as a butch or trans masc novel, but in fact the bar scene Feinberg writes into being presents multiple central cis femme, trans femme, and street queen characters within a

working-class scene made up of sex workers of all genders, working-class lesbians, femmes, and butches/he-shes. After she is expelled from school and
leaves home, bars like Tifka's, Abba's, and Malibou provide Jess with queer
comrades and a social scene. They invite her to stay with them until she finds
an apartment, help her find a motorcycle, and defend her when, inevitably,
the bars are raided by police. The people who frequent these bars are not all
butches and femmes: the clientele also includes sex workers "male and
female" (by which Feinberg seems to mean cis men, street queens, and cis
women) and drag queens, including Peaches, a queen who takes Jess to a
department store to buy her first men's suit. Peaches bails out Jess when she's
arrested in a bar raid, and comforts Jess after the police rape and assault her.
Peaches' trans femme mentorship is a crucial part of how Jess learns how to
be queer and trans in the context of criminalization, routine police violence,
and street harassment. While *Stone Butch Blues* points to the widespread
racial segregation of gay bars pre-Stonewall, Feinberg is also pointing to a
space in which multiracial working-class queer and trans people coexisted
and had to fight with and for each other against the cops. Other fiction about
pre-Stonewall butch-femme communities also places central importance on
bar culture; for example, Black and indigenous trans author Red Jordan Arobateau's novel *Lucy and Mickey: A Butch Trip through Life before Stonewall*
(1995) takes place in numerous working-class and racially mixed bars in Chicago, peopled by sex workers, hard femmes, and bar butches.[8] These fictional
accounts are consistent with scholarly historical accounts that locate the "association and camaraderie" found through bar culture as central to queer political mobilization (Boyd 2003: 10). Historical accounts of pre-1970s bar culture in Buffalo locate queer working-class bars as sites of occasional coalition
and coexistence, although by the 1960s (at the time when Feinberg might
have been around) these bars were in the minority (Kennedy and Davis 2014:
381). Nevertheless, at mixed bars "tough bar lesbians" would defend the men
(and likely street queens or trans women) who were present, who "used to
jump up on the tables" rather than fight (148).

  Stone Butch Blues narrates a shift in the early 1970s where deindustrialization and lesbian separatism both contribute to breaking up this coalitional
bar culture and butch-femme culture. The second half of *Stone Butch Blues*
maps a butch-femme bar community that has begun to fragment after lesbian
separatism and economic crisis, sending the inhabitants of that community
into atomized and geographically dispersed units, both couples and individuals. At the time, medical providers' fear of risk or litigation often meant that
hormone replacement therapy and trans surgeries often required a stated

renunciation of queerness and a desire to "go stealth," or blend into hetero-sexual, gender normative life (Velocci 2021; Irving 2008). After months of hormone replacement therapy and, finally, top surgery, Jess realizes that the absence of the queer bar community has left a hole in her life. Yet Feinberg shows how Jess cannot go back: eventually, Jess too leaves Buffalo to search for work in New York City. Feinberg's depiction of these events mirrors his-torical events: with increased queer resistance to criminalization and less police harassment in the 1970s and 1980s, lesbian bars and women's spaces across the United States multiplied (Wennerholm 2019: 19). Yet, specifically trans-friendly spaces were far less common, and many lesbian spaces rejected butches or trans men who had previously been a central part of les-bian culture. All these intra-community and trans-specific dynamics may help to explain why trans masc and SOFFA cultural production in the late 1990s tend to focus on the home or the clinic rather than bars or community spaces as sites of care, community, and relationality.

Yet into the 1990s broader historical shifts reflect the political ascen-dancy of homonormative and transnormative political logics, as calls for decriminalization of homosexuality and legalization of same-sex marriage deployed an understanding of sexuality (and to some extent, gender identity) as private matters. The historic moment of SOFFA mobilization happened just as the arrival of anti-retroviral therapies for those who could afford them meant HIV began to recede as a major political issue for mainstream LGBT movement. Instead, organizations like the Human Rights Campaign mobi-lized for same-sex marriage, consolidating homonormative claims for liberal inclusion (Duggan 2003: 65). The rise of campaigns for same-sex marriage in particular reflected widespread attempts at the privatization of social life through neoliberal economic policies. Clinton-era social policies weapon-ized marriage promotion and family responsibility, aimed at reducing reli-ance on welfare. These welfare reforms pathologized Black kinship forms via the specter of the welfare queen as a social problem of dependency, pro-viding a rationale for the introduction of workfare and withdrawal of social safety nets (Cohen 1997; Kim 2021). The enormous increase in incarcera-tion initiated by the war on drugs and intensified carceral logics such as bro-ken windows policing (Ansfield 2020) meant higher rates of incarceration of Black, brown, and immigrant queer and trans people, in particular sex work-ers and trans women of color. In terms of social reproduction, these policy shifts made family members, particularly women, responsible for "crimi-nal" behavior: both literal financial responsibility for bail, and symbolic responsibility to prevent re-offending (Page, Piehowski, and Soss 2019). All of these social policies weaponized the language of private responsibility to immiserate Black, Latinx, and immigrant communities.

As Melinda Cooper points out, these policies were about enforcing the family wage as an instrument of economic and social discipline. But although it had never extended to the entire population, the centrality of the family wage was in massive decline at the time. Cooper argues that in the context of these diminishing political horizons, left political movements were captured by more conservative demands: for instance, mainstream LGBT movements hung on to the last vestiges of the family wage through campaigns for same-sex marriage. Indeed, Cooper shows how the most conservative same-sex marriage advocates argued that marriage would enable queer people to reduce their reliance on welfare and to live more independently of the state (2017: 211). At the same time, property ownership posed the only real bulwark against dispossession through gentrification-related rent hikes—for many queers and trans people, a privilege only accessible via pooling resources with a romantic partner. In this context, perhaps it is not surprising to see a resurgence of focus on the nuclear family, couple-form, and private property within marginalized communities who were navigating their way through the 1990s welfare reforms and privatization. Here, the couple-form becomes a form of symbolic and material security against the depredations of capital.

Thus, rather than critiquing the transbutch/femme aesthetic dynamics of Lorenzo's "Domestic Bliss" as homo/transnormative, we could point to how marriage, monogamy, property, and coupledom appear to be a refuge for Lorenzo as the stability of her definition of herself in relation to her partner and her stable place in lesbian subculture unravel. These are, indeed, forms of flailing—the messy, provisional defenses invented when little else seems to be available. However, precisely because few of these tenuous entitlements were available to trans and gender nonconforming people in states of more direct criminalization or immiseration, denizens of the 1970s and 1980s queer bars, who might have attended True Spirit or contributed to *Your SOFFA Voice*.

Workplace Xeroxing and Word Perfect 5.1: Stratified Labor and Trans Post-Fordism

How were newsletters like *Your SOFFA Voice* produced, materially? It seems likely that similar to the lesbian feminist newsletter makers Cait McKinney documents in *Information Activism*, the editors of newsletters like *Your SOFFA Voice* clandestinely used their workplace xerox machines to produce issues of the newsletter (2020: 36). Covert use of Xerox machines is certainly refractory. Yet it also illustrates a particular position within the labor market that was available to white women clerical and administrative workers in particular. The newsletter design, laid out in columns with a variety of fonts and images, required expertise in word processing or design software which was most widely accessible through administrative or nonprofit work, on-campus participation in political movements, college courses, or a combination of all three. This reflected in the social composition of the regularly printed list of contacts in *Your SOFFA Voice*. Five out of seven local SOFFA coordinators in the contacts list had email addresses with suffixes indicating education institutions or tech companies. Cook-Daniels, who coined the term *SOFFA*, worked as a journalist and a nonprofit organizer throughout her involvement with American Boyz and True Spirit. The editor of *Your SOFFA Voice* worked as a software developer at the time she published *Your SOFFA Voice*; she later became an information technology professor and higher education administrator. We can't know whether those .edu email addresses indicate roles as students, faculty, or administrative workers. Yet this does give us some indication of the class composition of the social networks that newsletters like *Your SOFFA Voice* sustained. In the context of the receding horizon of social safety nets and focus on the family, this also gives us insight into a labor stratification that divided working-class queer and trans communities. Materially, the emergence of the newsletter as a form of community building sits at the intersection of higher education administration, nonprofit work, and the emergence of a trans community based on shared identity rather than inhabiting or surviving shared modes of criminalization or wealth redistribution. Clerical workers and administrative workers might often be paid at rates that immiserate them, but culturally they were and are understood as upwardly mobile, able to retrain on the job or perpetually reeducate for the purpose of employment flexibility.

It's instructive to return to *Stone Butch Blues* here, in which Feinberg outlines Jess's working-class butch career trajectory from factory work to the printing industry, as well as plotting femme trajectories from sex work and food service work to more white-collar forms of clerical and administrative work. The novel opens with Jess's letter to her lost femme lover Teresa, with whom Jess has her most formative relationship. Later in the novel, Jess will meet Teresa in the cannery where they both work, and they will end up part of the butch femme bar community before Teresa leaves Jess in what feels like a TERFy refusal to deal with Jess's emerging transmasculinity. (TERF stands for "trans exclusionary radical feminist.") The letter provides a vehicle through which the older Jess, narrating from the 1990s, returns to memories of her childhood and early adulthood. The older Jess has not seen Teresa since the early 1970s. What has happened to Teresa, Jess wonders: "Are you turning tricks today? Are you waiting tables or learning Word Perfect 5.1?" As Jordy Rosenberg points out in a meditation on this epistolary form, *Stone Butch Blues* maps a catalog of feminized service work onto the "chasm of love lost and industrialization offshored" (2021: 262)—that is, the ravages of neoliberalism in the post-1970s United States. After the disruptions experienced by the US working class through the 1980s, Teresa could be anywhere.

Feinberg's reference to Word Perfect 5.1 alerts us to the expansion of feminization of labor through the 1970s and 1980s, particularly clerical work embodying aspirations to upward mobility, which for women expanded into managerial and administrative work in higher education—and later, tech (England and Boyer 2009: 327). In the early 1970s of the novel, Teresa has already gained precarious access to this world. While she is living with Jess, Teresa leaves the cannery for a job as a secretary at the nearby state university. Teresa's job puts her in proximity with campus antiwar protests and feminist organizing, creating an opening for her newly found lesbian feminist consciousness and Teresa and Jess's simultaneous politicization around the Vietnam War and Black Power. However, Teresa's entry to campus political culture also functions to destabilize the cozy counterpoint of bar and factory as working-class social spaces. Feminist consciousness destabilizes her relationship with Jess, as Teresa comes to reject Jess's trans masculinity. Feinberg makes a subtle point here about the middle-class origins of lesbian separatism, which are fracturing the more working-class and previously coalitional queer bar community.

Stone Butch Blues captures the crises of capital of the 1960s and 1970s, but it also points to the events through which those crises were "recomposed into state, capital, and academy" (Ferguson 2012: 6) through reabsorbing demands for racial justice into workplaces, institutions, and higher education in particular. Ferguson, following Jodi Melamed, identifies aesthetic culture in particular as one of the avenues through which this takes place: the entry of Black, Latinx, Asian-American, feminist, and queer literature into a multicultural literary canon. The 1960s and 1970s campus protests resulted in the emergence Black studies programs, women's studies programs, and early ethnic studies programs; yet as universities recognized responsibility for minoritized knowledge production, they also became a site for disciplining epistemological frameworks around race, gender, and sexuality. As well as operating within the pedagogical locations of the university, these dynamics also played out in political movements and community build-ing: lesbian and gay rights movements largely institutionalized into a law reform lobby based on demands for liberal equality rather than social trans-formation (Spade 2015; Duggan 2003). This is related to the enormous growth of nonprofit organizations as social safety nets were withdrawn across the 1970s and 1980s: what Myrl Beam calls a narrative of "affirmative nation-alism centered on volunteerism and community" buttressed the narratives of welfare cheats and big government (2018: 23). So when Feinberg asks whether Teresa is using Word Perfect, we could argue that ze is also indicating the possibility of Teresa's absorption of the radical political imagination into cor-porate liberal feminist culture, homonormative lesbian and gay rights orga-nizing, or the institutionalization of feminist, queer, Black, Latinx, and indig-enous campus protest into liberal diversity and inclusion initiatives. Trans political movement and community building in the 1990s was undoubtedly influenced by these historical currents. The gendered division of labor within trans masculine organizing that designated SOFFA concerns as separate and less important—thus necessitating SOFFA-only networks—indicates a vision of identity-based community that has always been fragmentary and inade-quate. Despite the messiness of the SOFFA bill of rights, or Lorenzo's desire for her partner not to transition, the vision of trans masculine doing the "seri-ous" political work of advocating for health care while their partners network about how to support them reproduces an ideology that fundamentally deval-ues care, even as it is crucial for trans and queer survival.

Even working-class white femmes like Teresa, who could access pro-fessionalization of some form, were less likely to need to do sex work or other low-wage service work, whereas Black, Latinx, Asian, and indigenous queers were far more likely to be working in mass low-wage reproductive labor jobs that multiplied as deindustrialization took hold. Long into the 1980s and the 1990s, feminized labor markets continued to be more intensively stratified racially and on the basis of citizenship and immigration status (Colen 2016). The care economy (including health care and hospital work), as Gabriel Winant has shown, accounted for 74 percent of all job growth in the 1990s (Winant 2021: 3). Trans and queer people are to be found here, in particular trans women, working in call centers, hospitals, sex work, food service, domestic work, and other devalued forms of labor that both entrench racial and gender hierarchies and rely on racialization and the devaluation of fem-ininity to degrade the status of that labor itself.

This poses a problem for a trans analysis of labor that relies on a narra-tive of post-Fordism that locates a shift toward labor precarity in general, and which diagnoses the impediments (and sometimes openings) that historical shift poses for trans and gender nonconforming people. Jules Joanne Gleason and Elle O'Rourke argue that for trans workers, the casualization and precarity of twenty-first-century labor means the end of the restrictive temporal logic of a singular professional career and identity, but also the foreclosing of institutional protections from employer (or colleague) harassment and prejudices (2021: 22). Gleason and O'Rourke's parenthetical that Fordist employment is "a bargain offered to a select minority" in this passage alerts us to the necessity of understanding the secure, long-standing employment of the Fordist era and its disciplining of social reproduction through the family wage as a temporary gain extended mainly to white cis men and, through liberal feminist campaigns for workplace gender parity in the 1970s, begrudgingly extended to white cis women before it blew apart.

Following the openings made by Black and woman of color feminists, it is thus necessary to think social reproduction, reproductive labor, and indeed all labor within the span of the afterlife of slavery and transnational capital (Hartman 2016: 167). Even in the postwar ascendance of Fordist labor, the traditional gendered division of labor was impossible to access for most working-class households: in immigrant, Black, and indigenous households, men seldom earned a family wage; women and children often did paid labor, and Black women served as primary breadwinners in nonnuclear families. Traditional Marxist interpretations that focus on production, or even more narrowly on industrial waged labor, have also rendered domestic work and social reproduction invisible. This obscures the differently racialized and unvalued labor patterns of Black women, indigenous women, trans and queer people, and immigrants whose labor is feminized by virtue of a citizen/noncitizen racial order. Thus, if we talk about the labor market transformations of the long 1970s solely in terms of a meteoric rise in low-wage service work or casualized work, we risk neglecting the fact that prior to neoliberalism, informalized, privatized, or criminalized low-wage service work such as sex work, cooking, cleaning, and childcare propped up industrial production and the white nuclear family. That is, it doesn't serve trans critiques of labor history or movements to frame a singular professional career or industrial protections as benefits that extended to even a small percentage of trans workers, even at the height of Fordism, particularly when we're thinking of feminized work or workers.

This may seem a long way from debating the merits of SOFFA cultural production in the late 1990s and early 2000s. However, it teaches us some important lessons about the political accountability educated and/or intellectual trans communities carry to produce a history of labor and capital that can account for the contradictions and tensions that erupt in the reality of trans archives. To document SOFFAs or non-trans comrades in trans organizing and social publics is to question whether trans organizing need always only involve trans people. It is clear from looking at *Your SOFFA Voice* that non-trans partners and allies have always been central to trans cultural life. Additionally, within trans masc communities, it is often femme or cis women who raise the questions of labor division and the gendered distribution of emotional work. This is thankless work, barely acknowledged by many trans men publicly, and consigned to the private sphere precisely because of gendered divisions of labor. Clearly, the preoccupation with the couple-form as the crucible for trans becoming does not offer us an abundant enough vision for either being trans or creating trans care webs. Nonetheless, the vision of trans people as entirely autonomous is not sufficient either. Both obscure the patchwork, messy, and contingent passing-down of knowledge about how to practice community care, how to sustain trans communities and lives, and how to keep ourselves and our comrades safe. In order to fight the many threats to trans life that face us in the current decade, we need all the help we can get.

Notes

Thanks to Jordy Rosenberg, Jules Gill-Peterson, Cassius Adair, and special issue editors Jennifer Nash and Samantha Pinto for their helpful comments and enthusiasm for this essay.

1   In 1998 Cook-Daniels and her partner helped convene the first True Spirit conference, an East Coast convention for trans men and FTMs.

2   Nonetheless, I am in agreement with Amin's argument that the structure of inventing idealized normative categories like binary, cis, or heterosexual—through which nonbinary comes to be intelligible—has involved "the burial of gender deeper and deeper within the private recesses of the self, where it increasingly disavows any relation to the social" (Amin 2022, : 117).

3   The Stonewall Rebellion, the 1966 Compton's Cafeteria riot, and Sylvia Rivera and Marsha P. Johnson's formation of Street Transvestite Action Revolutionaries are among the crucial events in this historical timeline, as well as the formation of Transsexual Menace in the 1990s and Camp Trans, the camp set up to protest trans women's exclusion at the Michigan Women's Music Festival in the early 1990s.

4   Cassius Adair's forthcoming work looks at trans organizers and consultants who were involved in early Silicon Valley companies, in particular IBM.

5   The report comes in the Networking networking column of the magazine, separated from the than several much longer reports of the same conference by trans men, which that take up the first 10 ten pages of the magazine.

6   The exceptions are a regular column by a trans masculine partner of a trans man, who writes about the importance of support for trans partners of trans people, in the process inventing or contributing to the tradition of t4t.

7   Perhaps the most familiar recent example is Maggie Nelson's *The Argonauts*, which reproduces in literary memoir the generic conventions Lorenzo uses in her 1999 essay:

the second person address; the unselfconscious admission that a trans partner's identification as masculine may disrupt the partner's secure identification as queer or lesbian; the narrated desire to question whether surgery or hormones are "really necessary",," and (sometimes) the eventual arrival at reconciliation or "integrating" the partner's transness.

8   Red Jordan Arobateau's entire opus demands far more scholarly attention than it has received so far; however, this is a project for another publication.

References

Amin, Kadji. 2022. "We Are All Nonbinary: A Brief History of Accidents." *Representations* 158, no. 1: 30–38. https://doi.org/10.1525/rep.2022.158.11.106.

Ansfield, Bench. 2020. "The Broken Windows of the Bronx: Putting the Theory in Its Place." *American Quarterly* 72, no. 1: 103–27. https://doi.org/10.1353/AQ.2020.0005.

Arobateau, Red Jordan. 1995. *Lucy and Mickey: A Butch Trip through Life before Stonewall.* New York: Masquerade Books.

Aultman, B. 2019. "Injurious Acts: Notes on Happiness from the Trans Ordinary." *Writing from Below* 4, no. 2. https://writingfrombelow.org/happiness/injurious-acts-notes-on-happiness-from-the-tr.

Awkward-Rich, Cameron, and Hil Malatino. 2022. "Meanwhile, T4t." *TSQ: Transgender Studies Quarterly* 9, no. 1: 1–8. https://doi.org/10.1215/23289252–9475467.

Beam, Myrl. 2018. *Gay Inc.: The Nonprofitization of Queer Politics.* Minneapolis: University of Minnesota Press.

Berlant, Lauren. 2018. "Genre Flailing." *Capacious: Journal for Emerging Affect Inquiry* 2, no. 4: 156–62. https://doi.org/10.22387/cap2018.16.

Boyd, Helen. 2003. *My Husband Betty: Love, Sex, and Life with a Crossdresser.* San Francisco: Seal Press.

Brown, Nicola R. 2009. "I'm in Transition Too: Sexual Identity Renegotiation in Sexual-Minority Women's Relationships with Transsexual Men." *International Journal of Sexual Health* 21, no. 1: 61–77. https://doi.org/10.1080/19317610902720766.

Cohen, C. J. 1997. "Punks, Bulldaggers, and Welfare Queens: The Radical Potential of Queer Politics?" *GLQ: A Journal of Lesbian and Gay Studies* 3, no. 4: 437–65. https://doi.org/10.1215/10642684-3-4-437.

Colen, Shellee. 2016. "'Like a Mother to Them': Stratified Reproduction and West Indian Child Care Workers and Employers in New York." In *Feminist Anthropology: A Reader,* edited by Ellen Lewin, 380–397. Malden, MA: Blackwell Publishing.

Cook-Daniels, Loree. 1995. "Facing gender questions openly and honestly." *Washington Blade,* March 17.

Cooper, Melinda. 2017. *Family Values: Between Neoliberalism and the New Social Conservatism.* Princeton, NJ: Princeton University Press.

Duggan, Lisa. 2003. *The Twilight of Equality: Neoliberalism, Cultural Politics, and the Attack on Democracy.* Boston: Beacon Press.

England, Kim, and Kate Boyer. 2009. "Women's Work: The Feminization and Shifting Meanings of Clerical Work." *Journal of Social History* 43, no. 2: 307–40.

Fantasia Fair. 1990. *Fantasia Fair Participant's Guide.* Fantasia Fair: Programs, Participant Guides, and Directories Collection. University of Victoria Transgender Archives, Victoria, BC. https://www.digitaltransgenderarchive.net/files/2z10wq22z.

Feinberg, Leslie. 1999. *Trans Liberation: Beyond Pink or Blue.* Boston: Beacon Press,

Feinberg, Leslie. (1993) 2013. *Stone Butch Blues.* Twentieth anniversary author edition. https://www.lesliefeinberg.net/

Ferguson, Roderick A. 2012. *The Reorder of Things: The University and Its Pedagogies of Minority Difference.* Minneapolis: University of Minnesota Press.

FTM Newsletter. 1992. No. 20, July. University of Victoria Transgender Archives, Victoria, BC. https://vault.library.uvic.ca/concern/generic_works/8c63bf4b-e1e0-4bef-ac40-a7330070770e.

FTM Newsletter. 1995. No. 32, October. University of Victoria Transgender Archives, Victoria, BC. http:// https://vault.library.uvic.ca/concern/generic_works/5e4e63f6-dbc5-406d-a45c-f5a657c805eb.

Gleeson, Jules Joanne, Elle O'Rourke, Jordy Rosenberg, eds. 2021. *Transgender Marxism.* London: Pluto Press.

Halberstam, Judith. 1998. "Transgender Butch: Butch/FTM Border Wars and the Masculine Continuum." *Glq* 4, no. 2: 287–310. https://doi.org/10.1215/10642684-4-2-287.

Hartman, Saidiya. 2016. "The Belly of the World: A Note on Black Women's Labors." *Souls* 18, no. 1: 166–73. https://doi.org/10.1080/10999949.2016.1162596doi.org/10.1080/10999949.2016.1162596.

Hill, Robert. 2017. "'We Share a Sacred Secret': Gender, Domesticity, and Containment in Transvestia's Histories and Letters from Cross-Dressers and Their Wives." *Journal of Social History* 44, no. 3: 729–50.

Irving, Dan. 2008. "Normalized Transgressions: Legitimizing the Transsexual Body as Productive." *Radical History Review* 100, no. 100: 38–59. https://doi.org/10.1215/01636545-2007-021.

Kennedy, Elizabeth Lapovsky, and Madeline Davis. 2014. *Boots of Leather, Slippers of Gold.* New York: Routledge.

Kim, Jina B. 2021. "Cripping the Welfare Queen: The Radical Potential of Disability Politics." *Social Text* 39, no. 3: 79–101. https://doi.org/10.1215/01642472-9034390.

King, Michelle. 1998. "What SOs Forget They Have the Right To." *Your SOFFA Voice* 1, no. 1 (December). *Your SOFFA Voice* Collection, Louise Lawrence Transgender Archive, Vallejo, CA. https://www.digitaltransgenderarchive.net/files/ng451h61q

Lorenzo, Sonya. 1999a. "Domestic Bliss." *Your SOFFA Voice* 2, no. 1: 7 https://www.digitaltransgenderarchive.net/files/1r66j124j.

Lorenzo, Sonya. 1999b. "Loving Outside Simple Lines." *Your SOFFA Voice* 2, no. 3: 3–7. https://www.digitaltransgenderarchive.net/files/6969z084j

Lorenzo, Sonya. 1999c. "Loving Outside Simple Lines Part 3." *Your SOFFA Voice* 2, no. 4 (September): 1–3. *Your SOFFA Voice* Collection, Louise Lawrence Transgender Archive, Vallejo CA. https://www.digitaltransgenderarchive.net/files/vd66wooom

Malatino, Hil. 2020. *Trans Care.* Minneapolis: University of Minnesota Press.

McKinney, Cait. 2020. *Information Activism: A Queer History of Lesbian Media Technologies.* Durham, NC: Duke University Press.

Page, Joshua, Victoria Piehowski, and Joe Soss. 2019. "A Debt of Care: Commercial Bail and the Gendered Logic of Criminal Justice Predation." *RSF: The Russell Sage Foundation Journal of the Social Sciences* 5, no. 1: 150–72. https://doi.org/10.7758/RSF.2019.5.1.07.

Pfeffer, Carla A. 2014. "'I Don't like Passing as a Straight Woman': Queer Negotiations of Identity and Social Group Membership." *American Journal of Sociology* 120, no. 1: 1–44. https://doi.org/10.1086/677197.

Pratt, Minnie Bruce. 1995. *S/He*. New York: Firebrand Books.

Puar, Jasbir. 2017. *The Right to Maim: Debility, Capacity, Disability*. Durham, NC: Duke University Press.

Rosenberg, Jordy. 2021. "Afterword: One Utopia, One Dystopia." *Transgender Marxism*, edited by Elle O'Rourke and Jules Joanne Gleeson, 259–95. London: Pluto Press.

Schalk, Sami, and Jina B. Kim. 2020. "Integrating Race, Transforming Feminist Disability Studies." *Signs* 46, no. 1: 31–55. https://doi.org/10.1086/709213.

Smith, Brice. 2011. Oral History Interview with Loree Cook-Daniels, January 30, 2011. Oral History Interviews of the Milwaukee Transgender Oral History Project Collection. University of Wisconsin Milwaukee Library, Milwaukee, WI. https://collections.lib.uwm.edu/digital/collection/transhist/id/5

Spade, Dean. 2015. *Normal Life: Critical Trans Politics and the Limits of Law*. Durham, NC: Duke University Press.

Velocci, Beans. 2021. "Standards of Care: Uncertainty and Risk in Harry Benjamin's Transsexual Classifications." *Transgender Studies Quarterly* 8, no. 4: 462–80. https://doi.org/10.1215/23289252-9311060.

Ward, J. 2010. "Gender Labor: Transmen, Femmes, and Collective Work of Transgression." *Sexualities* 13, no. 2: 236–54. https://doi.org/10.1177/1363460709359114.

Wennerholm, Zoe. 2019. ""It's Your Future, Don't Miss It": Nostalgia, Utopia, and Desire in the New York Lesbian Bar." https://digitalwindow.vassar.edu/senior_capstone/897.

Winant, Gabriel. 2021. *The Next Shift: The Fall of Industry and the Rise of Health Care in Rust Belt America*. Cambridge, MA: Harvard University Press.

Ramzi Fawaz

Feminism Is for *Beginners*:
Learning from Straight Men
Doing Queer Feminism

> Though many of the chief producers of
> Unitedstatesean feminism are women with
> husbands, women with boyfriends, women who
> have sex with men, and women with sons, . . .
> there seems to be no urgent need in their
> feminism to understand women's version of
> what Leo Bersani . . . has called "love of the cock."
> —Janet Halley, *Split Decisions: How and Why to
> Take a Break from Feminism* (2006)

> If you hate what you desire . . . *that's tense.*
> —Hannah Gadsby, *Nanette* (2018)

The time has come to think about men. More than
a half century since the astonishing rise of US
women's liberation, feminism remains synonymous with *women's* oppression. Even though men
are directly implicated as both perpetrators *and*
victims of patriarchal conditioning in recent political catastrophes like the overturning of *Roe v.
Wade*; the increase in mass shootings carried out
by men; and the MeToo movement's meticulous
documentation of male sexual assault on women,
no robust feminist dialogue exists aimed at identifying the practical incentives that might encourage men to partner with feminists in combatting
these trends. And despite the growing conviction

The South Atlantic Quarterly 122:3, July 2023
DOI 10.1215/00382876-10644057   © 2023 Duke University Press

among many, and terrifying suspicion among others, that gender is a socially constructed phenomenon grounded in cultural inscriptions on the sexed body, popular feminisms focused on redressing women's trauma still frequently conceive men and women as diametrically opposed, and rigidly hierarchized, polarities in an intractable war rather than registering men as coproducers of a complex, often dysfunctional but also sometimes pleasurable, thrilling, and difficult-to-quit *arrangement* between "the sexes."

This essay seeks to better understand the role of cisgender men in the history of feminist theorizing: as feminism's most self-evident "bad object," as a site of meaningful knowledge about gendered performance, hierarchy, and socialization, and as ordinary persons whom feminists often love, desire, emulate, detest, struggle with and against. Toward this end, I flesh out a queer feminist theory of male masculinity that might sit productively alongside the sociological framework of men and masculinity studies, while rebutting the radical feminist contention that male feminists merely appropriate women's rightful intellectual and political territory. I aim to carve out renewed conceptual space for imagining men as critical interlocutors and potential comrades to feminist theory and practice, who may have something important to tell us about both the most gratifying *and* cruelest aspects of our long-standing gender and sexual dynamics.

One of the insights to be gleaned from paying attention to cis straight men in particular is that many frequently enact their own types of queer feminism. This is a consciousness born less from men's impeccable absorption of feminist and queer ideology critique, but more so as an organically evolving response to their commonplace relationships with the women, queer, and gender nonconforming people in their lives. This includes straight male resistance to heteronormative social and sexual regulations; the articulation of genuine care, investment, and affinity to women, other men, and gender and sexual outlaws who occupy significant roles in a given man's social universe; and men's capacity to recognize their own complex socialization into gender by way of conflicting familial, cultural, and social influences. Despite the vast structural inequality and brutality of a patriarchal culture, then, many men who understand themselves to be putatively cisgender and heterosexual are still directly, intimately, and positively shaped by the presence of other gender and sexual formations, including femininity and queerness, *without necessarily becoming them.*

Despite masculinity studies' nuanced unpacking of the social, cultural, and political dynamics of maleness—as a set of embodied behaviors, a site of vested power interests, a cultural lexicon of images representing "proper" manhood, or a social process of gender differentiation—an understanding of the *salutary* mutual influence between male masculinity, femininity, and queerness remains largely underexamined. Certainly, the interrelated subjects of men and masculinity constitute vast, variegated and interdisciplinary fields of inquiry, yet twenty-first-century queer and feminist interventions into the study of masculinity and male gender formation have tended to organize around three broad trends. Feminist sociologists like C. J. Pascoe (2007), Jane Ward (2015), and Vanessa R. Panfil (2017) have, respectively, conducted ethnographic research on high school teenagers, straight white men who have sex with men, and gay male gang members, to show how masculinity operates as a complex social process, or elaborated set of rhetorical and performative practices, for distinguishing proper masculine gender from "deviant" expressions. This includes the social rejection of perceived femininity and same-sex desire (such as the invention of the figure of the "fag," a mobile rhetorical placeholder for so-called failed forms of masculinity), or through intense forms of introjection and disavowal (such as some straight men's pursuit of violent, degrading same-sex eroticism paradoxically marked as "not gay" due to its lack of emotional intimacy). Simultaneously, queer of color scholars like José Esteban Muñoz (1999), Martin F. Manalansan (2003), Darieck Scott (2010), and Nguyễn Tân Hoàng (2014) have documented the diversity of racialized forms of gay male femininity, "feminization," and gender nonconformity, from the cross-dressing performances of gay Filipino "divas" to Asian American and Black gay men's reclamation of the sexual position of the penetrated "bottom" as a site of erotic power. These thinkers critique hegemonic forms of white gay male desire that erotically fetishize racialized men while devaluing racial and gender diversity within gay male community; and they develop concepts like "bottomhood," "disidentification," and "extravagant abjection" to describe the ingenious social and cultural strategies by which racialized queer subjects negotiate, and even wring pleasure out of, their knotty relationships to a dominant white patriarchal and homophobic US culture. Finally, Black male feminists like Mark Anthony Neal (2013) and Marlon B. Ross (2022) have reconstructed cultural and intellectual histories of nonnormative Black male masculinities that cannot easily be fitted into the categories of gay and straight. These include the Black "sissy," a highly educated and thus "effeminate" expression of Black masculinity born of the arrival of some Black men into middle-class status following Emancipation, and the range of Black men who nimbly combine aspects of normative male masculinity with feminine attributes (such as their pursuit of expressive arts or the performance of sartorial fabulosity), thereby inhabiting what Neal calls "illegible black masculinities."

All three of these approaches stress the fundamental diversity of masculinities (in the plural), commit to a critique of hegemonic masculinities that uphold heteropatriarchy and racism, and identify the logics that underly different performances of masculinity in distinct social and cultural contexts. Yet by placing focus on violent, racist, and heterosexist expressions of masculinity on the one hand, and illuminating multiply marginalized, queer, or "abject" masculinities on the other, this body of thought leaves neglected the life experiences, investments, and potential political commitments of straight cis men (from all races) who are nonviolent, and actually or *potentially* anti-sexist in their daily lives. Moreover, with the exception of Scott and Hoàng's provocative reclamation of gay male desire for sexual abjection, this work has not been as good at explaining how male masculinity, despite its association with a vast range of political and interpersonal horrors, on the whole remains an abiding object of erotic and social desire for many of us who claim feminist politics. In the drop-dead elegant deconstruction of toxic masculinity and the inspiring celebration of racialized queer male subjects and their lifeworlds, I read both a triumphant feminist rebuke of hegemonic masculinity, but also a melancholic resignation about the possibility that male masculinity, and those who inhabit it, could possibly be genuine allies to the queer feminist cause. Following Neal's moving impulse to make "illegible black masculinities" recognizable as part and parcel of the broader diversity of gendered existence, I seek to make male masculinity in its most prosaic, nontoxic forms legible again to feminist theory as a necessary comrade to cross-gender coalition. To this end, I ask: How can we better account for and amplify unexpected, quotidian expressions of male queer feminist consciousness in all its varieties (perhaps especially when that consciousness is not primarily enacted through a man's obviously divergent gender expression or sexual orientation)? Across the arc of this essay, I offer two answers to this query.

First, feminists must acknowledge and explain our enduring erotic, social, and affective desires for male masculinity, while crafting feminist theory attuned to the lived reality of our manifold associations and affinities with men. We feminists, women, and queer people of all stripes often want many things from men. And men just as frequently want many things from us. Our shared longings—for intimacy, sex, love, recognition, adventure, experimentation, accountability, ego support, and ego dissolution—are elaborated in complex scenes of agonistic exchange where we tailor various existing gender scripts to our unique circumstances, while inevitably altering them by virtue of our infinitely variable lived interactions. This fact demands a more supple attention to the ways that relationships across genders always constitute intricate psychological (as much as material) *arrangements*, or mutually constituted social and affective dynamics—some highly dysfunctional, others deeply satisfying—that require both individual and collective reorganization to be transformed (Dinnerstein [1976] 1999). Our goal should be to reinvent our relational scripts by literally inhabiting them differently, not simply exposing their ideological operation or endlessly cataloguing the list of privileges presumably afforded to one agent or group within that dynamic (men). If cis straight men might have any potential investment in queer feminism, it is in the co-creation of more life-affirming gender and sexual arrangements.

I look at the question of sexual arrangement through the insights of what I call *male affirmative feminist theory* written by people of all genders and sexualities, including cis straight men. I use this phrase to describe any form of feminist thought, writing, or political practice that (a) considers male perspectives on gender dynamics as critical to feminist knowledges and includes men as legitimate subjects of gender and sexual freedom; (b) apprehends the unequal power arrangements between men and women in a patriarchal society, but also takes seriously the ways men are distorted and injured by the very patriarchal privilege they wield; and (c) suspends, queries, or holds more lightly to the top-down structural critique of male power for the purpose of better understanding the mutual desire and attachment that flows between different gendered subjects. Male affirmative feminist theorizing acknowledges feminists as having split subjectivities, at once deeply critical of arbitrary gender hierarchies, while also often socially and erotically attached to male masculinity, in both its most virulent *and* humane forms. Rather than naturalizing the desire for male masculinity as God-given (à la the Christian right) or attempting to politically abolish it through ideological critique (ala the radical feminist deconstruction of patriarchal mystification), male affirmative feminist theory attempts to live and thrive within our split subjectivity, thereby developing healthier, more life-affirming approaches to our contradictory attachments to gender writ large. Moreover, this kind of feminist theorizing is male *affirmative* not in the sense of legitimizing toxic masculinity but because it argues for the importance of male positive self-perception as a building block toward men's potential investment in feminism, rather than masculinity's annihilation as a precondition of political transformation. Below, I clarify that much male affirmative feminism, especially that written by cis straight men, is also often *queer* (or queerly inflected), in that it considers the realm of sexuality and desire, namely its expansion into new territories of possibility beyond normative heterosexuality, as a key entry point into cis men's investment in feminist values. Instead of a fully formed position of structural power, a predetermined social role, or merely a set of interlocking privileged identities, male affirmative feminist theory reconceives masculinity writ large as a "constantly morphing," multidimensional composite of worldly variables that may sometimes congeal into the force we call patriarchy, though not always, or always in the same way (Saldanha 2006: 19). In this frame, even distinctly *male* masculinities—understood simply as the gendered self-perceptions or identities of male-bodied people who do not conceive themselves as necessarily gender or sexually divergent—become perpetually emergent, and thus open to transformation, rather than determined in advance either by patriarchal ideology or feminist critique.

Second, with a view of maleness as a form of becoming, and hence, contingent and mutable, we must invest in the *re-symbolization* and *multiplication* of male masculinity rather than its eradication. This would not involve a simple proliferation of prepackaged male "types" or identities, as Pascoe warns us against, but an encouragement for male-bodied people to expand their performative repertoire in relation to one another and to people of other genders and sexualities (7–8). From the perspective of sociology, R. W. Connell ([1995] 2005) argues that a de-gendering of patriarchal society would necessitate a wide-scale "re-embodiment for men," which would involve "a search for different ways of using, feeling, and showing male bodies . . . to develop capacities . . . other than those developed in war, sport or industrial labor [including the ability to] experience other pleasures" (233). From the perspective of feminist and queer cultural studies, however, such re-embodiment must go hand in hand with creative practices of projecting the male body into new contexts for socially, erotically, and affectively interrelating with others, which might facilitate material transformations in male masculinity's behavioral and emotional vocabulary. On this last score, cultural production remains one of our most indispensable tools for documenting the heterogenous masculinities we already encounter in our day-to-day experiences, as well as imaginatively figuring, and thus allowing us to directly see or vicariously experience, the aspirational possibilities for male masculinities yet to come.

I begin by distilling four lessons we can learn from male affirmative feminist theory. Among the most profound insights of this work is an insistence on a feminist *recommitment* to anti-essentialist thinking, not only refusing monolithic conceptions of women or female gender, but also of men, male gender, behavior, and being. In line with this view, it is the queerest aspects of feminist thought that have frequently inspired straight men to engage with its central insights, including the freedom to transgress gender conventions, the ability to express sexuality with greater emotional and erotic range, and the desire to be free of heteronormative policing, especially the threat of homosexual stigma. Rather than cynically treat these desires as indicating an imperious male patriarchal instinct to appropriate the hard-won freedoms of women and queer people, I join Marquis Bey (2017) in thinking of this set of queer feminist impulses as part of a widely shared male wish to be "fugitive from" toxic forms of masculinity, without eradicating one's own male gender.

To dramatize these insights, in the second half of the essay I conduct a close reading of Mike Mills's 2010 Academy Award–winning film *Beginners*, which narrates the unwitting evolution of a "lovable" but romantically bumbling straight man, Oliver, into a proto-queer feminist, following the revelation that his septuagenarian father Hal is gay. When Oliver learns his mother and father had made a pact to marry despite Hal's sexuality decades before, he brims with newfound empathy for both parents, as a straight woman and gay man forced by a heteropatriarchal society to choose the security of home and family above their personal desires. Through a series of dazzling montage sequences that render Oliver's interior life on-screen, the film graphically depicts one straight man's evolving attempt to integrate and make meaning of his queer parents' complex lives in relation to his own masculinity and heterosexual longings. *Beginners* offers a visual theory of male masculinity as a perpetually changing, combinatory formation that "builds upon a gradual, fragmented, and shifting sense of corporeal difference" (between men and women, children and parents, gay and straight people, even humans and dogs) thus rendering gender and sexuality "a lot less binary" (Saldanha 2006: 21). I conclude by returning to the concept of "beginning," asking what feminist and left social justice projects might gain by splitting their gaze between a focus on failed relations across gendered difference—grounded in the seemingly endless betrayal of women and queers by straight cis men—and a productive openness to the *inauguration* of unexpected relationships between all gendered subjects. Ultimately, contemporary feminisms of all varieties must conceive more expansive ideas of who men are and can be (in relation to women, one another, and queer people of all stripes) for the full force of feminism's transformative potential to be actualized.

Lessons from Male Affirmative Feminism(s)

At this point, however, some readers may be asking, who does this gay *man* think he is to tell feminist theory it needs to confront maleness? This essay is driven by three motives—personal, pedagogical, and political. Personally, as a single, Lebanese-American, gay male feminist pushing forty, I still desire erotic and emotional communion with men. Though so many gay men I encounter also seem to be seeking *something*, outside of extraordinary male friendships, the landscape of my romantic longings often looks like a desert of listless text exchanges, missed connections, and rolling dunes of indifference. Feminist and queer theory, the twin fields of knowledge I have built a career around, have had little helpful to say about this conundrum besides reminding me that male socialization is barbaric; that I am a victim of gender normativity; that gay male community is rigidly organized by hierarchies of masculine privilege; and that gay identity is grounded in a self-destructive erotic attachment to the sources of its subjection. Such claims have certainly affirmed my self-righteous rage at men, but it never did anything to help my sex life. I feel increasingly trapped by my own cruel optimism about the possibility that gay male affectional life can be genuinely fulfilling, on the one hand, and feminist and queer theory's even crueler *cynicism* about this potential on the other. So, motive one: how might a male affirmative feminist theory provide me more practical tools for negotiating my paradoxical, but real, desires so I can genuinely enjoy them without being swallowed up by my fantasies? That is, how can one live with one's cruel optimism in a better, more humane way?

Second, pedagogically I am alarmed that my most politically progressive students have become comfortable throwing out the phrase "cis straight white male" in everyday conversation as if it were a universally recognized epithet that appropriately describes a horde of "bad actors," *those people* we know are obviously the direct representatives of all things privileged and oppressive. Students frequently bandy this slogan about without self-consciousness, despite the fact that many of them sexually desire, are romantically involved with, or count cis-straight-white-males among their friends, peers, lovers, even family. My students conveniently forget that the formulation has no less than four axes of identity—referring (at least) to sexuality, gender expression, and race—each of which is riven by contradiction and multiplicity. Consequently, this seemingly impenetrable edifice of vested patriarchal interest could easily fall in and out of systems of domination, live in an ambivalent relationship to each of these seemingly self-evident categories, or count many other identities (like working class or disabled, not to mention qualities of personality, artistic or intellectual talent, or spiritual belief) as equally significant to their selfhood. So, motive two: figuring out how we might overcome the left progressive tendency to combat systematic oppression by using patriarchy's own bankrupt tools of flattening and homogenizing against its presumed emissaries.

Finally, politically, I am disheartened that the vibrant radical imagination of 1970s feminism, which was committed to expanding the possibilities of what women and gender outlaws could be or become, has been eclipsed by a popular feminism driven to the projects of publicly articulating women's trauma through MeToo and Title IX. The politicization of women's wounded identity has a long and storied history in feminist theorizing, galvanizing monumental and necessary transformations in law, social norms, and institutional practices. But to quote Donna Haraway ([1985] 2004), "we have *all* been injured, profoundly" by heteropatriarchy, not just or only women or queer people (38). Male pro-feminist Harry Brod urges us to consider that "it is the ability to take in and honor the pain men suffer that provides the surest foundation for the ability to oppose the pain men inflict" (1998: 205). The feminist ability to conceive men as multiplex beings capable of harming and being harmed—by systemic oppression as much as by women, other men, and gender nonconforming people—while still arguing for an account of women's and gender outlaws' infinite complexity *and* unjust subordination—can transcend the very reductive logic of patriarchy, which sees men and women as universally fixed types. I would love to see feminism revivified not only as a sustained attack on heteropatriarchy, but as an imaginative worldmaking practice continually inventing a different, more joyful, *yes even more erotically exciting* and *generally less miserable* way of living together (Zerilli 2005). So, motive number three: How might we consider the genuine diversity and plurality inherent to men as part and parcel of the diversity of all genders? What would it mean to look at a man and see a kaleidoscope, rather than a monolith? Let us begin to try by exploring some under-sung past theorists of male masculinity.

By now we are well versed in the monumental fact that 1970s women's and gay liberation movements produced a searing structural analysis of the system of heteropatriarchy, understood as the arbitrary production of sex-class distinction within the heterosexual nuclear family (Firestone [1971] 2003; Radicalesbians [1970, 1972] 1992; Rich 1980). In this same period, gay male liberationists borrowed feminist analytical tools to develop a complex account of what would later be called "hegemonic masculinity" (Wittman

[1972] 1992; Carrigan, Connell, and Lee 1987). This view recognized that male masculinity was structured by an internal hierarchy as starkly rendered as any between women and men, which upheld a widely accepted ideal of dominant or "normal" masculinity—associated with intense emotional repression, muscularity and athleticism, physical and sexual aggressiveness, acquisitiveness, and competition—even as most men failed to live up to this rigid archetype. These movements inspired diverse solutions to the problem of male masculinity's complicity with patriarchy. Lesbian separatists argued for complete divestment from patriarchal society, behavioral norms, and "thought patterns," and sometimes fantasized about male genocide (Solanos [1968] 2000; Gutter Dyke Collective 1973; Hoagland and Penelope 1988; Shugar 1995). The Black lesbian feminists of the Combahee River Collective urged political coalition with men in order to address the interlocking nature of racial and gender oppression among racially subordinated groups (Combahee River Collective [1981] 2015). Some gay liberationists like "The Effeminists" called for cisgender men to radically annihilate their masculinity by actively refusing to perform traditional "male" qualities (Dansky, Knoebel, and Pitchford [1973] 1997). Queer countercultural groups like the glam drag troupe The Cockettes threw traditional notions of binary gender into anarchy by combining fluid gender performances with psychedelic drug use (Weissman 2002). Both gay and straight male liberationists adapted the practice of feminist consciousness-raising to encourage men to confront their attachment to dysfunctional social roles (A Gay Male Group [1972] 1992; Fasteau 1974). And radical feminists often pretended that their own erotic attachments to men didn't exist, or arbitrarily exceptionalized their male partners as male feminist outliers impervious to critique (Morgan 1970).

Despite the variety of approaches to maleness, as the 1970s came to a close, the general consensus reigned that men could never be trustworthy or loyal allies to the project of dismantling their own power and privilege. If at the beginning of the decade Robin Morgan (1970) could righteously proclaim, "I haven't the faintest notion what possible revolutionary role white heterosexual men could fulfill, since they are the very embodiment of reactionary-vested-interest power" (xl), by decade's end, Marxist-feminist Heidi Hartmann (1979) would concur when she cautioned, "Women should not trust men to 'liberate' them 'after the revolution,' . . . [because] their immediate self interest lies in our continued oppression" (24). Yet scholar activists like Gloria Anzaldúa ([1981] 2015) would push back against this identitarian logic, admitting in an essay for the feminist anthology *This Bridge Called My Back*, "I do not exclude whites from the list of people I love, two of them happen to be gay males. For the politically correct stance we let color, class, and gender separate us from those who would be kindred spirits" (206). Similarly, Dinnerstein would take radical feminists to task for their blatant disinterest in understanding the psychic underpinnings of men's and women's shared "neurotic" sexual dynamics. Despite these latter pleas for a feminist politics attentive to the multiple cross-gender bonds that defined many women's lives, by the mid-1980s onward, as feminism became institutionalized in women's studies programs, the practical question of how men might take up feminist ideas, make common cause with women and gender outlaws, or expand the forms of feminist practice were abandoned and replaced with a mind-numbing epistemological debate about whether or not men could even be feminists if their existential being was an extension of patriarchy (Jardin and Smith 1987; Kauffman 1989; Boone and Cadden 1990). Amid this impasse, male affirmative feminists of all genders and sexualities continued to contribute to feminist theorizing, composing a diverse and inspiring archive of "feminism from its outside" (Halley 2006).[1]

The most recurrent theme in male affirmative feminist theory is the necessity of developing an androgynous view of gender, which involves understanding men and women as fundamentally sharing the same emotional and intellectual *capacities*, even if emanating from different kinds of bodies, while demanding the dissolution of culturally proscribed gender roles. As early as 1964, feminist sociologist Alice Rossi argued that the society-wide adoption of an androgynous view of gender would be a necessary precondition for making men and women equal participants in US civic life: "An androgynous conception of sex role means that each sex will cultivate some of the characteristics usually associated with the other in traditional sex role definitions. . . . [R]ather than a one-sided plea for women to adapt to a masculine stance in the world, this definition of sex equality stresses the enlargement of the common ground on which men and women base their lives together by changing the social definitions of approved characteristic and behavior for both sexes" (26–27). For male liberationists like Marc Feigen Fasteau (1974), androgyny was an aspirational ideal that would allow men access to a rich, interior emotional life previously denied them, and provide the opportunity for both men and women to become full social beings unrestrained by the demands of dimorphic gender scripts; this shift, he suggested, would infuse every aspect of social and affectional existence (from friendship, to sex, to child-rearing) with greater egalitarianism and spontaneity as polarized sex roles are reinvented or discarded. Androgyny then, has historically been a bedrock component of arguments for the ultimate *de-gendering* of human qualities. As feminist philosopher Patrick D. Hopkins (1998) explains, in this view, a human trait like "aggression" is neither understood as distinctly masculine or feminine, nor categorially "owned" by men or women, but rather a highly variable quality that people of all genders are capable of enacting, in both beneficent and destructive ways (46).

As these examples attest, androgyny is a deeply humanist value, which expands the feminist demand that women should have access to a broader share of worldly existence to everyone, including men. Queer anthropologist Gayle Rubin ([1975, 1991] 2012) articulates this inclusive vision of feminism as a cross-gender coalitional project to be free from "obligatory sexualities and sex roles" when she claims, "We are not only oppressed as women; we are oppressed by having to *be* women—or men as the case may be. . . . [the feminist movement] must dream of . . . an androgynous and genderless (though not sexless) society, in which one's sexual anatomy is irrelevant to who one is, what one does, and with whom one makes love" (61). Despite its utopian aspirations, the value of androgyny has recurrently come under attack as a male liberal sleight of hand intended to overlook men's significant structural power in relation to women (Carrigan, Connell, and Lee 1987). Yet its most progressive edge involves an acknowledgment of fundamental *similarities* between men and women that patriarchal logics frequently mask, which includes the mutual desire to express one's gender or sexuality more freely, but perhaps more radically to altogether reject the centrality of gender and sexuality to one's self-definition. Remarkably then, the contemporary project of imagining and cultivating nonbinary forms of gender expression finds one of its origins in distinctly *straight male* feminist arguments for an androgynous world.

Dinnerstein's *The Mermaid and the Minotaur: Sexual Arrangement and Human Malaise* (1976) presents us with one of the most ethical versions of androgynous thinking in all of feminist theory. Dinnerstein was interested in understanding the psychological underpinnings of modern "sexual arrangements," the complex emotional dynamics between men and women that drive them to consent to antagonistic interpersonal relationships, which form the basis for larger patriarchal norms. Dinnerstein argued that the systemic devaluation of women under patriarchy was a highly evolved *symptom* of a more fundamentally untenable psychological reality at the core of human development: the general rule of female headed child-rearing. For Dinnerstein, the fact that nearly all persons regardless of gender are raised by a single primary female parent means that young humans develop a distorted and internally contradictory relationship of intense attachment to *and* revulsion for, a god-like female figure who facilitates the conditions of their existence while becoming associated with every inhibition to their individuation, growth, and freedom (36–37). If men and women shared child-rearing coequally, she proposed, young humans of all genders would be forced to stop identifying a single category of people (women) as the universal scapegoat for their *"resentment of the human condition."* Dinnerstein simultaneously argues *from* an androgynous perspective (accounting for men and women's shared socialization in relation to primary female parental figures) as well as *for* a fully androgynous understanding of gender (through parenthood), where, without ever diminishing the especial toll this arrangement places on women, she bracingly argues "that the pressures [our sexual arrangement] imposes on men are at least as mutilating, distorting, and debasing as those it imposes on [women]" (234). At its most visionary then, an androgynous view of gender acknowledges the shared phenomenological and psychic conditions of men and women, thus providing a foundational argument for their mutual investment in destroying gender hierarchy. Its intended outcome is to cultivate in all humans their full repertoire of capacities toward collective flourishing, and away from deleterious behaviors, which may be inflected, but not wholly determined by, gendered performance.

Male affirmative feminist theory also offers one of the most convincing rebuttals to feminist essentialism in all of critical thought. Of course, second wave feminism was a full-throated assault on the rigid patriarchal view of women's so-called natural inferiority to men. Yet in working to dismantle this *negative* essentialist framing of women, feminists frequently imagined women as essentially sharing their own network of *positive* traits (like nurturance, generosity, and egalitarianism), while flipping the patriarchal script to produce an aggressively monolithic conception of man and male nature (as narcissistic, violent, and emotionally bereft) (Johnston 1973; Gutter Dyke Collective 1973; Cook-Daniels [1982] 2016; West 1999). In his essay "How Feminism Made a Man Out of Me," Hopkins (1998) confronts this paradox by comparing how conservative US evangelical views of the natural superiority (and unquestioned spiritual authority) of the male gender role ironically coincide with radical feminist assumptions about male bodies as innate vessels of patriarchal power. Hopkins explains how as a child raised in a highly gendered Christian school, whenever he questioned the church's rigid attachment to dimorphic gender scripts, he was derided as being either a feminist or gay (37). Years later, when he expressed his anti-sexist commitments as the only male feminist in a graduate seminar on lesbian feminism, he was perceived as an interloper in all-women spaces: "this cultural feminist ideology vilified masculinity (which was a nebulous collection of traits involving rationality, objectivity, and a propensity to dominate others) ardently . . . . [attempting to eliminate] the essentialist taint of . . . male-centeredness wherever it might be found" (39). Thus, Hopkins concludes, "Cultural feminism seemed do by fiat what Christian Family Living tried to do with education—stop me from being a feminist and make a man out of me" (41).

Building on Hopkins's insights, male pro-feminist thinkers like legal theorist Duncan Kennedy (1992), film scholar Scott MacDonald (1991), and philosophers Harry Brod and Tom Digby (1998) have offered anti-essentialist accounts of male masculinity that dismantle feminist orthodoxies about perceived male patriarchal nature on multiple fronts. In his groundbreaking essay "Sexual Abuse, Sexy Dressing, and the Eroticization of Domination," Kennedy (1992) asks what widespread social transformation would be required for men to perceive their own interests as aligned with the general reduction in sexual abuse and violation of women. Kennedy reminds us that while men benefit hugely from women's subordination, they also suffer profoundly when it comes to having noncoercive, erotically exciting, mutually beneficial relationships with women: "[The] reality of male abuse of women . . . discourages the activities of fantasy, play, invention, and experiment through which we have whatever hope we have of evolving or transcending our current modes of male and female sexuality. For this reason, men have at least a potential erotic interest in fighting against it" (1312). Here, Kennedy asks us to expand our feminist imaginative horizon, so we might conceive both men and women as sexually interested parties who, despite the ubiquity of patriarchal constraints, still desire one another, and might in fact have greater access to the full range of their fantasy life if structural forms of violence toward women were significantly reduced.

Similarly, in his autobiographical essay "Confessions of a Feminist Porn Watcher," MacDonald (1991) offers a nuanced portrait of the straight male porn viewer as a figure riven by ambivalence, rather than a confident wielder of sexual power over women as many essentialist feminist critiques claim. First, he reminds us that in a homophobic society, pornography is one of the only places that men are permitted to see visual images of other naked men's bodies in any sustained way (36). Second, he points out that the culture's general sexist expectation that women must be beautiful, and hence sexually available to men, finds a parallel formulation in the assumption that men are naturally ugly and revolting (41). Consequently, "from a male point of view, the desire [in watching pornography] is not to see women harmed, but to momentarily identify with men who—despite their personal unattractiveness by conventional cultural definitions . . . are adored by the women they encounter sexually. . . . [Pornography allows] men to periodically deal with the cultural context which mitigates against their full acceptance of themselves as sexual beings" (41). MacDonald never overlooks the potential conjoining of male pornographic fantasy with the material realities of rape and sexual assault; rather he loosens the presumed one-to-one fit between these realities, showing us how the realm of sexual *fantasy* captures a wide range of male vulnerabilities as much, if not more so, than their power and control. Ultimately, each of these thinkers commits to the feminist critique of patriarchal violence and misogyny, yet each also begins from the assumption that men are highly variegated social beings with multiplex interior lives and diversified motives. Each takes seriously men's stake in both the maintenance of patriarchy *and* its potential critique and dismantling. And all presume that men and women participate in a complex dynamic, rather than existing in an intractable polarity where each occupies an essential role whose privileges and disadvantages can be intellectually charted in advance. Precisely because it arrives from the perspective of feminism's perceived enemies, then, the anti-essentialism of male affirmative feminist theory offers one of the most powerful demands for feminist self-reflection and self-criticism.

Male affirmative feminist theorizing also assumes that men, like any other group with shared experiences, have a unique perspective that might provide valuable insights to the feminist project of better understanding the manifold dimensions of gender. For instance, in his essay "A Black Man's Place in Black Feminist Criticism," literary scholar Michael Awkward (1998) underscores that Black men have a distinct outlook on gender relations, which is crucial for the future success of anti-sexist coalitional work and the continued growth of Black feminist literary and cultural study:

> From my perspective, what is potentially most valuable about the development of a black male feminism is not its capacity to reproduce black feminism as it . . . is being practiced by black females who focus primarily on "the complexities of black female subjectivity and experience." Rather, its potential value lies in the possibility that, in being antipatriarchal, as self-inquiring about their relationship(s) to feminism . . . black men can expand feminist inquiry's range and utilization . . . as *comrades.* (158)

By valuing his own "perspective," Awkward literally takes up the Black feminist project of self-valuation famously articulated in the Combahee River Collective, neither lionizing nor denigrating Black male subjectivity but seeing it as one valuable dimension of gendered experience that can positively expand Black feminism's conceptual reach. This productive "outsider" critique of

Black feminist theory encourages the field to live up to its own ideals more fully, which includes taking seriously the unexpected uses of Black feminism by people who are not Black women, but are interested in their collective freedom.

Finally, male affirmative feminist theorizing emphasizes that while the feminist dismantling of male privilege represents a significant loss of power for men, it might also provide avenues for other kinds of gains, including the expansion of men's erotic lives, more fulfilling relationships with women and one another, and the freedom from coercive sexual and gender regulations. While some might immediately criticize this claim as a sentimental liberal pandering, male feminist theorizing compellingly argues that no radical movement can wage a successful campaign of dismantling an oppressive regime without gaining the consent of some of its antagonists to collectively forge a better world. One site for inspiring men to fight patriarchy is the freedom from the threat of homophobic policing, which would allow men to explore the full range of their affectional interests with partners of all genders, including intimacy with other men. Michael Warner's (1999) bracing description of "straight culture" as a heteronormative ideological system of practice that requires perpetual "terror to induce compliance," including threats of social shunning and physical violence for being perceived of as "queer," would suggest that a straight male feminism shares significant interests with a queer feminist politics, particularly in their mutual investment in throwing off the yoke of toxic masculinity (37–38). After all, many cis male feminist writers point out that the bundle of social privileges that come with being phenotypically male are offset by the experience of hegemonic masculinity as a living hell, "damage[ing] to our psyches" (Brod 1998: 199), transforming men into a category of "sub-humanity" (Dinnerstein [1976] 1999: 15), and turning affectively rich persons into "male machines" (Fasteau 1974). This is born out by the fact that cis men comprise the highest rate of reported "deaths of despair" (the combined fatalities of suicide, opioid overdoses, and alcohol related liver failure), and remain the dominant demographic of school shooters and sexual offenders, all forms of violent dysfunction deeply rooted in male anomie, sexual frustration, and self-hatred projected both inward at a devalued self, and outward at a despised world (Case and Deaton 2020). Against this nightmare, male affirmative feminist theorizing reminds us again and again that a queer feminist politics has much to offer men, including the possibility of "fighting [a sexual arrangement] that seems about to destroy everything earthly that you love . . . not with blind force . . . but with passionate curiosity" and we might add, *pleasure* (Dinnerstein [1976] 1999: viii). How then might we begin to imaginatively conceive a male masculinity positively inflected by feminist and queer identities, experiences, and worldviews and oriented toward collective flourishing rather than mutually assured destruction? I now turn to one striking cultural example of straight men doing queer feminism with precisely this intention.

Feminism Is for *Beginners*

In the MeToo era, Mike Mills's tender love story *Beginners* is an outlier. The film narrates the blossoming of a heterosexual romance between two thirty-something creatives—a melancholic but "lovable" graphic designer, Oliver, and a luminous French actress, Anna—from a straight male point of view. Yet the film is decidedly *not* about sexual trauma or violence. It depicts men and women engaged in a mutually pleasurable, if emotionally challenging, negotiation of desire. And it reveals the male gaze as an internally divided perspective fundamentally shaped by the lives, desires, and experiences of women and queer people. Shuttling rapidly and playfully back and forth across time, the film nests Oliver's developing romance with Anna within two broader frames of reference: his whimsical childhood relationship with his mother, Georgia, and the four short years he spent befriending his father Hal after Hal comes out as gay at age seventy-five. In Oliver's childhood, Hal had been an absent phantom, remembered only as the faceless man who anemically pecks Georgia on the cheek goodbye each morning before heading to work. Decades later, in the wake of her death, Hal becomes a vibrant, emotive figure of male queerness, pursing a nonmonogamous intergenerational relationship, developing a multiracial gay male friendship circle, and actively participating in the LGBTQ political life of Los Angeles. Bewildered but inspired by his father's late-in-life transformation, Oliver barely has time to synthesize this new side before Hal dies. Oliver meets Anna two months after his father's passing, and their relationship is shot through with Oliver's bifurcated memories of his mother's fanciful eccentricity and deep unhappiness alongside his father's emotional distance and later exuberance. The son of split subjects, Oliver is himself deeply torn between a desire to believe that "magic" can happen between people, and that "things will never work out." To capture this internal crisis, in between dramatic scenes, the film inserts a series of rapid-fire visual montages, which vividly depict the cognitive process by which a straight white man re-narrates his family history as a distinctly feminist and queer one against his traditionally held view of heterosexual sadness and anomie. The film then synthesizes the lessons of male affirmative feminist theorizing through the aesthetic experience of visually encountering one man's multiplicitous subjectivity. This project is accomplished through three key formal features.

First, the most visually striking element of the movie is its strategic use of kaleidoscopic montage sequences, in which Oliver interjects his voice into the frame to describe and display relevant bits and pieces of his past that shape his present identity. As a Los Angeles–based graphic designer, Oliver seems to see the world as a vast assemblage of creative materials always thinking of ways to rearrange the pieces so as to curate a story that would knit together the disparate parts of his fractured selfhood. In the first sequence, Oliver links his own identity as a straight man living in Southern California at the turn of the millennium to his parents' marital history at midcentury:

> This is 2003. This is what the sun looks like, and the stars, nature. This is the president. And this is the sun in 1955, and the stars, and nature . . . and movies, and the president. [This is] what it looked like when people kissed. . . . When they were happy. . . . [and] sad. . . . My parents got married in 1955. . . . They had a child, and they stayed married for 44 years. . . . Until she died in their bed, after four months of cancer and eating French toast for every meal . . . and skipping back and forth through time inside her head. Six months later, my father told me he was gay. He had just turned 75.

As Oliver speaks, each of his sentences is visually punctuated by corresponding images: telescopic snapshots of the night sky in 2003 and 1955; *Life Magazine* layouts of "happy" white Americans; black-and-white photographs of his family home; the visual confusion in his mother's mind when she was ill; and finally Oliver's father coming out to him while seated on their family couch. The sequence sets up his mother's illness and his father's gayness as disorganizing events that literally reorient his once seamless vision of the American good life toward the loneliness and dissatisfaction that was left unspoken, unpictured, or unimagined between the cracks (or edits) of his past. Though this initial loss of innocence is figured as a kind of psychic trauma, it ultimately grants Oliver access to the lifeworld of others, which facilitates his development of a distinctly queer and feminist consciousness.

As each of the five montages unfold, they successively become more intricate, braiding together Oliver's increasing awareness of gay history ("The first Gay Pride flag was made in 1978 by a man named Gilbert Baker"); his father's traumatic encounters with a homophobic psychiatric establishment ("The doctor told him that homosexuality was a mental illness, but it could be cured"); his mother's experience of stigmatization as a Jewish-American; and Anna's own personal history of familial trauma and a peripatetic existence as a traveling actor ("[This is what it looks like] when she tells me there's always a new empty room waiting for her"). As Oliver amasses these stories, they become occasions for making associational leaps between various experiences of marginalization. In one scene, he organically links Anna's childhood experience of being denigrated for her Jewishness to his mother's experience of anti-Semitism during WWII: "This is what it looks like when Anna tells me about being Jewish in 2003. And when I tell her my mother was Jewish. . . . My mother didn't know she was Jewish until she was 13. . . . It was 1938. . . . This was Man of the year [ADOLF HITLER ON TIME MAGAZINE COVER]. . . . This is the swim team that asked [my mother] to leave once they discovered that she was Jewish [GEORGIA'S SWIM TEAM PHOTO]." Later, Oliver compares the freedom he and Anna have to express their love in 2003 to his father's fear of being jailed for cruising public restrooms in the 1950s ("We didn't have to hide to have sex"). On one hand, in each subsequent montage, Oliver increasingly acknowledges that his distinct, evolving identity as a heterosexual male is inevitably a product of elaborate histories of sexist, racist, and homophobic exclusion (having been raised by parents who experienced these forms of oppression). On the other, as Oliver psychically incorporates the personal histories, creative products, and emotional landscapes of his mother, father, and lover into his imaginative flights, his straight maleness becomes an expanding gordian knot of interwoven ideologies, affective histories, broken memories, and explosive moments of insight forged *in relation* to others. By visually tracing the manifold idiosyncratic origins of Oliver's emergent feminist and queer sensibility, *Beginners* presents assemblage thinking, understood as the graphic artist's eye for juxtaposition, as a creative method for complexly describing organic feminisms born out of men's lived social relations with women and queer people.

Second, the film explicitly queers the male gaze by literally bisecting Oliver's point of view with images or memories of gay love, intimacy, and eros. A foundational visual motif in the movie is the recurring image of Oliver looking directly at his father as Hal kisses or cuddles with his boyfriend Andy, an eccentric Croatian physical trainer who loves "older men." Similarly, in numerous instances when Oliver looks at Anna, a memory of his father or mother explodes into the scene, visually interrupting or standing in the line of his heterosexual desire. Oliver first meets Anna at a Halloween party two months after Hal's death. He attends dressed up as Sigmund Freud (with a requisite white beard and pipe) while Anna appears costumed as the dissident radical Julius Rosenberg with a short black wig. Seeing Oliver seated glumly next to a couch, Anna plops down and playfully psychoanalyzes him. Unable to speak due to a bout of laryngitis, she writes on a pad of paper: "Why are you at a party if you're sad?" Taken aback by her piercing insight, Oliver replies: "I was doing such a good job of hiding it. How could you tell?" Anna responds by drawing two eyes above her question, while pointing two fingers back and forth from her line of sight to his. After this intimate exchange, Oliver leaves to get them drinks. Walking back, he looks wistfully at Anna from the kitchen doorway. Just as his (and our) gaze alights on her, however, Oliver is suddenly overtaken by a powerful memory of his father. In a moving flashback, we witness Hal wake Oliver from his sleep with a late-night phone call, in which he gleefully tells Oliver about his first visit to a gay bar. As Hal relates this story, Oliver imagines his father navigating the crowd, buying drinks, laughing with friends, experiencing moments of loneliness or rejection, but also joyfully taking in the convivial atmosphere. Finally he asks, "So did you meet anyone?" Hal replies subdued, "Young gay men don't go for older men. You have it easy." With these final words, Oliver's gaze returns to Anna, his father's words now carrying a far greater weight than before (see Figure 1).

In this breathtaking scene, Oliver's seemingly omniscient straight male look is cut through two ways: first, literally and figuratively seen by the object of his desire, a woman (dressed as a man no less) who reverses the classic fetishizing male gaze by reading back vulnerability in its stare, but then viewing his own developing experience of heterosexual potentiality through the prism of Hal's burgeoning gay desires. Here, Oliver is both remembering one of his first encounters with queer longing (captured in Hal's excitement over the possibilities of a new gay social scene) and empathizing with its thwarted energy in a homophobic and ageist culture. Through this "double consciousness," something about Oliver's worldview expands as he comes to realize that his father's gay desire is no different in intensity from his own straight one; rather, it is simply that Oliver's yearnings for a woman like Anna are granted free reign in a hegemonically straight society. In other instances, when Oliver contemplates Anna's features as she prepares her makeup, he recalls his mother doing the same in front of her vanity when he was a child. Just as he had empathized with Hal, here too he rereads his mother's careful beauty regimen as a fruitless effort to maintain her underappreciated looks for affection that was never forthcoming within her passionless marriage.

Figure 1. Top to bottom: Anna returns the classical male cinematic gaze by literally and figuratively "seeing" through Oliver's grief; Oliver stares at Anna from across the costume party only to be caught by a memory of his father's first time at a gay bar. *Beginners*, dir. Mike Mills (Universal Studios, 2010)

Over and over, then, when Oliver gazes at Anna he *re*-encounters his parents' distinct vulnerabilities and burning desires with greater clarity and compassion, at once acknowledging his privilege but also registering their distinctly feminine and queer imprint on his worldview. In these moments, the camera frequently puts us in Oliver's point of view—looking at or mentally picturing Anna laughing and crying, Hal and Andy kissing, Georgia listening forlornly to the blues—but then reverses the shot to reveal Oliver's face as he is visibly moved by each scene, variously brought to tears of joy, frustration, or sadness (see Figure 2). In *Beginners*, Mills intentionally undercuts the seeming singularity and violating potential of the classic cinematic male look, both by turning the camera upon it, and revealing this same gaze to be deeply affected by what its "eyes" light upon. Actor Ewan McGregor's heartrending performance as Oliver viscerally captures this sense of perpetual emotional impact, as he frequently appears on screen flush in the face and eyes wet with incipient tears. Oliver, then, is always on the cusp of being broken open by the swell of feelings that his network of queer and feminist relations incites within him; consequently, McGregor's material enactment of this sense of male emotional contingency literalizes a "different [way] of using, feeling, and showing male bodies," including the "experience of [non-violent] pleasures" (Connell 233). The film does not need Oliver himself to have same-sex desire for his gaze to be fundamentally feminist and queer; rather it suggests that one thing straight men do when they look at women and queers is identify with them, another is admire, another is desire, another is empathize. This queering of the male gaze reminds us that men, no less than any other gendered subject, introject competing, multiple identifications in their production of selfhood.

Third, the formal features of associational montage and a queered male gaze are expressive of the film's overall tone, which is simply *whimsical*. Whimsy is a quality or feeling state associated with childlike wonder and enchantment, the unraveling of certain norms or rules of conduct, and openness to imagination and play. Because of its ephemerality, in a patriarchal society, whimsy is a decidedly feminine-coded affect often denigrated as frivolous or superficial. Upending this logic, *Beginners* consistently treats straight male masculinity whimsically, thereby making it open for reinvention but also stressing its already contingent, socially constructed, and sometimes just plain silly aspects. This is playfully captured in Oliver's self-deprecating statement to his friend Eliot just days after meeting Anna: "It's embarrassing. I'm thirty-eight and falling for a girl again. . . . It's like I lost

Figure 2. Top to bottom: Hal cuddles with his younger boyfriend, Andy,
while playfully waving to Oliver; Oliver reacts with joy and affirmation
to this scene of same-sex affection; the camera captures Oliver on
the verge of tears as he faces the reality of his father's mortality.
Beginners, dir. Mike Mills (Universal Studios, 2010)

the instructions or I . . . never had them." Here, Oliver reminds us that the gendered scripts we assume are so readily available as ironclad command-ments and imprisoning identities never arrive to us immaculately, if they ever arrive at all. The whimsical nature of maleness recurs throughout the movie in numerous moments where hegemonic masculinity is presented as a fundamentally warped, unrealistic, or coercive "set of instructions," which the narrative systematically undermines through irony and irreverence. One site for this work is Oliver's relationship to his father's dog, Arthur, an aging Jack Russell terrier with whom he engages in a series of hilarious existential "conversations." When Oliver first takes Arthur to a dog park to play "with his own kind," he tells the dog: "You're a Jack Russell, that's a breed. Your personality was created by this guy John Russell, a hunting enthusiast, in the 1800s. . . . You think you're just you, and you want to chase the foxes, but other people planted that in you years ago. Now, somewhat arbitrarily, you are considered very cute." Immediately after this scene, the film cuts to Oli-ver in his drafting studio drawing an image of a T-shirt with the following words inscribed on it: "My personality was created by someone else and all I got was this stupid T-shirt." In each of these instances, straight male mascu-linity is comically represented, first as a failed set of "instructions," then a scientifically invented "breed," then a socially constructed "personality." Each version of masculinity fails to add up to a coherent self, and each rep-resents an abortive project that neither Oliver nor any other male character in the film ever live up to. Like the spontaneous, ludic flights of whimsy, masculinity in *Beginners* is always idiosyncratically divergent, proliferating various queer or proto-queer expressions, from Hal, the ebullient gay art his-torian, to Andy, the oddball daddy chaser, from Eliot the good-natured hip-ster best friend, to Juan, the nurturing male hospice nurse. Rather than rep-resenting fixed male types or identities, these various men—straight, gay, queer—literally inhabit or embody male masculinity in unexpected and enchanting ways: showing unrestrained physical affection and tenderness toward other men; crafting beautiful graphic artworks; nurturing household pets, plants, and furniture, with equal gentleness; and participating in forms of nonviolent, collective play with communities of fellow men.

This is perhaps no better captured than in British actor Christopher Plummer's tour de force (and Academy-Award winning) performance as Hal. In this utterly charming character, a classically straight male actor inhabits the most intricate and quotidian mannerisms, affectations, witti-cisms, and flirtatious innuendos of a gay septuagenarian, *without* stereotyp-ing those who make up this real-world demographic. Thus Plummer, like

Figure 3. Hal and Oliver hold hands at the edge of Hal's hospice bed, thus enacting alternative ways of inhabiting male masculinity. *Beginners*, dir. Mike Mills (Universal Studios, 2010)

McGregor, literalizes both a straight man professionally *acting as* gay, but also *enacting* or modeling for viewers a network of presumably "queer" gestures on screen (like kissing another man, or holding his son's hand, or dancing at a gay bar) that could potentially be taken up by any man, gay, straight, bisexual, or otherwise, as a meaningful expression of non-toxic male masculinity. At one point, Hal and Oliver tenderly hold hands while sitting on the edge of Hal's hospice bed (Figure 3). Hal admits: "You always wanted to hold my hand when you were little. I couldn't, you know. I was afraid it would look funny. I wanted to be close, you know and my father certainly was never close with me." Through an imagined "closeness" with gay male being and belonging, facilitated by the creative work of cinematic identification, two putatively straight male actors open up the space to occupy and vivify a broader male masculine desire for closeness and intimacy *across* sexualities, generations, and genders. The film then recurrently makes the case that gender is not something to be deconstructed as a psychic fantasy, known as a material or bodily truth, or exposed as ideology, but a lived practice that can be perpetually inhabited in new ways, expanded, and whimsically reimagined so that it might *do* different things in the world.

Simultaneously, whimsy functions throughout the movie as a kind of coping mechanism for the deeply painful reality of dysfunctional gender arrangements, including the presumption that love must make up for genuine loss, or that a shared home can permanently dispel loneliness. This is best captured by Anna when, after the first time making love to Oliver, she looks out her hotel room window and points to building across the street: "People in the building like us. Half of them think things will never work out. The other half believe in magic. It's like a war between them." Soon after, they share a moving exchange:

> ANNA: I used to love hotels. But now I'm always . . . in another hotel somewhere. . . . It makes it very easy to end up alone—to leave people.
>
> OLIVER: You can stay in the same place and still find ways to leave people.
>
> ANNA: You are like that? It's what you do? [Oliver nods yes] So we are the same?
>
> OLIVER: Yeah, I guess so. [The look to each other.]

Through an enchanted logic, the film reminds us that our obsessive attachment to gender dimorphism—reductively distinguishing people's personalities or behaviors on the basis of sexual difference—frequently masks other, perhaps far more salient categories or variables for adjudicating both similarity and distinction between so-called men and women. This includes people who "believe in magic" (Hal and Andy) and "people who think things will never work out" (Oliver); those who tend to "leave people" (Oliver and Anna) and those who stay (Hal and Georgia); those who grew up with both parents (Oliver) and those who didn't (Anna and Andy). Whimsy then, operates as a disorienting affective logic, which loosens the grip of sexual difference on human relationships, consequently facilitating an androgynous view of gender. In the course of the narrative both Oliver and Anna display emotional depth *and* recklessness, tenderness *and* coldness, generosity *and* selfishness. Both initiate sex and both interrupt it to address deep emotional conflicts. Both consent to, and both critically question, their reasons for falling in love. Consequently, Oliver and Anna's discovery that they are "the same" in their tendency to "leave people," is one outcome of their shared inhabitation of the of the full range of human vulnerability, which confirms the reality that men and women are capable of mutually loving, and mutually harming one another.

The film recognizes that achieving such an androgynous, associational, assemblage-like conception of gender comes with a significant loss: namely, the dissolution of security in performing normative gender roles, and the collapse of the aspirational stories we tell about idealized love, courtship, and fulfilling intimacy. It is fitting that Oliver meets Anna at the very moment that the loss of his father initiates a crisis of confidence in his own naive narratives about his family history and his relational fantasy ideals. When Hal is first diagnosed with terminal lung cancer, he asks Oliver to keep his prognosis a secret from his community of gay friends. Oliver interprets this request as an echo of Hal's decades-long secrecy about his sexuality, which in hindsight Oliver views as a kind of betrayal of their family, especially his mother. Having witnessed Georgia's sadness trapped in a listless marriage, Oliver now directly identifies with her as an adult worn down by Hal's self-delusions. Accordingly, when the Los Angeles–based indie band The Sads commission Oliver to draw their portraits for their upcoming album art, their name inspires him to produce an "impossibly long" flip-book narrating "The History of Sadness," a series of clumsy drawings graphically rendering the birth of heterosexual anomie: "Earth begins (sadness not yet invented) / first couple to marry for wrong reasons / invention of alcohol Ancient Egypt / first gay man diagnosed as mentally ill / first time an intense and difficult love revealed a person's shadow self to themselves." Though the band mates reject this idea, Oliver persists. Oliver's dogged commitment to selling this decidedly depressing version of The Sad's' potential CD case reflects a certain ambivalence, at once representing his increasingly feminist consciousness of the ideological ruse of heteronormativity, while also suggesting a narcissistic type of straight male melancholy. Here, Oliver is both feminist *and* straight male killjoy. *Beginners* then is an account of Oliver's reckoning with his own cruel optimism: torn between a desperate wish not to repeat the mistakes of his parents ("I just don't want to be like you and mom"), yet unable to release his fantasies of an ideal partner ("Hal: you can wait and wait for the lion or be with the giraffe; Oliver: I'd wait for the lion").

Yet Hal's sudden transformation into a loving, playful, erotically adventurous gay man in the wake of coming out disrupts Oliver's own melancholic narrative. When Oliver expresses shock that Hal would tolerate Andy's polyamorous relationships with other men, Hal retorts: "You want me to be with someone like me. I like Andy cause he's not like me . . . he's *fun*." The film then represents the clash between a normative conception of companionate love demanding a fixed, stable idea of how one is "supposed to feel" and a queer understanding of love and intimacy as fundamentally unpredictable experiences, much like the category of gender itself. To embrace that unpredictability requires a willingness to admit our lack of knowledge about the gender and sexual categories we hold so tightly to, that is, to become beginners or newcomers to what love, or desire, or intimacy is "supposed to feel" like. This Oliver can only do by releasing his claim to have ever transparently "known" his parents, which by extension means accepting his own subjectivity as an ever-evolving assemblage, rather than a seamlessly handed-down identity that cannot be reduced to the oedipal drama, hegemonic masculinity, or the gender norms of midcentury US culture.

In one of the film's most moving exchanges, Hal and Oliver disagree on the ubiquity of common knowledge about the gay pride flag. Oliver insists that "everybody knows" the rainbow flag means gay pride, while Hal continually rebuts: "No they don't. . . . Don't be ridiculous." Suddenly Hal reroutes the question of public queer knowledge to his relationship with Oliver:

HAL: Did you know, about me? [Oliver shakes his head no]

OLIVER: No, I just thought you and mom weren't in love.

HAL: Oh, we loved each other.

OLIVER: But you were gay that whole time.

HAL: I learned how not to be. . . . I knew I was gay, though . . . I couldn't have survived if I didn't know that. I just chose not to follow those instincts. . . . Look, I liked my life, the museum, our house, that's what I wanted.

OLIVER: And mom? You wanted mom too right? [Frustrated and angry]

HAL: Yes, stop that. She proposed to me you know. I said—look I love you and we're great buddies but you know what I am. And then she says, that doesn't matter. I'll fix that. . . . I thought, oh god, I'll try anything.

Here, Oliver is shocked to discover his parents' complexity on many scales and registers: the mutually destructive aspects of their compromised bond, the historical conditions that shaped their pact and limited their options, and their shared bending to normative gender and sexual expectations. In other words, their creation of a gendered *dynamic* that could never solely rest on any one person's shoulders. At the same time, this discovery forces Oliver to disentangle a series of false assumptions about the nature of emotional attachment, including the idea that authentic, companionate love can only emerge out of normative, sexual arrangements organized around the "truth" of one's sexuality that presumably produce pure and sustained joy and contentment. Instead, Hal offers a multi-dimensional, and perhaps more honest view, of love born out of highly compromised conditions, which often takes the form of deep friendship (even in the absence of sexual chemistry), shared values and aspirations, mutual experiences of oppression, even painful (if unintended) betrayal, hurt, and shame.

This realization transforms Oliver's affective orientation toward his father from resentment to curiosity. At first bewildered by the sense that he "never knew" his parents, he now becomes fascinated to perceive them from many new angles. This shift is graphically rendered in the visual movement away from Oliver's melancholic flip-book, "The History of Sadness," back toward the queer and feminist visual montages that anchor the larger narrative, where he incorporates more and more of his father's gay history. If "The History of Sadness" represents a self-pitying and solipsistic form of straight male melancholy, assemblage thinking is proper mourning, the working through of loss, and the recombination of its constituted parts, in order to invent a new relationship to oneself and the world. When the complex reality of his mother and father's arrangement becomes clear, an explosive full-screen image of the color pink appears on screen, breaking the emotional gravity of the scene with joyful queer energy. Rapidly we cycle through the colors of gay pride flag: red, orange, yellow, green, turquoise. As each flashes, we hear Oliver announce their corresponding terms: "Sex. Life. Healing. Sunlight. Nature. Spirit." The montage continues with his voice-over:

> The first Gay Pride flag was made in 1978 by a man named Gilbert Baker. He gave a meaning to each color. . . . On November 27th, 1978, Harvey Milk was shot and killed. One week later, my father opened his annual Museum Christmas Exhibit. He collected stuffed animals . . . and put them on display. My father printed a quote from The Velveteen Rabbit . . . on the wall . . . "'The stuffed rabbit asked—What is real?' And the Horse said, 'Real isn't how you're made. It's a thing that happens to you. When a child loves you for a long time not just to play with, but really loves you, then you become real. . . . Generally by the time you are real, most of your hair has been loved off, and your eyes drop out and you get loose in the joints. But these things don't matter at all because you are real and you can't be ugly, except to people who don't understand.

Just as Hal's disclosure about their family history expands Oliver's perspective, allowing him to see Hal and Georgia from a different point of view, now armed with his newfound insight, Oliver similarly expands *our* view of gay history, returning the gay pride flag to us as a visual prism composed of enchanting hues that alter our mood and perception while reconnecting them to Gilbert Baker's life-affirming queer vision. The scene visually depicts the slow, steady, sometimes painful but also beautiful process by which a straight white man comes to perceive his gay elderly father as "real" by genuinely learning to love him, which is another word for *understanding*. And so too, even those feminist and queer viewers thoroughly convinced of their own organic knowledge of

LGBTQ cultural history now are quite literally compelled to see this iconic gay emblem anew, as though they were encountering it for the first time, through the unique graphic design sensibility of this particular cis straight man, himself a neophyte student of the queer past.

As this shift occurs, the film's core question comes to the fore: What does it mean to really know someone, to understand them, to commune with them across differences of gender, sexuality, personality, and worldview? Moreover, how do you come to know someone you desire? As Oliver and Anna first achingly drift apart, then gingerly reknit the fabric of their relationship, it is fitting he finally shares with her Hal's personals ad for *The Advocate*. Anna marvels at the erotic boldness and emotional authenticity of Hal's photo. She reads part of the ad aloud: "I'm looking for sex with the hope it turns into friendship or a relationship. But I don't insist on monogamy. I'm an old senior guy, 78, but I'm attractive and horny. I'm an art historian, now retired. . . . I have a nice house with food, drinks, friends and me. If you are willing to try an older guy, let's meet and see what happens." In the moving image of Hal emotionally exposed—vulnerable, authentic, erotic— Anna finally inhabits Oliver's queered gaze, seeing their relationship in and through Hal's gay desire (see Figure 4). This is an image of a man who was once one thing (seemingly straight, monogamous, professional, buttoned up) and then became another (publicly gay, nonmonogamous, experimental, ebullient). *Or perhaps Hal was simply always many things*: the absent father, the talented museum curator, the playful gay man, the loyal but emotionally distant husband, the older boyfriend, and more. Thus, in the wake of Oliver and Anna's brief separation, Hal returns as a figure of the newly thinkable for two putatively straight people whose attachment to gendered scripts have utterly failed them. Hal's advertisement represents the new script he invented for himself when the horizon of possibility for becoming something else, something queer and alive, finally arrived. "He never gave up," Anna says hopefully. Sitting side by side on Oliver's bed, the two look at one another with nervous anticipation. "What happens now?" Oliver asks. "I don't know," Anna replies. Oliver delivers the film's last line: "How does that work?" They look at each other and smile.

Beginners then, ends with playful uncertainty, leaving us with a picture of men and women looking toward one another to decide how to move forward into an uncharted future. Perhaps one of the most unexpected and moving elements of the story is that it presents a straight man who comes to see traditional male-female sexual arrangements as intolerable, as much if not more so, than any woman or gender outlaw. The film suggests that when

Figure 4. Oliver shares Hal's personals ad with Anna, which inspires a renewed openness to the unpredictable possibilities of their bond beyond the norms and expectations of marriage, traditional gender roles, and idealized companionate love. *Beginners*, dir. Mike Mills (Universal Studios, 2010)

we try to conceive or make sense of the intricate workings of male masculinity individual psychology matters, family history matters, the contexts of space, place, and time matters, networks of relationships matter, how people move through and inhabit the world matters, as much as any ideological system or structure. *Beginners* offers both a representation, and theory, of a male affirmative queer feminism born not from ideological education but from an affective vulnerability, which includes the willingness to admit that we simply do not know what shape or form our genders, our sexualities, our arrangements might take because they are always emergent, rather than fixed in advance. The crisis of knowing that sits at the core of *Beginners*, the question of how we come to know who people are and the manifold ways they continue to slip from our grasp, is ultimately an allegory for the crisis at the core of all feminist theorizing (and perhaps all social justice–oriented theories of power): namely, that an ideological critique of men, male being or nature, does not ultimately grant us transparent access to who men are individually or collectively. And so too with "white people," "straight people," "cisgender people," "white feminists," or any other broadly defined group of perceived oppressors that our most cherished theories convince us we have all figured out. Our crystalline analyses of these various groups' complicity in producing and maintaining elaborate systems of top-down power tell us much about the mechanisms by which domination is enacted and achieved, but so very little about the complex lives, motives, interests, investments of the actual flesh-and-blood humans that compose them beyond their presumed bid for godlike power.

Could a more humane feminist theory admit to the wish to learn more about men, our desire for them, and our shared potential for liberation and communion, rather than presume to know men in and through our exquisite critique of them? As Linda Zerilli (2005) has compellingly argued, to do so requires that we revivify feminism not as an ironclad theory of patriarchal oppression, but as an imaginative worldmaking project committed to the perpetual process of *beginning* anew, including forming novel and unexpected associations across gendered difference. This necessarily demands a feminist practice in which we recurrently admit to being novices in our attempts to understand the sources of our subjection, or even one another. The consequences of failing to learn this lesson are vast, if not nigh catastrophic: expanding forms of right-wing psychopathy combine with a form of recalcitrant left moralism unwilling to imagine or entertain any bond with one's perceived enemies. I remain completely uncertain about the potential for men's widescale, collaborative participation in the dismantling of the very dysfunctional systems we all seem to be suicidally clinging to. Yet I have also seen deep humanity, loving kindness, generosity, self-reflexivity, and awareness in men of all stripes; I love many of them; I erotically desire more than a few; and I want to commune freely with others. I want a feminism that can account for these truths, and so much more. What I have offered, then, is not a reparative reading of male masculinity, but a *pragmatic* one, attentive to those lived reali-

ties about our relationships with men that our awe-inspiring critiques of heteropatriarchy sometimes miss. Can we reclaim the passionate curiosity that
Dinnerstein argued was necessary for our earthly survival? To do so would
demand that we extend the kind of play, inventiveness, irreverence, and uncertainty of our everyday attachments across gender to our feminist politics.
What kind of feminism might be willing to respond to those perennial questions "What is a man?" "What is a woman?" "What is gender?" "What does
freedom look like" and answer, "I don't know. How does that work?"

Notes

This essay is dedicated to Richard Hutson, my first, most cherished, and enduring model of
a straight male feminist. Thank you for sharing with me your unrestrained love of the world.

1   An abbreviated genealogy of male affirmative theorizing since the 1970s might include
     the anthologies: Snodgrass 1977; Kauffman 1987; Boone and Cadden 1990; Kimmel
     1990; and Digby 1998; feminist writing about male interpersonal and social dynamics,
     such as Fasteau 1974; Dinnerstein 1975; Segal 1990; Kennedy 1992; Connell 2005
     [1995]; Ehrenreich 1983; Faludi 2000; hooks 2004; and Digby 2014; and male feminist
     cultural criticism like Ikard 2007; Neal 2013; Poulson-Bryant 2011; and Ross 2022.
     Digby's *Men Doing Feminism* remains the most nuanced, multi-dimensional and
     frankly hopeful anthology of cis and trans male writers thinking through the practical
     role that men can play in the advancement of feminist political transformation. To date,
     Digby, Kimmel, Neal, and Michael Awkward are among the most sustained cisgender
     male scholars who write about the value of male feminist or pro-feminist perspectives.
     Cynthia Barounis's recent monograph *Vulnerable Constitutions* offers a theoretically
     innovative account of US-American male masculinity as heavily shaped by queer and
     disabled embodiment.

References

Anzaldúa, Gloria. (1981) 2015. "La Prieta." In *This Bridge Called My Back: Writings by Radical
     Women of Color*, edited by Cherríe Moraga and Gloria Anzaldúa, 22–29. Albany: SUNY
     Press.
Awkward, Michael. 1998. "A Black Man's Place in Black Feminist Criticism." In Digby 1998:
     147–67. New York: Routledge.
Barounis, Cynthia. 2019. *Vulnerable Constitutions: Queerness, Disability, and the Remaking of
     American Manhood*. Philadelphia: Temple University Press.
Boone, Joseph A., and Michael Cadden, eds. 1990. *Engendering Men: The Question of Male
     Feminist Criticism*. New York: Routledge.
Brod, Harry. 1998. "To Be a Man, or Not to Be a Man—That Is the Feminist Question." In Digby
     1998: 197–212.
Carrigan, Tim, Bob Connell [R. W. Connell], and John Lee. 1987. "Hard and Heavy: Toward a
     New Sociology of Masculinity." In Kaufman 1987: 139–92.
Case, Anne, and Angus Deaton. 2020. *Deaths of Despair and the Future of Capitalism*. Prince-
     ton, NJ: Princeton University Press.

Combahee River Collective. (1981), 2015. "A Black Feminist Statement." In *This Bridge Called My Back: Writings by Radical Women of Color*, edited by Cherríe Moraga and Gloria Anzaldúa, 210–18. Albany: SUNY Press.

Connell, R. W. (1995) 2005. *Masculinities*, 2nd ed. Berkeley: University of California Press.

Cook-Daniels, Carol. (1982) 2016. *In a Different Voice: Psychological Theory and Women's Development*. Cambridge, MA: Harvard University Press.

Dansky, Steven, John Knoebel, and Kenneth Pitchford. (1973) 1997. "The Effemenist Manifesto." In *We Are Everywhere: A Historical Sourcebook in Gay and Lesbian Politics*, edited by Mark Blasius and Shane Phelan, 435–48. New York: Routledge.

Digby, Tom, ed. 1998. *Men Doing Feminism*. New York: Routledge.

Digby, Tom, ed. 2014. *Love and War: How Militarism Shapes Sexuality and Romance*. New York Columbia University Press.

Dinnerstein, Dorothy. (1976) 1999. *The Mermaid and the Minotaur: Sexual Arrangement and Human Malaise*. New York: Other Press.

Ehrenreich, Barbara. 1983. *The Hearts of Men: American Dreams and the Flight from Commitment*. New York: Anchor.

Faludi, Susan. 2000. *Stiffed: The Betrayal of the American Man*. New York: William Morrow.

Fasteau, Feigen Mark. 1974. *The Male Machine*. New York: McGraw-Hill.

Firestone, Shulamith. (1971) 2003. *The Dialectic of Sex: The Case for Feminist Revolution*. New York: Farrar, Straus and Giroux.

A Gay Male Group. (1972) 1992. "Notes on Gay Male Consciousness Raising." In *Out of the Closets: Voices of Gay Liberation*, edited by Karla Jay and Allen Young, 293–300. New York: NYU Press.

Gutter Dyke Collective. 1973. *Dykes and Gorgons* 1, no. 1 (May–June).

Halley, Janet. 2006. *Split Decisions: How and Why to Take a Break from Feminism*. Princeton, NJ: Princeton University Press.

Haraway, Donna. (1985) 2004. "A Manifesto for Cyborgs: Science, Technology and Socialist Feminism in the 1980s." [1985]. In *The Haraway Reader*, 7–46. New York: Routledge.

Hartmann, Heidi. 1979. "The Unhappy Marriage of Marxism and Feminism: Toward a more Progressive Union." *Capital and Class* 3, no. 2: 1–33.

Hoagland, Sarah Lucia, and Julia Penelope, eds. 1988. *For Lesbians Only: A Separatist Anthology*. London: Onlywomen.

Hoàng, Nguyễn Tân. 2014. *A View from the Bottom: Asian American Masculinity and Sexual Representation*. Durham, NC: Duke University Press.

hooks, bell. 2004. *The Will to Change: Men, Masculinity, and Love*. New York: Washington Square Press.

Hopkins, Patrick D. 1998. "How Feminism Made a Man Out of Me: The Proper Subject of Feminism and the Problem of Men." In Digby 1998: 33–56. New York: Routledge.

Ikard, David. 2007. *Breaking the Silence: Toward a Black Male Feminist Criticism*. Baton Rouge: Louisiana State University Press.

Jardin, Alice, and Paul Smith, eds. 1987. *Men in Feminism*. New York: Methuen.

Johnston, Jill. 1973. *Lesbian Nation: The Feminist Solution*. New York: Simon & Schuster.

Kauffman, Linda, S. ed. 1989. *Gender and Theory: Dialogues on Feminist Criticism*. Oxford: Wiley-Blackwell.

Kaufman, Michael. 1987. *Beyond Patriarchy: Essays by Men on Pleasure, Power, and Change*. Oxford: Oxford University Press.

Kennedy, Duncan. 1992. "Sexual Abuse, Sexy Dressing, and the Eroticization of Domination." *New England Law Review* 26: 1310–89.

Kimmel, Michael ed. 1990. *Men Confront Pornography*. New York: Plume.

MacDonald, Scott. 1990 "Confessions of a Feminist Porn Watcher." In Kimmel 1990: 34–42. New York: Plume.

Manalansan, Martin F. 2003. *Global Divas: Filipino Gay Men in the Diaspora*. Durham, NC: Duke University Press.

Morgan, Robin. 1970. "Introduction: The Women's Revolution." In *Sisterhood Is Powerful: An Anthology of Writings from the Women's Liberation Movement*, xv–xlvi. New York: Vintage.

Muñoz, José Esteban. 1999. *Disidentifications: Queers of Color and the Performance of Politics*. Minneapolis: University of Minnesota Press.

Neal, Mark Anthony. 2013. *Looking for Leroy: Illegible Black Masculinities*. New York: New York University Press.

Panfil, Vanessa R. 2017. *The Gang's All Queer: The Lives of Gay Gang Members*. New York: New York University Press.

Pascoe, C. J. 2007. *Dude, You're a Fag: Masculinity and Sexuality in High School*. Berkeley: University of California Press.

Poulson-Bryant, Scott. 2011. *Hung: A Meditation on the Measure of Black Men in America*. New York: Crown.

Radicalesbians. (1970, 1972) 1992. "The Woman-Identified-Woman." In *Out of the Closets: Voices of Gay Liberation*, edited by Karla Jay and Allen Young, 172–76. New York: NYU Press.

Rich, Adrienne. 1980. "Compulsory Heterosexuality and Lesbian Existence," *Signs* 5, no. 4: 631–60.

Ross, Marlon B. 2022. *Sissy Insurgencies: A Racial Anatomy of Unfit Manliness*. Durham, NC: Duke University Press.

Rossi, Alice. (1964) 1988. "Equality between the Sexes: An Immodest Proposal." *Daedalus* 117, no. 3: 25–71.

Rubin, Gayle. (1975, 1991) 2012. "The Traffic in Women: Notes on the 'Political Economy' of Sex." In *Deviations: A Gayle Rubin Reader*, 33–65. Durham, NC: Duke University Press.

Saldanha, Arun. 2006. "Reontologizing Race: The Machinic Geography of Phenotype." *Environment and Planning D: Society and Space* 24, no. 1: 9–24.

Scott, Darieck. 2010. *Extravagant Abjection: Black, Power, and Sexuality in the African American Literary Imagination*. New York: New York University Press.

Segal, Lynne. 1990. *Slow Motion: Changing Masculinities Changing Men*. New York: Rutgers University Press.

Shugar, Dana. 1995. *Separatism and Women's Community*. Lincoln: University of Nebraska Press.

Snodgrass, Jon. 1977. *A Book of Readings for Men Against Sexism*. New York: Monthly Review Press.

Solanos, Valerie. (1968) 2000. *S.C.U.M. Manifesto (Society for Cutting Up Men)*. In *Radical Feminism: A Documentary Reader*, edited by Barbara Crow, 201–22. New York: NYU Press.

Ward, Jane. 2015. *Not Gay: Sex between Straight White Men*. New York: New York University Press.

Warner, Michael. 1999. *The Trouble with Normal: Sex Politics and the Ethics of Queer Life*. Cambridge, MA: Harvard University Press.

Weissman, David, director. 2002. *The Cockettes*. Strand Releasing.

West, Robin. 1999. *Caring for Justice*. New York: New York University Press.

Wittman, Carl. 1992 [1972]. "A Gay Manifesto." In *Out of the Closets: Voices of Gay Liberation*, edited by Karla Jay and Allen Young, 330–41. New York: NYU Press.

Zerilli, Linda. 2005. *Feminism and the Abyss of Freedom*. Chicago: University of Chicago Press.

Abolition Politics

Marquis Bey, Editor

Marquis Bey

Introduction: Abolition Politics

We hear the word uttered in streets, on signs, in think pieces. We see it used as an analytic through which to understand how the radical among us seek to initiate change. It is on the cover of books and in course titles. It is a politic, a modality of living and relating, a call, a demand, an invitation, a wish.

Abolition.

With such an increase in its utterance, it grows more and more imperative that we come to a clearer understanding of what abolition is and seeks. Certainly, the clarification here will not settle the record on abolition's meaning, nor is that the aim; instead, we seek only to supplement abolition with a multifaceted articulation of additional ways—philosophical, geographical, and historical—the term can resound. In this contemporary moment, which is fed and sustained, fractured and cohered, by an assemblage of other moments, *abolition* as a term and practice has become, to say the least, a hot button issue. Often when it is discussed, it is in the context of prisons, and perhaps police, conversation often bearing the scope of should we or should we not get rid of prison/police? What will replace them if we got rid of them? In other words, abolition is a fulcrum around which questions of harm reduction, and specifically the institutions that proliferate harm, are debated.

Let us, then, think intentionally about the terms under which we gather for this discursive occasion. Abolition, to introduce for the uninitiated and perhaps clarify for the already on board, has a history often rooted— which is too often to say, immobilized—in particularity, namely the particularity of the cessation of slavery. Narrowly and simplistically, *abolition* is the term used for when slavery has ended, but we might begin to rethink the

The South Atlantic Quarterly 122:3, July 2023
DOI 10.1215/00382876-10644076   © 2023 Duke University Press

term in light of its use by activists and scholars in Black, Indigenous, queer, trans, and feminist thought. It serves to raise a different set of questions, ones that inquire into the shape and duration of enslavement, the conditions under which enslavement shifts or lessens, the various ways enslavement manifests, the effects of it; and it rethinks the operative terms we ought to use to make sense—or *non*sense—of what exists and, importantly too, what might exist, such as carcerality, dispossession, and the like. It is, in short, to struggle over the terms and tenor, and possibility, of that which might come (see Haley 2018: 9).

But in the contemporary moment, abolition has drawn from, departed from, and expanded on its context of enslavement and has taken on a differently textured meaning. Today, abolition is most often a call for the abolition of the prison industrial complex (PIC). Understood as a bastion of privatized and sequestered resources better used in service of communities; unmitigated violence in the form of assault, surveillance, and disciplining; the gender binary and gendered harm and circumscription; the *reduction* of safety by way of its proliferation of force and police and criminality and resource scarcity and severing of kinship ties, the PIC is the primary aim of abolitionist efforts, for abolition, in large part, seeks the elimination of the violence and harm characteristic of prisons.

And it is quite sensible for many to ask, as they have, what this looks like. How might this be actualized, how does it work, when have people done this? *What does abolition look like?* And we could respond in myriad ways: Surely we can respond very specifically, with avowedly organizationally abolitionist projects like cutting police and prison budgets, shrinking the size of those employed for carceral punishment, closing detention and immigration centers, developing networks of care in communities, and a host of other practices. These are things that organizations like BYP100, We Charge Genocide, Critical Resistance, No Cop Academy, and Project NIA, among others, have been enacting and agitating for years. But additionally, and in line with the ways this dossier seeks to expand our notion of what abolition can be and in what realms it might travel, we can note as abolitionist, too: when they insurrect and smash windows and burn buildings because those sites serve as edifices of racial capitalist empire; when they circulate tips for extinguishing tear gas and use lasers to foreclose the sight of police and law enforcement during the riot; when they loot; when they skip class and drive downtown to give out water and carpool protestors back home because cops have shut down the city and bus lines; when they open up schools and hotels to temporarily or permanently house unhoused people; when they push and push for reparations in the city in which your university is located and actually get those reparations; when they shut down prisons and steal money from government agencies. In short, one need not deem oneself abolitionist to do, and to have been doing, abolitionist work. Because when they love even when it is hard; when they watch *Criminal Queers* and read *Captive Genders* together; when they refuse to dispose of, exile, punish anyone, no matter whom; when they feed you and clothe you and hug you because *everybody need some loving sometimes*—that, too, is an abolitionist project in all but name. When they keep the underground party going. When not even the threat, pervasive as it always is, of death will stop their living.

We might also respond less helpfully, though perhaps a bit more honestly: abolition looks like nothing at all, nothing in particular. Because abolition, to enact its politics, is to refuse to predetermine, to prefigure the future since such predetermination would belie its capacity, its breadth, its imaginative scope and possibility to be anything at all, primarily something we have not yet conceptualized. If it is about futures—futures that are, still, here and now—and in particular futures that radically rethink what ought to be, we cannot shuttle in extant regulations and grammars, for we would recapitulate the same logics that got us into this. So we imagine, we dream, we let the windows stay broken, unrepaired and unreformed, because "they are a living, breathing archive of a shared grammar of insurrection" (Hwang 2021: 92). If "to be anti-abolitionist" is "to exhibit a kind of preservative concern for the disruption of the structures, effects, and affects that accrue to the system of slavery," of captivity and, too, carcerality; if "it is to be nervous about—and moreover to attempt to discipline and contain—the forces that fugitivity unleashes," then abolition, in the way we move through it in these pages, is precisely the unleashing of such unruly fugitivity—in the realm of history, of the contemporary, of the ontological, of the geographical, of the terrestrial (Moten 2018: 109).

And now, *politics*. When one hears the word, it is almost rote by now to immediately imagine the partisan, the governmental, the policy-oriented, elections, voting, step-by-steps, and the like. Politics has become the name for a very specific sector with clearly demarcated criteria for behavior and inhabitation. It could then be misunderstood that our occasion for gathering in this particular forum seeks to bring abolition to such a sector and attempt to advance its demands on such a terrain, wanting Congress and senators to vote on its merits, trotting it out on a tour with podiums and debates. Instead, we wish to offer a very different conception of politics as we assert "abolition politics"; we wish to offer abolition's politics as a modality that undermines the logics of the aforementioned way of conceiving of politics. Here, we will be concerned with thinking about politics and the political as a nebulous and ongoing terrain of struggle and expanding, cultivating a different terrain on which to indeed *do*. This forum concerns the various ways abolition is done and lived and engendered in the quotidian, the ethical, the relational. Surely, this is not to the exclusion of prisons and police; it is instead a shift in the scope through which we conceptualize how abolitionist work is carried out at the level of ontology and epistemology, of affect and coalition. So, rather than asserting the importance of abolition and supporting its proliferation by running for office or appealing to courts, as some who wish to initiate change seek to do, which would be a kind of politics that lambastes abolition's radicality, we want to ask how might we engage politically the abolition of things like whiteness or borders; or, indeed, how might we think about gender as carceral, or abolition's relationship to (de)coloniality. It is, in short, the *other things* subject to abolition that fall under the capacious heading of the political that this forum seeks to examine.

Because the former definition of politics as adhering always and already to the government and electoral is a type of carcerality, one predicated on unimpeachable regulatory criteria unable to be gotten outside of, and indeed punished for being attempted to be breached. Such a politics places alternative possibilities for relationality in captivity; it demands specific checked boxes, prerequisites, an outness after three (or fewer) strikes, an individuated subject capable of speaking on certain terms, demographic and delimited thinking. On this, we can of course turn to Jacques Rancière, who provides an articulation of the narrow definition of politics characterized here as that which "exists when the figure of a specific subject is constituted, a supernumerary subject in relation to the calculated number of groups, places, and functions in a society," which is to say that politics, properly understood, emerges when an unrecognized subject seeks equal recognition within an order already established to bestow such a status on the grounds of its extant criteria. Politics and the political, in other words, as the democratic pursuit of equality for human subjects (Rancière 2006: 51; Olivier 2015). For our purposes, "politics" cannot abide this because the affixed "abolition" is an abolition, a subversive vitiation, a making impossible the conditional violence, of the conceit of a singular and coherent self, the assumption of ownership, the binarity that inheres in the "bi" of bipartisan, the totality touted by the logics of the world. We desire here a certain reworking of the very landscape for what is possible, thinkable, doable, and what exists—a reconfiguration of the very terrain on which we relate to others. For our purposes, once more, the politics of abolition politics is not the domain of the governmental or the ontological, nor is it concerned with pluralism or egalitarianism. Our aim is perhaps more radical. We venture forth with an understanding of the political, the politics of abolition politics, as the insistent, quotidian engendering of different conditions for the cultivation of other possibilities that exceed what currently reigns as normative and "real." Politics and the political as intellectual, ethical, social, and relational provocations, subtle and small as they may be, that promote the emergence of altered terrains of encounter.

Abolition's politics, its politicality, and the political's abolitionism incite for us a steadfast and concerted intellectual, philosophical, historical, geographic, and relational ethic that is broad and imaginative. The commingling of the terms insists that abolition does not merely take place in movement or organizing spaces, nor is it simply about prisons; it is not simply to be in the streets demanding non-reformism and being unwavering in the demand for the end of police and carceral institutions; nor is it to be fixed into an appeal to policy and lawmakers, a valorization of voting, or a reprising of tenets of past movements as templatic doctrine for contemporary movements. "Abolition politics" seeks to undercut *all* modes of carcerality, via myriad means, and it understands carcerality as any form of (non)relation that necessitates the circumscription, punishing, or disposing of any one and non-one. Prisons, detention centers, immigration camps, militarized borders are all, deeply, instantiations of carcerality. So, too, however, are racializing categorizations, the gender binary, liberal democracy, food deserts, privatized property, "law" and "order," miseducation. It is this expansive definition of carcerality that abolition politics sets its sights on, because abolition politics is a political and politicized abolition of the very grammars of existence and relationality, necessitating not mere eradication but imagination, an imaginative politics that predicates its vision—and its listening, its feeling, its taste, its smell—on so many other things here and now, yet also neither here nor now. "Abolitionist praxis," writes Ren-yo Hwang, though it is also a thought, a politics, an expansive Foucauldian and Derridean "way of life," must "always be and remain in relation to not just those behind cages and institutional walls but, to quote Foucault, to be concerned about any shared practice in which one tolerates the '[pushing of] a portion of the population to the margins'" (Hwang 2021: 91). These populations are not always legible; at times, and perhaps in the most radical of times, these populations are not even conceptualized as such because they have not been made legible by extant grammars of life and relationality. Think of the beaver and the dam (Guenther), the trans (Hewitt), the non- and un-white "white" accomplice workers (Cutrone), the radically autonomous (Bey-West).

That abolition as a discourse gaining in legitimacy is undeniable, as activists and thinkers, even politicians, begin using its language and seeing it as, if not a viable option (with all the accusations of "idealism" and impossibility, and non-practicality, ascribed to it), something that demands being acknowledged. Indeed, even in the sphere of the literary there are more and more books with *abolition* in their titles, more and more publishers dedicated to publishing and promoting abolitionist literature—most notably Haymarket Books, which has routinely published texts on leftist and abolitionist ideas and has recently established the Abolitionist Papers book series with titles such as *Abolition. Feminism. Now*; *We Do This 'Til We Free Us: Abolitionist Organizing and Transforming Justice*; *Rehearsals for Living*; and *Change Everything: Racial Capitalism and the Case for Abolition*. Such growth is significant, if ostensibly small in the grand scheme of a cultural landscape hostile to the radical imaginative call of abolition, precisely because abolitionist discourse promotes and expands and, importantly, makes more possible and thinkable abolitionist politics (though, of course, the two—discourse and politics—are not mutually exclusive). The more others understand that doing and thinking abolition is possible and being done, the more likely it is that they will, as it were, get on board. Changing the conditions, material surely, but also intellectual and ethical and relational, will permit the capacity for others to change themselves, their ways of moving and being and feeling. And that is at the heart of abolition, its optimism (see Kaba 2021; Taylor 2021).

In this Against the Day, abolition is multifaceted and is approached from a number of angles—indeed, not only approached but enacted and made manifest via a number of intensities, inflections, and with a number of aims. Hence, even though I have attempted to invite readers into a general understanding of abolition and its politics, politics and its abolition, I will not attempt to give the final word on abolition or abolition politics, as that might very well belie its aims, and certainly the aims of this dossier. These entries inflect abolition politics historically, culturally, philosophically, and ethnographically, and this range is indicative of its aims. It is this breadth, a coalitional and non-hierarchized breadth, that illuminates abolition politics so well, so generatively, so, if you will, abolitionistly.

The South Atlantic Quarterly · Against the Day · July 2023

Haley, Sarah. 2018. "Abolition." In *Keywords for African American Studies*, edited by Erica R. Edwards, Roderick A. Ferguson, and Jeffrey Ogbonna Green Ogbar, 9–14. New York: New York University Press.

Hwang, Ren-yo. 2021. "Abolitionist Broken Windows and the Violence of Power Relations." *Foucault Studies* (December): 89–93. https://doi.org/10.22439/fs.vi31.6462.

Kaba, Mariame. 2021. *We Do This 'til We Free Us: Abolitionist Organizing and Transforming Justice*. Abolitionist Papers. Chicago: Haymarket Books.

Moten, Fred. 2018. *Stolen Life*. Durham, NC: Duke University Press

Olivier, Bert. 2015. "Rancière and the Recuperation of Politics." *Phronimon* 16, no. 1): 1–17.

Rancière, Jacques. 2006. *The Politics of Aesthetics: The Distribution of the Sensible*. Translated by Gabriel Rockhill. New York: Continuum.

Taylor, Keeanga-Yamahtta. 2021. "The Emerging Movement for Police and Prison Abolition." *The New Yorker*, May 7, 2021. https://www.newyorker.com/news/our-columnists/the-emerging-movement-for-police-and-prison-abolition.

Andrew Cutrone

Beyond Distinctions:
A Treatise on Abolition and Accomplice Work

> The institutions that we are fighting are not just the school, the police, the clinic, and the jail. It is also the self—the subject.
> —Fred Moten, "the university: last words" (2020)

This essay is an experiment in mutinous ideas, tethered to the notion that in order to fight for the possibility of life on earth, white people *must* radically reorganize our politics toward the abolition of ourselves and welcome the unexpectable subjectivities to come in light of our abolition. If we are to do this, we must dispense entirely with "allyship" as a desirable subject-force and theorize white radical intentionality otherwise. Indeed, I want to insist upon a future whose contours we do not yet know, and by this I mean a sociality that is livable for everyone on a planet that sustains our fullest lives; one whose ethic is black trans feminist abolition, and whose abolitionist efforts are aimed at, which is to say *against*, the ontological. Again, to begin, these politics require us to dispense with allyship.

To be an ally, and a "white ally" in particular, is to join with others in a social movement—those who are non-white—because of some common interest expressed within the liberal grammar of rights, but often for selfish reasons that makes the alliance worthwhile. The diplomatic history and etymology of the word *alliance* suggests that white allies come to the fight with interests of their own to protect. In my mind, one such "interest," perhaps its most deeply seated, is the preservation of whiteness as a conditioning force for their understanding of self; for the *very notion of the "self."* However, these

The South Atlantic Quarterly 122:3, July 2023
DOI 10.1215/00382876-10644090   © 2023 Duke University Press

interests diminish the capacity for radical work to be done by these actors as they run counter to the liberatory project.

Allies congeal as Subjects by way of allyship. Allyship mobilizes and conditions the subject position "ally." Allies are inert[1] political units, and allyship functions as a vacuous, though not meaningless, pathogen, seizing a home in a variety of actors (who Shannon Sullivan [2014] calls "good white people") as well as in symbolic gestures, such as those perennial lawn signs that rehearse neoliberal multicultural slogans, such as "Kindness Matters," "Science is REAL," and "Black Lives Matter." These gestures are necessarily performative; allies neither affect the materialities of anti-blackness, nor disrupt the ideological conditions that engender normative subjectivity. These considerations, along with showing up to the ballot box to "vote blue no matter who," seem to be the tasks as well as the limit of allyship. Nevertheless, framing allyship as a force that subjectivates allies is consistent with my broader theoretical perspective that political-ethical labor shapes the subject position and structures it. This formulation will become more precise as I elucidate the argument that the figure of the accomplice emerges out of what I call "accomplice work."

What do abolitionists mean *exactly* when they say they want accomplices to show up, not allies? And how can we think more productively about this distinction ("Accomplices NOT Allies") by harnessing the politicality of its black and indigenous assertions rather than its more paltry assertions by liberal allies? It is not enough to say that accomplices are simply more radical than allies, or that accomplices show up more earnestly than allies who are merely performing their politics. We must dig deeper than these simple identitarian binaries and move beyond the performance of comparing the ways in which they are both similar to and different from one another.

To be sure, we must distinguish accomplice work from allyship—for the accomplice is "the being who is not there and yet by being there makes us more and less of ourselves, unsafe, in danger" (Desideri and Harney 2013). The accomplice does not simply "advocate" within preordained structures in order to reform them, but aims to unstructure and do away with them. The accomplice is animated by a "notion of fugitivity that is not simply an opposition to power but a refusal to even accept the validity of the terms of power" (Bey and Sakellarides 2016).[2] Ultimately, however, we must retire the tendency to place them in contradistinction. Not only because allyship is a liberal formulation that desires normative categories of difference, but also because serially theorizing accomplice work in relation to allyship reduces its ethical and political radicality into a lateral move between supposedly comparable identities.

Accomplice work is the radical, chronic refusal of the ontological scene that claims (to benefit) the normative Subject *by* those purportedly normative Subjects.[3] This scene is almost banal and quotidian, yet it remains violent because it is privilege laden, biologistic with respect to racial as well as gender and sexual formations, aggressively identitarian, and thus, individuating. If these are the pillars of a violent scene that enables allyship, then its fixedness must also be contended with. If we understand "trans" as an insurgency indexing movement away from imposed, regulatory norms, then the ontological scene is structured by transantagonism as well. Accomplice work, as the appellation for the political and ethical labor to desubjectivate from whiteness, aims to dissolve the self-possessed individual as the consummate achievement of the human, proliferating instead a practice of study that is entirely unbound from any individuated precepts. Its unit of analysis is the gathering, or the collective. Its mood is the subjunctive, the fugitive, and the nonnormative. In study, accomplice work shapes an ethical mode of subjectivity whose central tenets are radicality, care, liberation, and abolition. I view it as an expression of fugitive subjectivity that refuses the anti-black regime of the Subject; the paraontological distinction; a necessary component of genuine coalitional possibility (Campt 2014; Bey 2020b).

Accomplice work is abolitionist—it is work that "promotes a dismantling of [oppressive] systems in search of life and livability by other means not predicated on violence" (Bey 2020a). It is an assuredly quotidian practice against imposed ontology, which is the philosophically and politically hegemonic domain of *being* "predicated on violence," and organized through supremacies (and, therefore, normativities) of whiteness and cisheteropatriarchy. bell hooks, for example, names an ontological scene when she theorizes "white supremacist capitalist patriarchy" (hooks 1992). Signally, this ontology makes real particular renditions of social life and denigrates and denies the capacity of others. While archival traces such as federal court opinions and runaway advertisements might suggest a contextual magnitude that does not easily square itself with "the quotidian," I want to point out that the dominant, who control archival production, were mounting an enclosure of space in order to eradicate the fugitive impulse. In the context of extreme domination, the archive distorts accomplice work's everydayness.

Ontology thrives on anti-blackness and thus maligns a range of blackness's self-determined conceptualizations. One way that "ontology distorts blackness" is by reducing it into a sedimented epidermal notion, and therefore subsuming it under the colonial grammar of "race" (Warren 2017). Under this grammar and its logic, raciality is categorical—that is, "determinable" and "separable" according to hegemonic parameters (Ferreira da Silva 2016: 57). Identity, as a conceptual frame, becomes the vector within which raciality is expressed, and "racial identity" entrusts its hefty metaphysical status on the plane of the body, in the epidermis. The body ultimately cannot bear this intense ontological bestowal. It is no surprise, then, that oppressive machinations exact themselves on people given to specific identificatory lodgings—it is precisely these identities that oppressive power forms in the service of its continuance. In much the same way that Marquis Bey posits blackness, transness, and feminism not as "tied to a specific kind of body or identity" but, rather, as "inflections of mutinous subjectivities that have been captured and consolidated into bodily legibilities," I want to make an inverse-parallel argument about whiteness—that whiteness is a political subjectivity historically affixed to specific kinds of bodies, and its overdeterminative power in the ontological domain obfuscates the process by which whiteness subjectivates epidermally white people (See Bey 2021, esp. 9). This is a violence whose magnitude is incomprehensibly large. But what would it mean, and what would it look like, to recognize and *refuse* this violative processual arrangement? If the categorical identities to which we relate are not serving our liberatory project, what good are they?[4] If racial identity is normativity's vector that secures subjection as the basis of social relation, then we must abolish it—full stop. At a higher level of abstraction, we must, too, dispense with ontology with abolitionist regard, because ontology dampens the ethical and social possibilities exuding from blackness that normative metaphysical and ontological structures are bent on regulating (Warren 2017; Bey 2020c). Paraontology is one of abolition politics' strategies to elide ontology's grasp on identitarian modes of social relation. A paraontological rendering of blackness conditions accomplice work, a traitorous, mutinous project to abolish the normative Subject by those who have been prefigured as these very normative Subjects.

But how is this possible? In "Blackness and Nothingness (Mysticism in the Flesh)," Fred Moten argues, "On the one hand, blackness and ontology are unavailable for one another; on the other hand, blackness must free itself from ontological expectation, must refuse subjection to ontology's sanction against the very idea of black subjectivity." Moten's point is that blackness is incompatible with ontology, with the very capacity that black beingness can be enclosed within ontology in any normative capacity; that black subjectivity in any ontological scene manifests through anti-blackness. By way of Chandler, he posits a *paraontological distinction*, and asks us to "think otherwise" in an effort to eclipse the ravages of ontology:

> The paraontological distinction between blackness and blacks allows us no longer to be enthralled by the notion that blackness is a property that belongs to blacks (thereby placing certain formulations regarding non/relationality and non/communicability on a different footing and under a certain pressure) but also because ultimately it allows us to detach blackness from the question of (the meaning of) being. (Moten 2013: 749)

Presuming the nonproprietarity of blackness is an intimidating proposition, for what it could suggest and open, namely that *others, especially whites*, might find, claim, and expropriate blackness, and thus ravage it from the inside. By expressing this move, I do not mean to exact what can be understood as a colonial move to dispossess black people of their blackness. That is not my intention here at all. Instead, I want to consider deeply the implications of blackness's *non-exclusivity* to people racialized as black. Caring for its open aesthetic ground, I want to consider what an ethical encounter with blackness looks like—an engagement with the aesthetic sociality of blackness as someone not prefigured, or racialized, as black. In my view, I (and the "we" not racialized as black) have an ethical obligation to open ourselves to such an encounter. If this is possible, it is, then, necessary for white people to subjectivate, or *de*subjectivate, themselves through blackness, such that *white people are no longer moving through whiteness, are, perhaps, very tentatively, no longer white*. Accomplice work invites and makes an ethical demand to refuse whiteness such that white people are rendered un-white—indeed, the abolition of whiteness.

Accomplice work also rejects—and proliferates the rejection of—the idea that ontology can be beneficial for anybody by taking up the politics behind what is arguably Harney and Moten's most famous statement in *The Undercommons*.

> The coalition emerges out of your recognition that *it's* fucked up for you, in the same way that we've already recognized that *it's* fucked up for us. I don't need your help. I just need you to recognize that *this shit* is killing you, too, however much more softly, you stupid motherfucker . . . (Harney and Moten 2013: 141; emphases added)

So, the task of accomplice work, before accomplice work can happen, is recognizing that "it," "this shit"—the world, anti-blackness, cisgender supremacy, heteropatriarchy; ontology—hardly confers an ethical program to the Subject, hardly a genuine possibility for livingness for everyone, including those who are said to benefit from such configured realities.

Accomplice work emerges into the social as an ethical *disposition* on the edge of black study's critique of ontology. Accomplice work, indeed, breaks ethics away from ontology by striking at the very heart of the anti-blackness of ontology's quintessential Subject and its figuration of the world. If the production of a world—an ontology—presumes an array of normativities that give us something like the Subject, accomplice work constitutes a fugitive disposition *already given* in black study that is radically open, "available to *anyone*, or more pointedly, *any* posture, that is willing to take on the formidable task of thinking as a willful act of imagination and invention" (Spillers 2003: 5). The point is that accomplice work *might* index that ethical, laborious disposition *with* which white folks might take on the "formidable task" of abolishing whiteness. I use *"with* which" to denote a working-through, whereas *"from* which" might denote that accomplice work comes from somewhere, say, a fixed, habitable position. "From which," then, anticipates a positionality discourse that I ultimately seek to discard, yes, abolish—because it presumes identitarian logics within its frame, logics that, as I have detailed, are not conducive to the kind of politico-ethical interventions that blackness and accomplice work—as appositional formulations—seek.

I ultimately want to unsettle the effects that positionality discourses have on the extent to which we mobilize ourselves in the service of living otherwise. Blackness is the conduit for this mobilization; and whiteness might very well be said to be its inverse—the brutal imposition of identity categories and regimes of thinking and being whose intent and effect is a stalled, fixed understanding of thinking and being. Accomplice work, therefore, is an engagement with the entropic capacities of blackness to dislodge insurgent social desire from something that might be understood under the rubric of identity. It hinges on the idea that the desire to produce a black world must not only be desirable to black people. Accomplice work is the work of breaking down the strictures of thought that convince, for instance, white folks that a black world is undesirable. A black world, where blackness releases itself into the social, where blackness breaks the social down and then back up again, where blackness means something like abolition, might enable *all of us* to actually live—or "live otherwise." This work defies the logics of position and positionality as methodological, and thus conceptual, apertures *from* which to build a legible social movement. Accomplice work cannot live in or with these delimiting frames, frames that I think find their root in the dominant ontological scene. It works toward their abolition, the abolition of positionality.

Notes

1   In chemistry, an inert chemical is one that is stable and unreactive under specified conditions.

2   In Harriet Jacobs's *Incidents in the Life of a Slave Girl*, a portion of chapter forty tells of Mrs. Bruce, a woman who harbors Jacobs away from Dr. Flint. Mrs. Bruce's husband is irate at the fact that she is harboring a slave and that she is "violating the laws of her country." When asked if she knew the penalty for harboring a fugitive, she said: "I am very well aware of it. It is imprisonment and one thousand dollars fine. Shame on my country that it is so! I am ready to incur the penalty. I will go to the state's prison, rather than have any poor victim torn from my house, to be carried back to slavery" (Jacobs 2005 [1861]: 211). I read a kind of accomplice ethicality, which is a refusal of the terms of order, undergirding her rebuttal.

3   In this sentence, I want the reader to consider what it means for a given ontology to make a claim that it benefits the normative Subject and abjectifies "others," and have this be understood as the "source" of inequalities expressed in socialities organized by capitalist, white, and cisgender supremacies. But I also want the reader to consider, perhaps more emphatically, what it means for the given ontology to *claim subjects* who will go to work on behalf of the given ontology, and consider this a kind of (spiritual, metaphysical) theft. This is really how I want to understand whiteness, cisgender, and other fonts of supremacy—as permitting the theft of life and livability of, really, everyone. In this respect, I agree with and am making recourse to the oeuvre of afropessimist thought that emphasizes the ways in which the given ontology sanctions (Black) social death, though I ultimately yearn to refuse this ontological scene by way of a paraontological abolition politics.

4   The logic of this argument is akin to Baldwin's critique of the Christian God: "If the concept of God has any validity or any use, it can only be to make us larger, freer, and more loving. If God cannot do this, it is time we got rid of him" (Baldwin 1963: 57). If hegemonic renditions of race, identity, and racial identity do not work in the service of abolition, which they do not, then we must dispense with them and find new, unlimiting frameworks with which to participate in sociality.

References

Baldwin, James. 1963. *The Fire Next Time*. New York: Dial Press.

Bey, Marquis. 2020a. *Anarcho-Blackness: Notes Toward a Black Anarchism*. Chico, CA: AK Press.

Bey, Marquis. 2020b. "Incorporeal Blackness: A Theorization in Two Parts—Rachel Dolezal and *Your Face in Mine*." *CR: The New Centennial Review* 20, no. 2: 205-41.

Bey, Marquis. 2020c. *The Problem of the Negro as a Problem for Gender*. Minneapolis: University of Minnesota Press, 2020.

Bey, Marquis. 2021. *Black Trans Feminism*. Durham, NC: Duke University Press.

Bey, Marquis, and Theodora Sakellarides. 2016. "When We Enter: The Blackness of Rachel Dolezal." *The Black Scholar* 46, no. 4: 33–48.

Campt, Tina. 2014. "Black Feminist Futures and the Practice of Fugitivity." https://www.you tube.com/watch?v=2ozhqw84oPU&feature=youtube_gdata_player

Desideri, Valentina, and Stefano Harney. 2013. "A Conspiracy without a Plot." In *The Curatorial: A Philosophy of Curating*, edited by Jean-Paul Martinon, 125–136. London: Bloomsbury.

Ferreira da Silva, Denise. 2016. "On Difference without Separability." In *Incerteza Viva: 32nd Bienal de São Paulo*, edited by Jochen Volz and Júlia Rebouças, 57–65. São Paulo: Fundação Bienal de São Paulo.

Harney, Stefano, and Fred Moten. 2013. *The Undercommons: Fugitive Planning and Black Study*. New York: Minor Compositions.

hooks, bell. 1992. *Black Looks: Race and Representation*. New York: Routledge.

Jacobs, Harriet. 2005 [1861]. *Incidents in the Life of a Slave Girl*. New York: Barnes and Noble Classics.

Moten, Fred. 2013. "Blackness and Nothingness (Mysticism in the Flesh)." *South Atlantic Quarterly* 112, no. 4: 737–80.

Moten, Fred, and Stefano Harney. 2020. "the university: last words." YouTube Video. July 9. https://www.youtube.com/watch?v=zqWMejD_XU8

Spillers, Hortense. 2003. *Black, White, and In Color: Essays on American Literature and Culture*. Chicago: University of Chicago Press.

Sullivan, Shannon. 2014. *Good White People: The Problem with White Middle Class Anti-Racism*. Albany: SUNY Press, 2014).

Warren, Calvin. 2017. "Black Mysticism: Fred Moten's Phenomenology of (Black) Spirit." *Zeitschrift für Anglistik und Amerikanistik* 65, no. 2: 219–29.

Huey Hewitt

Gender Is Carceral:
On Racialized Gender Criminalization
and Abolitionist Cis-Trans Coalitions

On May 8, 2022, Alabama Senate Bill 184 went into effect.[1] Under the law, doctors who provide trans health care to patients under the age of nineteen can face up to ten years in prison. Upon signing the law, Alabama governor Kay Ivey stated, "I believe very strongly that if the Good Lord made you a boy, you are a boy, and if he made you a girl, you are a girl" (Migdon 2022a). After being signed in April, the law was immediately challenged in several suits by Alabama families, physicians, and LGBTQ+ rights groups, though US district judge Liles Burke did not grant a preliminary injunction to halt the law's enforcement while the suit is ongoing (Migdon 2022c). But a federal judge did block the enforcement of a governor's directive in Texas that defined trans health care for minors as a form of child abuse pending the outcome of another ACLU suit (Goodman 2022). Soon after, the Texas Supreme Court lifted the injunction in claiming that lower courts had overstepped by trying to block the child abuse investigations from going forward. Parents of openly trans children in Texas thus continue to be investigated by the Texas Department of Family and Protective Services (DFPS).

Similar anti-trans bills have been introduced in the last few months in Arkansas, South Carolina, Idaho, Tennessee, Missouri, Oklahoma, Kentucky, Pennsylvania, Arizona, Iowa, Ohio, Mississippi, Louisiana, and several other states (thirty-four in total, according to the Freedom for All Americans legislative tracker ["Legislative Tracker" n.d.). While many of these bills target transgender youths' access to medical and social transition, others target

The South Atlantic Quarterly 122:3, July 2023
DOI 10.1215/00382876-10644104 © 2023 Duke University Press

trans youths' participation in sports, the availability of multi-gender or gender-neutral restrooms, and any existing state-protected civil rights for trans people. This recent wave of laws criminalizing transgender life is but one part of a broader genealogy of the criminalization of gender nonconformity in the United States. And we know, too, that the history of criminalization in this country has been unfailingly racialized—that the social science inherited from the postbellum period and Progressive era produced enduring discourses of Black criminality that explicitly relied on notions of gendered and sexual pathology (Muhammad 2010: xiv). Practices of policing and incarceration continue to rely on the conjunctional pathologization of sexual and gender nonconformity as well as racial difference. From municipal and state anti-cross-dressing laws to sex segregation within prisons, racialized gender regulation has been a consistent feature of the US carceral state since at least the nineteenth century (Sears 2015). Any coherent vision of abolitionist politics must therefore resist today's newest wave of anti-trans panic and propaganda.

Before World War I, at least forty-five US cities had anti-cross-dressing laws on the books. The policing of gender nonconformity frequently went hand in hand with efforts to clean up so-called vice: sex work, queer bars, and drug use. Even when anti-cross-dressing laws could not be used to justify arrest, police discretion often translated into arresting people whose appearance did not match the name or gender designation on their IDs for impersonation or suspected prostitution, as well as vagrancy, loitering, and other racialized crimes (Stryker 2017).

The 1965 Moynihan Report and the emergence of mass incarceration in the second half of the twentieth century elevated and intensified the stakes of a US criminological discourse that had always been raced, sexed, and gendered. Black feminist and Black trans studies scholars like Hortense Spillers, Sarah Haley, and C. Riley Snorton have all illuminated the ways in which Black people have been constructed outside of the white, cisgender, heteronormative gender binary since the days of slavery—with Snorton going furthest in reading the "trans in transatlantic" in his groundbreaking monograph *Black on Both Sides: A Racial History of Trans Identity* (Spillers 1987; Haley 2016; Snorton 2017). But even reactionary masculinist thinkers like Eldridge Cleaver have been sensitive to the ways in which a grammar of Black ungendering has been deployed to justify anti-Black violence (Cleaver 1968). Hence, while for much of US legal history, states and municipalities explicitly criminalized and policed practices of gender transgression, the criminalization and policing of Black people has also consistently been justified and shaped by ideas about the non-normativity of Black genders. In my remarks here, I reflect on how abolitionist praxis is and can be responsive to the reality that all of these histories have accumulated such that today, in this settler colony we call the United States, gender is carceral.

While Judith Butler's classic *Gender Trouble* is frequently understood to be an argument for the denaturalization of sex and gender, the book's Foucauldian register readily implies—for the reader willing to pay close attention—that gender is carceral. As Butler writes in a preface to the 1999 edition of the book:

> I grew up understanding something of the violence of gender norms: an uncle incarcerated for his anatomically anomalous body, deprived of family and friends, living out his days in an "institute" in the Kansas prairies. . . . It was difficult to bring this violence into view precisely because gender was so taken for granted at the same time that it was violently policed. . . . What would the world have to be like for my uncle to live in the company of family, friends, or extended kinship of some other kind? How might we rethink the ideal mor-phological constraints upon the human such that those who fail to approxi-mate the norm are not condemned to a death within life? (Butler 1999: xx–xxi)

Butler was (and is) interested in imagining alternative life-worlds in which gendered incarceration is impossible. But I want to suggest here that, with most other forces remaining constant—that is, with the world itself remain-ing relatively the same—the life of Butler's uncle as lived out among family and friends may well have been just as carceral his life in a prison. This is where Michel Foucault's ideas prove to be useful.

For Foucault, places like schools, hospitals, and workplaces function in conjunction with prisons to form a carceral network: a series of institutions that are not all formally affiliated with the state, but which nonetheless serve, expand, and embody state power (Foucault 1979). Foucault coined the terms *biopolitics* and *anatamo-politics* in an effort to explain how everyday people enforce laws and norms, beyond the formal structures of the state, which gov-ern the terms of not just who lives and dies but also precisely *how* people are *made to live* (e.g., in a dress or in a suit). In abolitionist circles, Foucault has rightfully faced criticism for not appropriately citing some of the thinkers who influenced his ideas, including militant imprisoned intellectual George Jackson (Heiner 2007). Nonetheless, Foucault's contributions to post-struc-turalist theory are useful tools for analyzing the state and extra-state violence faced by gender-nonconforming people of color. Following Foucault, I con-tend that non-state actors frequently perform a carceral function in uphold-ing gender norms. From parents who discipline the genderqueer practices of their children to catcallers who harass passersby for so-called cross-dressing, everyday people routinely appoint themselves as gender pigs: gender police. Even George Jackson, in one of his less noble moments, described people who did not subscribe to gender norms as "confused psychotics" (Jackson, Genet, and Jackson 1994: 48). To be gender nonconforming under gendered racial capitalism is to be constantly subjected to policing by the state and everyday citizens alike.

Before elaborating on the extra-state policing of racialized gender-non-conforming subjects—and its implications for the abolitionist movement—I want to note that, like Butler, I have my own personal investments in this issue. Early on in my transition as a Black transgender man, like many trans people, I found myself fearing everyday people almost as much as I feared the police. My body sent to outsiders what many would interpret as mixed signals regarding my sex and gender: a voice seemingly deepened by testosterone, some facial hair, masculine clothing, and breast tissue (albeit compressed by a binder). These signals left people feeling confused and outright tricked during ordinary daily interactions with me. In 2017, just one day after a New York Police Department officer randomly stopped me on the street, asked me for my ID, and sadistically questioned me regarding the "F" gender marker I had not yet changed, I was approached by a random man in a subway station who continually asked me, "Are you a man or a woman?" His voice got louder and louder as my train got later and later. Eventually, I simply left the subway station and decided to get home another way. Such occurrences were not rare before I got top surgery, after which I was more frequently (mis)perceived to be a cisgender man in the public sphere. But these two specific back-to-back interactions facilitated within me an organic intellectual instinct concerning the nexus of race, gender, and carceral violence. For both the cop and the man in the subway station, questioning who I was in relation to normative gender categories became a means of reasserting the fact that I was untenable. Despite later claiming that he knew I was "a transgender," the cop initially feigned ignorance so as to imply that I was inherently disorderly, potentially criminal, and therefore a justified target for being brought to the precinct. Of course, he never took me there, just as the man in the subway station did not escalate his harassment to the level of physical violence. Both men, nonetheless—even if unwittingly—performed a carceral function: acts of psychological warfare that functioned to police, and potentially rein in, gender nonconformity (or at least its presence in the public sphere). Even though I was not as proximate to policing, poverty, and street harassment as many other Black transgender people—in part because

I was not fully locked out of the formal, overground economy—I still witnessed gender as a carceral project well before I could understand or affirm this experiential instinct through historical or theoretical analysis.

Unfortunately, enemies of trans freedom and self-determination also seem to have an organic intellectual understanding of how extra-state gender policing functions. Texas governor Greg Abbott's directive to the state's Department of Family and Protective Services (DFPS) to investigate the parents of children who receive transgender health care *relies on* everyday citizens' willingness to report violations of the cisnormative social contract to the state.[2] In a word: the directive deputized cis people. But while the Texas governor's directive deputized vigilante observers to aid in the criminalization of parents who support their transgender children, parental support of trans kids is, unfortunately, quite rare. More common is the strict gender socialization to which most of us were subjected by our families while growing up: being taught what to wear, how to talk, how to walk, how to eat, how to sit, where to go to the bathroom, and so on. Those of us who systematically failed our gender assignments as youths were also systematically punished for these deviations—typically until at least some level of conformity, or a general commitment to attempting conformity, could be extracted from us. In countless cases, when trans youth have courageously refused to conform, their families have abandoned them, and they have been forced onto the streets and into underground economies for survival—leaving them even more vulnerable to criminalization. In this way, extra-state gender policing frequently bears a direct relationship to gender policing by the state. Gender policing by family and community members is a key component of a broader carceral superstructure—a superstructure being expanded by people like Greg Abbott and egged on by political candidates like Pastor Mark Burns, who advocated for the relaunching of the House Un-American Activities Committee to investigate and execute teachers who educate youth on queer and trans issues for "treason" (Roos 2022).

I linger on the matter of extra-state policing because I think the issue is absolutely central to the question of coalition building between cis and trans abolitionist organizers. Such coalitions are imperative for building up enough power to defeat contemporary fascism. Extra-state policing is the zone wherein people we might otherwise assume to be natural allies in the fight against the carceral state demonstrate a complicity with anti-trans state violence. It is noteworthy that in Black communities—where there is nominal distrust of the police—many gender-conforming individuals continue to enact carceral violence through the extra-state policing of Black queer and trans community members. And policing, as we know too well in the United States, is deadly. In this light, we may be able to make sense of the reality that in the contemporary crisis of Black trans murders cisgender Black men are frequently found responsible for taking Black trans lives. While some have extrapolated from the work of C. Riley Snorton and other Black trans studies scholars the claim that "there are no cis black people"—a claim meant to emphasize shared stakes between all Black people who have been, wittingly or not, constructed outside of white, heteronormative gender ideals—such a claim obfuscates real differences in material conditions and relations to violence between cis and trans Black people. Our coalitions can and must simultaneously be attuned to shared stakes as well as real differences in our vulnerabilities to specific forms of violence. In this way, we can come to understand gender as a carceral phenomenon that influences the ways in which *all* of us are surveilled and policed, while also being honest about *who* faces the brunt of gendered violence such that we can collectively craft more successful anti-violence interventions.

Black trans organizers are at the forefront of crafting such interventions. Ky Peterson, a formerly incarcerated Black transgender man, cofounded Freedom Overground to support incarcerated trans and gender-nonconforming people—those who know perhaps most intimately that gender is carceral. In New York City, Black trans organizers cofounded the Black Trans Travel Fund, a collective that redistributes funds to Black trans women to self-determine safer travel options for them so as to limit their interactions with police or non-state street harassers. In Texas, organizations like allgo mobilize queer youth of color to build power and communities of care in the face of threats like Governor Greg Abbott's directive criminalizing transgender health care. The Knights and Orchids society, based in Alabama, works to provide transgender health care in a state in which only three endocrinologists offer hormone therapy to trans patients (Nast 2022).

All of these organizations work to protect and empower trans people of color amid a white power structure dedicated to repressing Blackness and gender variance. Black trans organizers, especially in the South, remind us of the intensity of our current political moment: that, despite our efforts, we are losing, that fascism continues to grow and threaten our livelihoods, and that collectively, we need to find a way to do more. The criminalization of all transgender health care—at any age—is clearly on the fascist agenda. (The slippery slope fallacy is only a fallacy if one's enemy does not sincerely plan on sliding all the way down the slope.) We must be prepared to resist the criminalization of trans life at every stage: on the streets, in classrooms, in medical offices, and in our own homes. Doctors, teachers, and parents must be prepared to break laws; the abolitionist movement must be prepared to strategize concomitant jail and prison support. As we renew our commitment to the sanctity of Black trans life, we must vow to conspire together in this moment without hesitation, against fear, against comfort, and for freedom.

Notes

I am grateful for the feedback of Phil Deloria and editor Marquis Bey on multiple drafts of this essay.

1   I use the term *transgender* health care rather than *gender-affirming* health care because cisgender people receive gender-affirming health care—from birth control not aimed at contraception to testosterone therapy in cis men—all the damn time. If a young cis boy whose body was not naturally producing the hormone were to receive testosterone therapy as "gender-affirming" health care in Alabama under the current law, his doctor would not be criminalized. Trans health care specifically is what is being targeted.

2   I do, here, mean citizens, and not just "people"—holding citizenship to be a violent category.

References

Butler, Judith. 1999. *Gender Trouble: Feminism and the Subversion of Identity.* New York: Routledge.

Cleaver, Eldridge. 1968. *Soul on Ice.* New York: Dell.

Foucault, Michel. 1979. *Discipline and Punish: The Birth of the Prison.* New York: Vintage Books.

Goodman, J. David. 2022. "Texas Court Halts Abuse Inquiries into Parents of Transgender Children." *New York Times,* March 11, sec. U.S. https://www.nytimes.com/2022/03/11/us/texas-transgender-child-abuse.html.

Haley, Sarah. 2016. *No Mercy Here: Gender, Punishment, and the Making of Jim Crow Modernity.* Justice, Power, and Politics. Chapel Hill: The University of North Carolina Press.

Heiner, Brady Thomas. 2007. "Foucault and the Black Panthers." *City (London, England)* 11, no. 3: 313–56.

Jackson, George, Jean Genet, and Jonathan Jackson Jr. 1994. *Soledad Brother: The Prison Letters of George Jackson.* Chicago: Review Press.

"Legislative Tracker: Anti-Transgender Legislation Filed for the 2022 Legislative Session." n.d. *Freedom for All Americans* (blog). Accessed May 14, 2022. https://freedomforallamericans.org/legislative-tracker/anti-transgender-legislation/.

Migdon, Brooke. 2022a. "Alabama Gov. Ivey Signs Bill Criminalizing Gender-Affirming Care into Law." *The Hill* (blog), April 8. https://thehill.com/changing-america/respect/equality/3262961–alabama-gov-ivey-signs-bill-criminalizing-gender-affirming-care-into-law/.

Migdon, Brooke. 2022b. "Florida Health Dept. Says Gender-Affirming Care Should Not Be Provided to Minors." *The Hill* (blog), April 20. https://thehill.com/changing-america/respect/equality/3274150–florida-health-dept-says-gender-affirming-care-should-not-be-provided-to-minors/.

Migdon, Brooke. 2022c. "Gender-Affirming Care Ban Goes into Effect in Alabama." *The Hill* (blog), May 9. https://thehill.com/changing-america/respect/equality/3481830–gender -affirming-care-ban-goes-into-effect-in-alabama/.

Muhammad, Khalil Gibran. 2010. *The Condemnation of Blackness: Race, Crime, and the Making of Modern Urban America*. Cambridge, MA: Harvard University Press.

Nast, Condé. 2022. "The Advocates Helping Trans Alabamians Fight for Their Right to Healthcare." *Them*, June 13. https://www.them.us/story/the-knights-and-orchids-alabama -organization-trans-healthcare-now-awards-2022.

Roos, Meghan. 2022. "Pro-Trump Pastor Wants LGBTQ 'Indoctrinators' Executed for Treason." *Newsweek*, June 10, 2022. https://www.newsweek.com/pro-trump-pastor-wants -lgbtq-indoctrinators-executed-treason-1714767.

Sears, Clare. 2015. *Arresting Dress: Cross-Dressing, Law, and Fascination in Nineteenth-Century San Francisco*. Durham, NC: Duke University Press. https://doi.org/10.2307/j.ctv1220nx9.

Snorton, C. Riley. 2017. *Black on Both Sides: A Racial History of Trans Identity*. Minneapolis: University of Minnesota Press.

Spillers, Hortense J. 1987. "Mama's Baby, Papa's Maybe: An American Grammar Book." *Diacritics* 17, no. 2: 65–81. https://doi.org/10.2307/464747.

Stryker, Susan. 2017. *Transgender History: The Roots of Today's Revolution*. Second edition. Berkeley, CA: Seal Press.

Lisa Guenther

#AbolishCanada:
Breaking Down the 2022 Freedom Convoy

In early 2022, hundreds of right-wing activists got in their trucks and drove to Ottawa, the capital of so-called Canada, and occupied the city for almost four weeks straight. They called themselves the Freedom Convoy. They were fed up with Covid mandates and angry about government mismanagement of the pandemic. They were also fired up about "political Islam," the "Great Replacement," carbon taxes, and Western Canadian separatism (or Wexit). Between January 22 and February 21, 2022, thousands more people would join the convoy, some in spite of the right-wing agenda, others because of it.

Freedom looked like different things to different people in different moments of the convoy. It looked like bouncy castles and hot tubs and bonfires in the street. It looked like Confederate flags and swastikas. It looked like honking horns and fake Indigenous drum circles and singing "O Canada" in the face of an arresting officer. It looked like the righteous indignation of white people who were sick and tired of being told what to do, standing up to fight for their human right to eat in restaurants and play indoor sports.

Not everyone felt so free, though. BIPOC residents reported being harassed and assaulted by convoy protesters. The incessant honking and fumes from idling trucks made everyday life a nightmare for people and pets. Some Ottawa residents demanded that police "do their job" and forcibly clear the occupation; some filed a class action lawsuit against convoy organizers because of the noise; and some organized counter demos to reclaim their neighborhoods and block weekend convoy enthusiasts from joining the party.

The South Atlantic Quarterly 122:3, July 2023
DOI 10.1215/00382876-10644118 © 2023 Duke University Press

Between the calls to Make Canada Great Again and to Make Ottawa Boring Again, my students and I tried to make sense of what was happening, and what a decolonial abolitionist response to the convoy might look like. It was clear that while the organizers framed the occupation as a peaceful, family-friendly event to celebrate freedom and human rights, they were also motivated by a toxic blend of white supremacist, Islamophobic, anti-immigration, settler nativist, and pro-pipeline politics and conspiracy theories. A lot of this is just a remix of Trumpist memes and themes. But there's also a very specific history driving both the occupation of Ottawa and the colonization of Canadian psychic space.

The Freedom Convoy grew out of Yellow Vests Canada, a spin-off of the French Yellow Vest movement that blended their opposition to carbon taxes with a rejection of "foreign oil" from Muslim countries in the Middle East and a celebration of "ethical oil" from Alberta (Tewksbury 2021). Ethical oil is the brainchild of Ezra Levant, who also runs a far-right media outlet called Rebel News. It's a rebranding of the tar sands mega-project that *National Geographic* calls "the world's most destructive oil operation" (Leahy 2019), built on Cree, Dene, and Métis land around Fort McMurray. This is where my dad worked as a crane operator for most of my life growing up. The tailing ponds are so large around Fort Mac, they can be seen from outer space (Leahy 2019; Preston 2017: 14). Tens of thousands of "temporary foreign workers" (TFWs) are employed to work in the oil patch and related service industries, then expelled from the country when they're no longer needed (Preston 2017: 15). Downstream from the oil fields, Athabasca Chipewyan First Nation report high rates of cancer, including a rare form of bile duct cancer (Lawrynuik 2019; Preston 2013: 54). And man camps in the oil and gas industry are notorious as sites of sexual violence against Indigenous women, contributing to what the National Inquiry on Missing and Murdered Indigenous Women and Girls calls a "deliberate, often covert campaign of genocide" (National Inquiry 2019: 5; see also 584–86). In other words, ethical oil is a thick slurry of violence marketed as a peaceful alternative to Islamic "Conflict Oil regimes" who "support terrorism" and violate the human rights that Canadians hold so dear (qtd. in Preston 2013: 53).

In 2019, Yellow Vesters joined with other pro-pipeliners to organize a truck convoy to Ottawa called United We Roll, which functioned as a trial balloon for the 2022 Freedom Convoy. One of the ironies of this moment is that the federal government under Prime Minister Justin Trudeau, whom right-wingers like to mock as a treasonous coward and pedophile, used public money to keep the TransMountain pipeline project alive in 2018, in the face of ongoing opposition from Indigenous nations, environmental groups, and the BC provincial government. For over a decade, the RCMP has run surveillance programs targeting Indigenous peoples and environmentalists as potential threats to "critical infrastructure" such as pipelines (Preston 2013: 51–53; see also Bosworth and Chua 2021: 9–11). It would be hard to find a liberal government more open to oil and gas development and pipeline expansion.

Given this context, what's an abolitionist to do when a revanchist petrostate movement rolls into town and occupies your capital city, celebrating freedom and demanding the end of public health mandates in the midst of a global pandemic? And what does a situation like this teach us about the meaning of abolition?

On one hand, it makes no sense from a decolonial abolitionist perspective to call for the police of a settler state to crack down on unruly settlers for the sake of restoring peace, order, and good government on stolen Indigenous land. This is precisely the tag-team operation that sustains settler colonial logics: the state upholds "the rule of law" while settlers push the boundaries of legal occupation on the ground. In the end, both sides of the settler equation benefit from the way internal squabbles naturalize the settler occupation of Indigenous land as "our streets."

On the other hand, it isn't clear how to organize effective grassroots resistance against a well-funded group of possibly armed right-wing protesters in large vehicles who decide to occupy a small, liberal city in the middle of winter, and very quickly set up a military-style supply chain of fuel, food, and entertainment to keep them going, thanks in large part to a friendly response from local police (at least in the first few weeks). And even when people do take matters into their own hands, as in the Battle of Billings Bridge, where Ottawa residents came together in −22 °C weather to confront convoy weekenders on the ground, the problem of "whose streets" does not magically dissolve.

Whether you rely on the police or not, the fact remains that the city of Ottawa is built on unceded Algonquin Anishinaabe territory. And so, even if grassroots efforts were successful in ousting the settlers who illegally occupied the city of Ottawa for three weeks, the settlers who have illegally occupied these Indigenous lands for over three hundred years would still remain. This dilemma recalls the "ethic of incommensurability" between abolition and decolonization that Tuck and Yang identify as both a problem and a possibility for radical politics (2012: 29–36). Every prison, jail, and detention center could be shut down in so-called Canada, and the country would still remain a settler colony on a patchwork of unceded, purchased, and treaty land. Every police force could be defunded and abolished, and settlers could still informally police Indigenous peoples and extract wealth from Indigenous lands.

But this is precisely the lesson of the Ottawa occupation: there can be no meaningful abolition without decolonization and Indigenous resurgence. This does not necessarily mean that every settler leaves Turtle Island, although it does not rule it out. Either way, abolitionist movements must go beyond dismantling carceral institutions, and even beyond dismantling the state. We must also care for the land upon which prisons and pipelines, but also community gardens and yoga studios, are constructed.

As Robyn Maynard argues, "One opposite of policing is Land Back, which is, after all, an end to the imposition of private property regimes and the carceral technologies developed to enforce them" (Maynard and Simpson 2022: 204). Before colonial invasion, Indigenous peoples on what the Algonquin and Haudenosaunee call Turtle Island kept each other safe and held each other accountable without prisons or police. This means that a world without prisons is not just a utopian future to be imagined here, but a plurality of practices and legal orders to be *remembered and reimagined.* White settlers like myself are not keepers of these memories, but we can play a role in helping the colonial-carceral world to die so that other, more life-giving worlds may flourish (Oliveira 2021). Part of this process involves un-learning the history of the death-dealing world we have inherited and continue to inhabit.

A Canadian Heritage Minute

It all began with the beaver. Europeans admired their waterproof pelts, so they killed most of them, then crossed the Atlantic looking for more. The French were first off the mark, but the English were not far behind. In 1670, King Charles II granted the Hudson's Bay Company exclusive trading rights on 1.5 million square kilometers of Indigenous land in what is now known as Canada, and he appointed his cousin Rupert as governor of this land. The position of governor was a strange combination of CEO and political leader, empowered to "enact any laws and regulations not repugnant to the laws of England," as long they increased the flow of beaver pelts to Europe, and guns, wool, and other manufactured goods to Rupert's Land (Smandych and Linden 1996: 21). The Hudson's Bay Company was, in effect, a venture capitalist enterprise attached to an increasingly elaborate security force. It made trade deals with Indigenous nations, invented its own currency called the "made beaver," and in time even established its own police force and court system in the Red River settlement (Baker 1999).

The first penitentiary in Canada was built in 1835 on Anishinaabe and Haudenosaunee territory in Katarokwi/Kingston, where I now teach. A hundred acres of land north of the prison became a farm where prisoners grew food for their own consumption and fertilized with their own waste. They dug limestone out of quarries and used the stone to build Canada's first asylum for the "criminally insane" and, decades later, the first prison for women. Today, the university's football stadium sits in the former prison quarry and the prison for women is being converted into luxury condos. Kingston Penitentiary is up for grabs as a film set and potential yacht club.

These are just a few of the flows and accumulations that eventually morphed into the Canada whose greatness the Freedom Convoy was hell-bent on remaking: a massive fur warehouse with an ad hoc assemblage of governors, constables, and carceral enclosures to stabilize trade relations and secure what would later be called the "critical infrastructure" of global capitalism. But there's more to the story than this.

In 1869, the newly repackaged Dominion of Canada purchased Rupert's Land from the Hudson's Bay Company and began clearing the plains for agriculture, railways, resource extraction, and settlement. Just a few years later in 1873, Canada's first police force, the North-West Mounted Police (NWMP), was created to control Indigenous peoples on their own lands and secure territory for further development. This included forcing open a corridor for the construction of the Canadian Pacific Railway and operating an illegal pass system to control the movement of First Nations people off-reserve.

None of this capitalist-colonial violence went uncontested. The Red River Rebellions and North-West Rebellion are just two examples of large-scale coordinated resistance by Métis and Plains Indigenous nations against the corporation-turned-nation-state of Canada. But this resistance was met by an increasingly well-armed and tightly organized carceral apparatus. In 1885, Métis leader Louis Riel was executed for treason against the Crown in Regina, and less than two weeks later, six Cree and two Assiniboine leaders were executed in Battleford. This was the largest mass execution in Canadian history. Prime Minister John A. MacDonald explained: "The executions of the Indians . . . ought to convince the Red Man that the White Man governs" (qtd. in Monaghan 2013: 504). Chiefs Big Bear and Poundmaker were also convicted of treason and incarcerated at the newly built Stony Mountain Penitentiary in Manitoba, a province that Riel had helped to found.

Today, almost 150 years after the creation of the NWMP, Indigenous women make up 50 percent of the population in federal prisons for women, and just 5 percent of the overall population. Already in 1989, the Aboriginal Women's Caucus saw this as a structural feature of the settler state: "All Aboriginal, First Nations citizens are in conflict with the law . . . [insofar as they are subject to] a system of laws to which we have never consented" (qtd. in Nichols 2014: 453).

The same RCMP force that was empowered to use "lethal overwatch" in 2019 against Wet'suwet'en matriarchs defending their unceded land against a gas pipeline (Dhillon and Parrish 2019) offered handshakes and hugs to white protesters in 2022 after an eighteen-day blockade of the Alberta-Montana border connected to the Freedom Convoy. Four of these white protesters were arrested for conspiring to murder RCMP officers, and a cache of guns, ammunition, a machete, and body armor with the Diagolon insignia were seized from their trucks (National Post staff 2022).

One of the lessons of the convoy—we could miss it if we focus too narrowly on those three weeks of honking in Ottawa—is that Canada has always been a colonial resource extraction project backed up by state violence, from the early days of the fur trade to the clear-cuts, agribusiness, mines, and oil fields of the settler colony today (Pasternak 2022). For over three hundred years, carceral power in so-called Canada has been driven by racial capitalism. The truck convoy is just a particularly obnoxious expression of a more basic logic of extraction and destruction that crisscrosses not only the continent but the globe.

So what would it take to dismantle this "criminal empire" (Stark 2016)? Let the beaver be our guide.

Learning from the Beaver

In her 2020 lecture, "A Short History of the Blockade," Michi Saagiig Nishnaabeg writer Leanne Betasamosake Simpson reflects on the world-building power of Indigenous blockades against "the colonial machinery of elimination," which includes everything from police and prisons to universities and museums (2021: 4). Writing in support of the Wet'suwet'en people's refusal of a gas pipeline on their unceded land and the many solidarity actions that #ShutDownCanada for three weeks in February 2020, Simpson calls blockades "both a refusal and an affirmation. An affirmation of a different political economy. A world built upon a different set of relationships and ethics. An affirmation of life" (56).

The Freedom Convoy demonstrated loud and clear that the tactic of the blockade could be appropriated for settler world-building projects. But it also challenges us as decolonial abolitionists to reclaim the tactic of generative refusal, following the teachings of the beaver, or *Amik,* who builds "dams that create deep pools and channels that don't freeze, creating winter worlds" that sustain multiple forms of life rather than securitizing its own self-enclosed domain (14). Simpson asks:

> And who is the first back after a fire to start the regeneration makework?
>
> *Amik* is a world builder.
>
> *Amik* is the one that brings the water.
>
> *Amik* is the one that brings forth more life.
>
> *Amik* is the one that works continuously with water and land and plant and animal nations and consent and diplomacy to create worlds, to create shared worlds. (15)

Simpson contrasts the life-giving infrastructure of a beaver dam with the critical (read: colonial capitalist) infrastructure of the Trent Severn Waterway, which channels waters between Chi-Nibish (Lake Ontario) and Odawa Wiik-wwedong (Georgian Bay) into a canal system to support industrial development. While the Trent Severn Waterway is a simple negation, "an ending of life" (32), the beaver dam is "both a negation and an affirmation" (20).

This is not to say that Amik is incapable of doing wrong or harming others, whether by accident or on purpose. Simpson shares a story of the Giant Beaver who once roamed the earth, wrecking havoc for Nokomis and their grandchild Nanabush. Giant Amik builds a giant dam that raises the water levels between Gichi Gaming (Lake Superior) and Odawa Gaming (Lake Huron). In Simpson's version of the story, Nokomis and Nanabush hack into Amik's social media accounts and start deleting their posts until Amik comes crashing into their encampment between the lakes. A fight ensues for two days and nights, and in the end Amik bursts through their own dam to escape, releasing the water and creating thirty thousand islands with the wreckage of the dam (Simpson 2021: 21–3). And so, a giant dam that once threatened to destroy a campsite creates thirty thousand new dwelling places for two-legged and four-legged creatures through its generative destruction. After the battle, Giant Beaver runs off to the ocean, but Nanabush calls them back and invites them to what we might now call a community accountability process. Eventually, they learn "to use their beaver skills for good," thanks to "a little patience, a little resistance, some community, and a considerable reduction in size to the Amik we know and love today" (23).

This story of the Giant Beaver reminds us that a world without prisons or police is not a world where nothing harmful can happen, but rather a place where harm, accountability, and repair are all part of a process of learning how to share the earth and build worlds with others. The destructive activities of Giant Amik are neither tolerated nor demonized, but rather scaled down to the point where they may support life rather than undermining it.

This is not to say that the Freedom Convoy or the tar sands of Fort McMurray could become life-giving if they were scaled down and befriended by a twenty-first-century Nanabush. Some projects are just incommensurable with decolonial abolition—with life itself. Simpson's story doesn't tell us whether or not to call the cops on big rig blockaders, although she does "give thanks to Nokomis and Nanabush for not arresting Giant Beaver, destroying the blockade, and going back to business as usual" (32). A part of me also wonders what might happen if Giant Beaver kept their size but used their mighty tail to bust up pipelines and convoys with their new friends.

If we understand Canada as both a liberal democracy committed to the rule of law and—precisely as such—a "criminal empire" (Stark 2016) willing to destroy the earth along with the Indigenous nations who care for it, then Robyn Maynard is right: Abolition means Land Back. The question for decolonial abolitionists then becomes not just how to shut down this particular institution or dislodge that annoying right-wing occupation, but rather how to work together to stanch the flows of colonial racial capitalism, deepening pools that support diverse forms of life and busting up blockages of accumulated wealth to create islands of refuge for sharing the earth.

Note

Thank you to Marquis Bey, Bettina Bergo, Melissa Folk, Sheena Hoszko, and Adele Perry for feedback on this essay.

References

Baker, H. Robert. 1999. "Creating Order in the Wilderness: Transplanting the English Law to Rupert's Land, 1835–5." *Law and History Review* 17, no. 2 (summer), 209–46.

Bosworth, Kai, and Charmaine Chua. 2021. "The Countersovereignty of Critical Infrastructure Security: Settler-State Anxiety versus the Pipeline Blockade." *Antipode* (October). https://onlinelibrary.wiley.com/doi/abs/10.1111/anti.12794.

Dhillon, Jaskiran, and Will Parrish. 2019. "Exclusive: Canada police prepared to shoot Indigenous activists, documents show." *Guardian*, December 20. https://www.theguardian.com/world/2019/dec/20/canada-indigenous-land-defenders-police-documents

Lawrynuik, Sarah. 2019. "Downstream of oilsands, death by cancer comes too often." *National Observer,* December 17. https://www.nationalobserver.com/2019/12/17/news/downstream-oilsands-death-cancer-comes-too-often

Leahy, Stephen. 2019. "This Is the World's Most Destructive Oil Operation—And It's Grow-ing." *National Geographic,* April 11. https://www.nationalgeographic.com/environment /article/alberta-canadas-tar-sands-is-growing-but-indigenous-people-fight-back

Maynard, Robyn, and Leanne Betasamosake Simpson. 2022. *Rehearsals for Living.* Toronto: Alfred A. Knopf Canada.

Monaghan, Jeffrey. 2013. "Settler Governmentality and Racializing Surveillance in Canada's North-West." *The Canadian Journal of Sociology / Cahiers canadiens de sociologie* 38, no. 4: 487–508.

Murray, Laura J. 2018. "Settler and Indigenous Stories of Kingston/Ka'tarohkwi: A Case Study in Critical Heritage Pedagogy." *Journal of Canadian Studies / Revue d'études canadiennes* 52, no. 1 (winter/hiver): 249–79.

National Inquiry into Missing and Murdered Indigenous Women and Girls. 2019. "Reclaim-ing Power and Place: The Final Report of the National Inquiry into Missing and Murdered Indigenous Women and Girls." https://www.mmiwg-ffada.ca/wp-content/uploads/2019 /06/Final_Report_Vol_1a-1.pdf

National Post staff. 2022. "Police Hug Protesters as They Roll Out from Coutts, Alberta Border Crossing." *National Post,* February 15. https://nationalpost.com/news/canada/police -hug-protesters-as-they-roll-out-from-coutts-alberta-border-crossing

Nichols, Robert. 2014. "The Colonialism of Incarceration." *Radical Philosophy Review* 17, no. 2: 435–55.

Oliveira, Vanessa Machado de. 2021. *Hospicing Modernity: Facing Humanity's Wrongs and the Implications for Social Activism.* Berkeley, CA: North Atlantic Books.

Pasternak, Shiri. 2022. "Canada is a Bad Company: Police as Colonial Mercenaries for State and Capital." In *Disarm, Defund, Dismantle: Police Abolition in Canada,* edited by Shiri Pasternak, Kevin Walby, and Abby Stadnyk, 66–73. Toronto: Between the Lines.

Preston, Jen. 2013. "Neoliberal Settler Colonialism, Canada and the Tar Sands." *Race and Class* 55, no. 2: 42–59

Preston, Jen. 2017. "Racial Extractivism and White Settler Colonialism: An Examination of the Canadian Tar Sands Mega-projects." *Cultural Studies* 31, no. 2–3: 1–23.

Simpson, Leanne Betasamosake. 2021. *A Short History of the Blockade: Giant Beavers, Diplomacy, and Regeneration in Nishnaabewin.* CLC Kreisel Lecture Series. Edmonton: University of Alberta Press.

Smandych, Russell, and Rick Linden. 1996. "Administering Justice without the State: A Study of the Private Justice System of the Hudson's Bay Company to 1800." *Canadian Journal of Law and Society* 11, no. 1 (spring): 21–62.

Stark, Heidi Kiiwetinepinesiik. 2016. "Criminal Empire: The Making of the Savage in a Law-less Land." *Theory and Event* 19, no. 4. muse.jhu.edu/article/633282.

Tewksbury, Doug. 2021. "Petro-Nostalgia and the Politics of Yellow Vests Canada." *Canadian Journal of Communication* 46, no. 4: 939–59.

Tuck, Eve, and K. Wayne Yang. 2012. "Decolonization is not a metaphor." Decolonization: Indi-geneity. *Education and Society* 1, no. 1: 1–40.

S. B. West

U jeets'el le ki'ki' kuxtal:
A Hemispheric Meditation on
Abolition and Autonomy

On April 13, 2021, the Campeche-based campaign "U jeets'el le ki'ki' kux-tal"[1] held a press conference that highlighted a series of events, talks, and gatherings organized around establishing a collective push toward autonomy as the response against the so-called and poorly named Tren Maya (Maya Train). As the most publicly visible portion of the massive infrastructural project known as the South-Southeastern Territorial Reordering Project and one leg of Mexican president Andrés Manuel López Obrador's National Development Plan (PND), the Maya Train has been fervently critiqued by environmentalists, scholars, activists, and community members of the region, where this latter group mostly identifies with or are identified as "maya."[2] The Maya Train is marketed to propel the PND's six-part plan conceived to "guarantee employment, education, health, and wellbeing" by "modernizing" turistic and socioeconomic frameworks in Mexico's Southeast (Adrián, Yannick, and Sergio 2019). Organizers of U jeets'el le ki'ki' kuxtal urge the Southeast's maya rural population to reject the "colonization that has slipped in and deeply embedded itself in our territory, our minds, and our hearts" and begin work toward an autonomous community. Autonomy is understood as the possibility of "wellbeing, living with dignity, and a free life," and is part of a long-standing practice of sociopolitical self-determination mobilized through the exercising of the second article of the Mexican constitution.[3] The dialogues that comprised the press conference centered on autonomy as a framework to create "un mundo donde quepan muchos mundos," *a world where*

The South Atlantic Quarterly 122:3, July 2023
DOI 10.1215/00382876-10644132 © 2023 Duke University Press

many worlds might fit, as a response that might halt the mass appropriation of maya territory and destruction of fragile ecosystems by the Mexican state as it begins its mega project (Campaña U Je'ets'el le ki'ki kuxtal 2021b).

A world where many worlds might fit. This utterance stems from the EZLN movement and beautifully expresses U je'etsel's position on autonomy as I experience it through their virtual presence, including communiqués, press releases, and Facebook Live events. I contend that U je'etsel's autonomy also speaks to forms of radical abolitionist politics currently taking shape in the region from which I currently write, and offer an example of these nested worlds.[4] My first goal in this meditation is to think alongside U je'etsel's campaign as a budding autonomous movement to learn from their concept of autonomy and how it enacts forms of what might be understood as abolition in the United States—that is, to consider how these two worlds fit together. And so, what is abolition as it is imagined and enacted in the US setting? My intervention into these politics is perhaps best captured by Catherine Walsh's decolonial posture of "thinking-otherwise" (2012: 55) and Charles Sepulveda's "life beyond" (Wilson Gilmore et al. 2020)—I think through abolition as a possibility of living that takes up, from its very organization, a radical refusal of oppression and white supremacy. Indeed, while abolition—and trans abolitionist feminisms in particular—defies categorization and fixity, abolition is rooted in the axiom that enslavement is not yet abolished in the United States (Dillon 2012). Enslavement today manifests in prisons, in policing, and in the penal codes that entrap human life and enact social oppression—namely, racism, classism, gendered violence, ableism, etc.—through myriad reconfigurations of hegemonic logics. Abolitionist politics emphasize that these institutions dehumanize us all; they mobilize and maintain legalized racial genocide, feminicide, class struggles, homophobia, cisheteronormativity, and other forms of dehumanization (Gossett 2011: 324). Further, another portion of abolitionist roots is located in the refusal of myriad forms of social and structural enslavement that affect those currently exterior to the prison system, as well, an extension of prison enslavement defined through the *mundane*: those quotidian practices of living articulated—and *inescapably* so—through systems that harm: lives lost to clocking in and clocking out; love, acceptance and wellbeing sacrificed to unattainable norms of beauty, of "health"; interest payments and overdrafts; commutes to places we don't want to be in order find jobs that provide survivability, the curated impulse to consume, etc. These habits or behaviors—often perceived as inevitable, if perceived at all—cause us to lose the possibility of multiplicity, of living in other ways. I use the term enslavement purposefully: we currently experience these virtually ineludible systemic harms that rob us of choice and subsequently, the experience of knowing ourselves and what we are capable of.

Abolitionist stances are active, both physically and intellectually, and do not merely "sit with" these realities. Radical or revolutionary trans feminist abolitionisms as I experience them seek opportunities to destabilize, imagine, and *act upon those imaginings in another way*, a way in which we learn to care for ourselves and each other, take accountability for our (in)actions and those of the past, and design social systems that provide resources and frameworks that meet those ends (Bey 2022; Boellstorff et al. 2014; Giroux 2004; Lamble 2011; Lamble n.d.). Those goals drive abolitionism to seek an opening-up of the "us," one that goes beyond the ways the modern colonial system has divided "us," be that in gender, in race, in class—toward an imagining of "us" that takes into account, and radically so, how these preconfigured identities have shaped us and enable certain behaviors, but harken us to be traitorous to those forms. In a word, I follow Dylan Rodríguez's definition that the abolitionist stance seeks to "build a different set of historical and political assumptions that recast our understanding of the prison regime as a focal point of a collective, radical political creativity—abolitionism—that takes seriously the monumental challenges of freedom, liberation, self-determination, and anti-violence" (Gossett 2011: 361).

Thus, from Rodríguez's definition to my own conjectures on abolition, self-determination—or in other words, autonomy—plays a central role in an abolitionist stance, and vice versa (Hasta Muerte Coffee 2021). If we return now to the "Mexican" southeast, we might think about how abolition is employed in the autonomy of U je'etsel's movement. The hegemonic response to U Je'etsel's declarations for autonomy were swift. Less than one month after the Facebook Live press conference, President Andrés Manuel López Obrador (AMLO) traveled to Yucatán for an event planned by his administration to formally request forgiveness from the mayan people for the centuries of "terrible abuses" committed (past tense) by colonial and national regimes. Replete with a display of Authentic Mayan Traditional Ceremonies, the event culminated in a speech delivered by the president before an emblem that read "Petition for Forgiveness for the Harms Caused to the Mayan People / Ending the Caste War" (Osorio 2021). Even during the speech, the response to the petition was exceedingly clear through the shouts and interruptions from the protests surrounding the event (Pie de Página [@PdPagina] 2021). Shortly after, U je'etsel le ki'ki kuxtal mobilized against AMLO's "false apology," highlighting through various communiqués that while AMLO (vaguely and loosely) denounced the liberal politics of Porfirio Díaz, or the Porfiriato,[5] and subsequent neoliberal policies, he continues to move forward with the very sort of project for which he claims to seek forgiveness (Campaña U Je'ets'el le ki'ki kuxtal 2021a; Indignación 2021). In one such communiqué, U je'etsel indexes the political orientations of the Porfiriato as they appear today in their neoliberal form. They state, "What comes with forgiveness? While one part of this speaks of asking forgiveness, the other part commits the same acts that Porfirio Díaz did back then. With forgiveness comes big companies, the loss of our land, the accumulation (of wealth) for the few and misery for the people. [With it comes] The military: agents of violence and the cruelest disappearances of our recent history." They earmark the notion of "progress" as one that stems from a "western perspective" that provides "wealth for the few" and has caused "exploitation and expropriation that prioritizes death," that "enslaves and kills," and "destroys others' forms of living." They highlight that what is in "dispute [are] the possible futures of the many ways of living and organizing of the people, of the children, of nature, and of life itself," that "when large projects come and snatch away our land, the peace of our people is transformed to terror [. . .] because [our land] has become regional, national and even global sites of labor exploitation, of general lack of safety, of femicides and murder, of drug and human trafficking" (Cortés and Fernando 2021).

What this brief vignette illustrates is how autonomy and abolition share multiple points of struggle. The maya and other oppressed peoples of Latin America possess decades and centuries of experience carving out autonomous zones that are independent of the colonial-liberal state. Even within the last fifty years, from Zapatista autonomous municipalities in Chiapas to the Cherán K'eri movement in Michoacán, autonomy encapsulates a right to live outside the social-institutional totality of the nation-state that continues its process of global universalization. Like abolition, there are myriad approximations, understandings, and deployments of autonomy, but the form of autonomy here enacted emphasizes (and is often spurred by, as is the case here) the state-sanctioned theft of the land and unchecked (neoliberal) capitalist extractivism, which autonomy understands as a deeply dehumanizing endeavor. The U Je'etsel movement, like other Indigenous or native autonomous movements, emphasizes independent decision-making structures, economic alternatives to capitalism, and territorial restructuring that permits collective rights to land and natural resources, all of which sharply diverge from the PND and its train. Additionally, autonomy, especially in the "Mexican" southeast, has historically prioritized the independent implementation of other important social structures, such as medical and educational systems, that support self-determination outside the systems of the state (Mora 2017). So, where abolition might first turn to the abolishment of police and carceral violence (and the systems such violence proliferates) as its center, autonomy centers the abolishment of legalized and illicit land appropriation and ecocide. This variance illustrates the centrality of each movement's locus of enunciation (Mignolo 2000), where in the context of mayan resistance, there is a continued, historical struggle of land appropriation that, like enslavement in abolition in the US context, has changed shapes many times (Desinformémonos 2020). In the colonial moment, such land theft began via terra nullius claims by European colonizers; in the nineteenth century, *terreno baldío* (vacant land) claims mobilized the theft of indigenous lands by the early iterations of the nation-state; today, neoliberal law and ideology facilitates land-grabs by a state increasingly intertangled in multinational mega companies. In US abolition, on the other hand, land has become the meeting place of productive conflict, in the case of indigenous sovereignty versus land reparations and ultimately, commensurability (King, Navarro, and Smith 2020), for example. Land is thus the place where abolition and decolonization show their intimate entanglement, demonstrating how the end of the consumption of the land benefits all, and conversely, white cisheteropatriarchy, that which propagates that consumption, will end us all, even those that currently benefit from its proliferation (for indeed, what will even those in power consume once all is consumed?). While this differing point of entrance addresses how state systems cause harm in different political contexts, what both orientations share is the deep and profound refusal of state/hegemonic logics that promote harm (the language of abolition) and the loss of dignity (the language of autonomy).

During U Je'ets'el's press conference, representatives there noted that they chose to have their event on that precise day because 88 years ago, in 1933, the "Last Mayan Rebel" was vanquished in Dzulá by the Mexican state, thus closing the door on a mayan autonomy that had lasted more than fifty years in Noj Kaaj Santa Cruz X Balam Naj, known also as Felipe Carrillo Puerto, the same city where AMLO held his own press conference a few weeks later. In other communiqués, U je'etsel's campaign gestures toward a reclaiming of Yucatán's so-called Caste War as part of its ideological roots. Where historical configurations define the fifty-four-year uprising (1847–1901) as connected to local *caudillos*, disagreements regarding federalism, and "Maya bigmen" (Rugeley 2009: 2) occurring during the extension of liberal politics and capitalist extractivism into rural areas of the peninsula, U je'etsel's estimation of the conflict differs significantly from other interpretations of the historical register. Curiously, AMLO also lays claim to the Caste War move-

ment, evoking it in his presidential backdrop during his petition for forgiveness: "Ending the Caste War." In response, one protester yelled, "If [the rebel
leader] Jacinto Pat were alive today, he would be embarrassed of this display"
(Osorio 2021). What, then, might this battle for meaning-making mean?
What is the importance of historical autonomous movements that have sought
to halt land appropriation and enclosure of the commons, and what might be
found in the apposition of US abolition and indigenous autonomy?

I proffer that the so-called Caste War is a historicized form of radical
autonomy and a project of abolition subject to forces that seek to vacate it of its
liberatory power. This substantiates the symbolic importance of the Caste
War in both AMLO's forgiveness tour and in U je'etsel's autonomy campaign.
Indeed, control of Caste War discourse constitutes a decades-long battle.[6]
Nineteenth-century newspapers, narratives, and historical accounts talk of
rebel leaders and their rebel troops attacked white-owned haciendas and set-
tlements, killing, raping, and plundering as they went. Eyewitness reports tell
tales of rebels taking hacienda owners' wives as concubines; of houses and
possessions burned; of entire towns of white families—including women
and children—murdered, their bodies left to decay in the aftermath (Ancona
1878, 4:5–14). In all, it was reported that more than half of Yucatán's white
population either fell victim to the rebels or fled the peninsula: casualties are
estimated from 250,000 to 360,000 throughout the course of this fifty-five-
year war (Reed 1964; Rugeley 2009). A militarized mayan independent state
called Chan Santa Cruz formed in the 1850s, encompassing the majority of
what is today called Quintana Roo. Chan Santa Cruz was recognized as a de
facto independent country by the British government, which reflected the
intimate ties between the former and British Honduras (Dumond 1997).

The rebels themselves tell a strikingly different tale in the epistolary
accounts that they left behind. "Indio"-identifying leaders maintained that
the war was not one of racial antagonism; and if it was being conceptualized
as such, it was because "the whites began it" (Rugeley 2001). Leaders repeatedly state that the rebellion reflected a response to the loss of life caused by
poverty, cultural control, and labor exploitation, a response taken to after
exhausting all other possibilities. Indeed, the rebels' perspective reflects
much more accurately what is known of the period: Yucatán's nineteenth
century was defined by white politicians attempting to bring the lofty
charges of order and progress—the credence of modernity—to the region
via institutionalized and epistemic violence. The maya, in turn, paid the cost
in land expropriation, exorbitant taxation, and cultural oppression all in the
(white European) hopes to mold Yucatán into a racially homogenous, liberal,

capitalist state. Rebel epistolary accounts reflect a push against the biological essentialism of blanco racial discourse, or the imagining of the Caste war as an antagonism based on skin color and the meanings assigned to phenotypic difference as exemplified above. To them, the Caste War was not about the accumulation of rights under a white regime, but rather, the right to live otherwise, outside of capitalism, and outside of state participation, and outside of social articulation. As one general succinctly expresses, "it will not be necessary to buy land, the white, the black, or the Indian can plant their milpa wherever he wants, and no one will prohibit it" (Kazanjian 2016). That is, Caste War rebels were imagining a world-otherwise at the metonymic nexus of capitalism and land—the very rejection of land as ownable, its surplus, its enclosure, its sale, the radical refusal of the chattelizing of the earth—which attests to a pushing away from wanting "more" or "better" rights in a world organized by whiteness, and toward a world that abolished the very systems that oppress in the first place.

An invasion by Porfirio Díaz's troops in 1902 is often considered the end of the so-called Caste War—incredibly, an invasion motivated by the establishment of a *railway* that would facilitate the shipment of chicle sap to use in the booming chewing gum industry (Redclift 2004). However, some scholars account for the decades of struggle that took place after Díaz's invasion, including the above-cited "last battle" of Dzula in 1933 (Kaeding 2013). However, it is clear that the continued battle over meaning-making and discursive control lies at the heart of two diametrically opposed movements: autonomy and the PND. Indeed, if AMLO seeks to discursively end the war to ideologically clear the way for the PND, this constitutes an admission that the Caste War movement continues on as U je'etsel asserts: "the [so-called Caste] war continues. We live in one of the most critical moments of the history of mayan territory." And at the center of this contention, I find *a world where many worlds might fit*. Where institutions and individuals complicit with white cisheteronormative patriarchy seek to create narrative logics that claim that no other way is possible, that there has never been and never will be any other way to live and organize our social and political worlds, U jeetsel asserts that this is not the case: there have already been worlds within worlds, as evident in the living memory of the so-called Caste War. Abolition and autonomy, while experiencing moments of convergence and departure, share similar struggles in the face of naturalized, overpowering narrative logics in a struggle for making the world. As Bassichis, Lee, and Spade claim, "To chart a different course for our movements, we need to understand the road we've traveled" (Bassichis, Lee, and Spade 2011: 19):part of U jeets'el's emancipatory project is a radical reclaiming of autonomy's historicity.

Notes

1   Establishment of the Good Life / Autonomy (Asentamiento de la buena vida/autonomía). This campaign forms part of the collective Rebirth of Collective Work, or Ka Kuxtal Much Meyaj. Translations to English from Spanish and Maaya T'aan resources are my own throughout. Speakers at the press conference included Manuel May, Ángel Sulub, Álvaro Mena, Nora Tzec, Wilma Esquivel, Letina Cruz Velasquez, and Selena Uc, many of whom are also involved with the collective Ka kuxtal much meyaj (Kuxtal 2021).

2   Following Juan Castillo Cocom, the notion of "maya" came to being via its relationship to state-building, institutionalized hegemony, and westernizing knowledge crafting. On the other hand, the term *maya* is also an identitary category under which many find political power and belonging. As such, it can both "interpellate and exceed the mayan realism created in the long night of the times of the anthropological romance" (Castillo Cocom and Castañeda 2021). It is of note that many people who are deemed "maya" by the state and cultural institutions in fact identify otherwise, as, for example, masewuales, indios, campesinos, mayeros, etc. I opt to not capitalize the word maya or any currently popular identificatory category, following, for example, Samuel Delany's considerations on the word *black* (2000). See also Whittaker 2021.

3   The Mexican Constitution of 1917 "recognizes and protects the indigenous peoples' right to self-determination and, consequently, the right to autonomy." Regionally, other legislatures exist that might create the legal groundwork for mayan autonomy, including the 1998 Ley de Derechos, Cultura, y Organización Indígena del Estado de Quintana Roo, and the 2011 Ley para Protección de los Derechos de la Comunidad Maya del Estado de Yucatán.

4   Chicago is the stolen land where the Ojibwe, Odawa, and Potawatomi Nations reside and resided. It is the stolen land where the Miami, Ho-Chunk, Menominee, Sac, and Fox reside and resided. It is land enslaved under capitalism; capitalism makes chattel slavery of the land. It is also one of the US urban centers, with Minneapolis as its epicenter, that saw significant abolitionist activity via the uprisings of the summer of 2020, the year of George Floyd's murder (Nevada 2022).

5   The Porfiriato is the de facto dictatorship of Porfirio Díaz, lasting from 1876 to 1911, or seven "elections." During his reign, he sought international foreign investment in Mexico and directly contributed to the mass accumulation of land in the hands of the wealthy and the widespread suffering of his impoverished, rural, and racialized constituents. While widely hailed as the elite golden age of the Mexican economy, Díaz' massive "modernizing" projects—including the construction of railways and landmark buildings—required the widespread dispossession of peasant lands and the poorly remunerated labor, indentured servitude, or enslavement of those dispossessed.

6   The "Caste War" is a near permanent presence in peninsular politics, evoked often in major political shifts in the Yucatán peninsula, especially those referring to changes in land tenure. See Fallaw 2012.

References

Adrián, Flores, Deniau Yannick, and Prieto Sergio. 2019. "El Tren Maya. Un nuevo proyecto de articulación territorial en la Península de Yucatán." México: GeoComunes / Consejo Civil Mexicano para la Silvicultura Sostenible.

Ancona, Eligio. 1878. *Historia de Yucatán, Desde La Época [Sic] Más Remota Hasta Nuestros Días: La Guerra Social.* 5 vols. Mérida: Impr. de M. Heredia Argüelles. http://catalog.hathi trust.org/Record/007032688.

Bassichis, Morgan, Alexander Lee, and Dean Spade. 2015. "Building an Abolitionist Trans and Queer Movement with Everything We've Got." In *Captive Genders: Trans Embodiment and the Prison Industrial Complex,* edited by Eric A. Stanley, Nat Smith, and CeCeMc-Donald. Chico, CA: AK Press.

Bey, Marquis. 2022. *Black Trans Feminism.* Durham, NC: Duke University Press.

Boellstorff, Tom, Mauro Cabral, Micha Cárdenas, Trystan Cotten, Eric A. Stanley, Kalaniopua Young, and Aren Z. Aizura. 2014. "Decolonizing Transgender: A Roundtable Discussion." *TSQ: Transgender Studies Quarterly* 1: 419–39. https://doi.org/10.1215/23289252-2685669.

Campaña U Je'ets'el le ki'ki kuxtal. 2021a. "Pronunciamiento de la Campaña U Jeets'el le Ki'ki kuxtal en el aniversario del inicio de la lucha social maya de 1847." *Radio Zapatista,* July. https://radiozapatista.org/?p=38831&lang=en.

Campaña U Je'ets'el le ki'ki kuxtal. 2021b. "Conferencia de prensa; Campaña por la autonomía en Facebook Live." https://www.facebook.com/watch/?v=2875628566019008.

Castillo Cocom, Juan A., and Quetzil E. Castañeda. 2021. "Visión etnográfica: Imaginar el *iknal* maya." *The Journal of Latin American and Caribbean Anthropology* 26, no. 1: 10–24. https://doi.org/10.1111/jlca.12543.

Cortés, Andrade, and Luis Fernando. 2021. "Campaña U Jeets'el le ki'ki' kuxtal Territorio Maya en Resistencia y Rebeldía Contra el falso perdón y por las Autonomías." *Ke Noticias con Sol de Abril,* May. https://kenoticiasconsoldeabril.com.mx/index.php/2021 /05/06/campana-u-jeetsel-le-kiki-kuxtal-territorio-maya-en-resistencia-y-rebeldia -contra-el-falso-perdon-y-por-las-autonomias/.

Delaney, Samuel R. 2000. "Racism and Science Fiction." In *Dark Matter: A Century of Speculative Fiction from the African Diaspora,* edited by Sheree R. Thomas. 383–97. New York: Warner Books.

Desinformémonos, dir. 2020. *La Palabra Del Monte.* https://www.youtube.com/watch?v =p6dLF5JKvsw.

Dillon, Stephen. 2012. "Possessed by Death: The Neoliberal-Carceral State, Black Feminism, and the Afterlife of Slavery." *Radical History Review* 12: 113–25. https://doi.org/10.1215 /01636545-1416196.

Dumond, Don E. 1997. *The Machete and the Cross: Campesino Rebellion in Yucatán.* Lincoln: University of Nebraska Press.

Fallaw, Ben. 2012. "Primitive Revolution: Restorationist Religion and the Idea of the Mexican Revolution, 1940–1968." *Hispanic American Historical Review* 92, no. 3: 566–68. https://doi.org/10.1215/00182168–1600515.

Giroux, Henry. 2004. "When Hope Is Subversive." *Tikkun* 19: 38–39.

Gossett, Che. 2011. "Abolitionist Imaginings: A Conversation with Bo Brown, Reina Gossett, and Dylan Rodríguez." In Stanley and Smith 2011: 323–42. Oakland, CA: AK Press.

Hasta Muerte Coffee. 2021. *No Abolition without Autonomy.* Oakland, CA, Huichin Village, Lisjan Ohlone territory. https://hastamuertecoffee.com/wp-content/uploads /2021/05/hastamuerte-booklet-online-v05212021.pdf.

Indignación, Equipo. 2021. "Carta del Chuunt'aan maya de Yucatán ante la petición de perdón al pueblo maya y el fin a la guerra de la mal llamada 'guerra de castas.'" https://twitter. com/indignacion_dh/status/1389273858679705606/photo/1.

Kaeding, Adam R. 2013. "Negotiated Survival—An Archaeological and Documentary Investigation of Colonialism in Beneficios Altos, Yucatan, Mexico." PhD diss., Boston University.

Kazanjian, David. 2016. *The Brink of Freedom: Improvising Life in the Nineteenth-Century World.* Durham, NC: Duke University Press.

King, Tiffany Lethabo, Jenell Navarro, and Andrea Smith. 2020. *Otherwise Worlds: Against Settler Colonialism and Anti-Blackness.* Durham, NC: Duke University Press. https://muse.jhu.edu/book/75685.

Kuxtal, Ka. 2021. "'Campaña u jeets'el le ki'ki kuxtal por una vida digna ¡vamos por la autonomía!'" April 2021. https://www.kakuxtal.org/post/campa%C3%B1a-u-jeets-el-le-ki-ki-kuxtal-por-una-vida-digna-vamos-por-la-autonom%C3%ADa.

Lamble, Sarah. "Transforming Carceral Logics: 10 Reasons to Dismantle the Prison Industrial Complex Using a Queer/Trans Analysis." In *Captive Genders: Trans Embodiment and the Prison Industrial Complex,* edited by Eric A. Stanley and Nat Smith, 235–66. Oakland, CA: AK Press, 2011.

Lamble, Sarah. 2020. "Practicing Everyday Abolition." *abolitionistfutures.com,* August 19. https://abolitionistfutures.com/latest-news/practising-everyday-abolition. Accessed April 18, 2022.

Mignolo, Walter. 2000. *Local Histories/Global Designs: Coloniality, Subaltern Knowledges, and Border Thinking.* Princeton, NJ: Princeton University Press.

Mora, Mariana. 2017. *Kuxlejal Politics.* Austin: University of Texas Press.

Nevada. 2022. *The Abolition of Law.* Minneapolis, MN: Stolen Dakota Land.

Osorio, Camila. 2021. "López Obrador pide perdón a los mayas por los abusos contra ellos a lo largo de la historia." *El País,* May. https://elpais.com/mexico/2021-05-03/lopez-obrador-pide-perdon-a-los-mayas-por-los-abusos-contra-ellos-a-lo-largo-de-la-historia.html.

Pie de Página [@PdPagina]. 2021. "#AlMomento | En Tihosuco, municipio de Felipe Carrillo Puerto, está a punto de empezar la ceremonia de petición de perdón al pueblo maya del presidente @lopezobrador_ por los agravios cometidos en la colonia y en el México independiente Reportan @danielapastrana e @ignaciodealba https://t.co/DkcQdF1tlq." Tweet. *Twitter.* https://twitter.com/PdPagina/status/1389280315554807810.

Redclift, Michael. 2004. "Chicle and Social Revolution in Yucatán." In *Chewing Gum: The Fortunes of Taste,* 43–81. London: Routledge.

Reed, Nelson. 1964. *The Caste War of Yucatán.* Stanford, CA: Stanford University Press.

Rugeley, Terry. 2001. *Maya Wars: Ethnographic Accounts from Nineteenth-Century Yucatan.* Norman: University of Oklahoma Press.

Rugeley, Terry. 2009. *Rebellion Now and Forever: Mayas, Hispanics, and Caste War Violence in Yucatán, 1800–1880.* Stanford, CA: Stanford University Press.

Walsh, C. 2012. "Interculturalidad y (de)colonialidad. Perspectivas críticas y políticas." *Visao Global, Joacaba* 15, nos. 1–2: 61–74.

Whittaker, Nicholas. 2021. "Case Sensitive: Why We Shouldn't Capitalize 'Black.'" *The Drift,* September 17. https://www.thedriftmag.com/case-sensitive/

Wilson Gilmore, Ruth, Nick Estes, Sarah Haley, and Charles Sepulveda. 2020. "Abolition on Stolen Land with Ruth Wilson Gilmore." *Challenge Inequality.* https://challengeinequality.luskin.ucla.edu/abolition-on-stolen-land-with-ruth-wilson-gilmore/.

Notes on Contributors

Aren Aizura is Associate Professor in Gender, Women and Sexuality Studies at the University of Minnesota. His first book, *Mobile Subjects: Transnational Imaginaries of Gender Reassignment* (2018), won the Sylvia Rivera Award in Transgender Studies in 2019. He coedited the *Transgender Studies Reader 2* (2013) and *Keywords for Gender and Sexuality Studies* (2021), as well as a special issue of *Transgender Studies Quarterly* on Decolonizing the Transgender Imaginary (2013). His most recent work appeared in *TSQ: Transgender Studies Quarterly*.

Leticia Alvarado is Associate Professor of American Studies at Brown University. She is the author of *Abject Performances: Aesthetic Strategies in Latino Cultural Production* (2018). Her current book project, *Cut/Hoard/Suture: Aesthetics in Relation*, has been supported by The Andy Warhol Foundation Arts Writers Grant and the American Association of University Women.

Heather Berg writes about sex, work, and social struggle. Her first book, *Porn Work* (2021), explores workers' strategies for navigating—and subverting—precarity. Her writing also appears in the journals *Feminist Studies*, *Signs*, and others. She is Assistant Professor of Women, Gender, and Sexuality Studies at Washington University in St. Louis.

Marquis Bey is Assistant Professor of African American Studies and English, and Gender & Sexuality Studies and Critical Theory, at Northwestern University. They are the author, most recently, of the books *Black Trans Feminism* and *Cistem Failure: Essays on Blackness and Cisgender*, both published with Duke University Press in 2022.

Andrew Cutrone is a PhD Candidate in Sociology and a Graduate Affiliate of the Rapoport Center for Human Rights and Justice at the University of Texas, Austin. He writes about and studies Black social theory and abolition politics. His research examines, but ultimately seeks to dispense with, the regime of the normative subject, preferring, instead, to induce and honor instances of fugitive coalition. Specifically, Andrew reads a range of archival materials to theorize the radicality underpinning the relationship between fugitive enslaved people and those who aided in their escape.

Ramzi Fawaz is a Romnes Professor of English at the University of Wisconsin, Madison. He is the author of *The New Mutants: Superheroes and the Radical Imagination of American Comics* (2016) and *Queer Forms* (2022). With Darieck Scott he coedited a special issue of American Literature titled "Queer

About Comics," which won the 2019 best special issue of the year award from the Council of Editors of Learned Journals. Alongside Deborah E. Whaley and Shelley Streeby, he coedited *Keywords for Comics Studies*, which was selected as a Choice Outstanding Academic Title of 2022. Fawaz is currently at work on a new book project titled "Literary Theory on Acid," in which he argues for the necessity of literary and cultural studies approaches to the contemporary psychedelic renaissance.

Lisa Guenther is Queen's National Scholar in Political Philosophy and Critical Prison Studies at Queen's University in Canada. She is the author of *Solitary Confinement: Social Death and its Afterlives* (2013) and co-editor of *Death and Other Penalties: Philosophy in a Time of Mass Incarceration* (2015).

Huey Hewitt is a Doctoral Candidate in the Department of African and African American Studies at Harvard University, where he is also a Harvard Presidential Scholar and Prize Fellow. He holds an MA in history from Harvard and a BA in black studies and history from Amherst College. His dissertation is an intellectual history of black anarchism in the United States in the twentieth-century.

Candice J. Merritt is a PhD Candidate in the Department of African American Studies at Northwestern University. She holds an MA in Women's, Gender, and Sexuality Studies from Georgia State University and a BA in Women's Studies from Emory University. Her dissertation project, "In Search of Our Mothers' Freedom: Examining the Felt Life of Black Motherhood," centers Black women's disavowals of motherhood in the late-twentieth and twenty-first centuries and theorizes its implications for Black feminist theories of mothering and reproductive freedom. Her essay "Trapped in the Political Real: Imagining Black Motherhood Beyond Pathology and Protest" is included in *The New Feminist Literary Studies,* edited by Jennifer Cooke (2020).

Durba Mitra is the Richard B. Wolf Associate Professor of Women, Gender, and Sexuality at Harvard University. She is the author of *Indian Sex Life: Sexuality and the Colonial Origins of Modern Social Thought* (2020). Her current project explores the history of Third World feminist thought.

Jennifer C. Nash is the Jean Fox O'Barr Professor of Gender, Sexuality, and Feminist Studies at Duke University. She is the author of *The Black Body in Ecstasy: Reading Race, Reading Pornography* (2014); *Black Feminism Reimagined* (2019); *Birthing Black Mothers* (2021); and the forthcoming *How We Write Now: Living with Black Feminist Theory*. She is the editor of *Gender: Love* (2016) and a coeditor (along with Samantha Pinto) of *The Routledge Companion to Intersectionalities* (2022).

Emily Owens is the David and Michelle Ebersman Assistant Professor of History at Brown University, where she does research on and teaches about US slavery, the legal history of race and sexual violence, and the intellectual history of American feminisms. Her work broadly considers the ways that racism and misogyny get expressed in ordinary—and intimate—life. She is the author of *Consent in the Presence of Force: Sexual Violence and Black Women's Survival in Antebellum New Orleans* (2023), and her writing can also be found in *Signs: Journal of Women, Culture and Society, The Black Scholar, Literary Hub,* and *Louisiana History.*

Samantha Pinto is Professor of English, director of the Humanities Institute, core faculty of Women's and Gender Studies and affiliated faculty of African and African Diaspora Studies at the University of Texas at Austin. She is the author of *Difficult Diasporas: The Transnational Feminist Aesthetic of the Black Atlantic* (2013) and *Infamous Bodies: Early Black Women's Celebrity and the Afterlives of Rights* (2020).

S. B. West is Assistant Professor in Gender, Women's and Sexuality Studies and is affiliated faculty in Latinx and Latin American Studies at Northeastern Illinois University in Chicago. Their research and intellectual production is focused on breaking away from traditional approaches to the study and engagement of the "Latin American" literary and cultural canon. West's work is organized around theoretical frameworks—specifically, those with roots in abolitionist, decolonial and trans feminisms—that question and challenge the always already colonial, cisheteronormative underpinnings of gender, class and race relations. While "Caste War Textualities," their current project, is a rereading of Yucatán's nineteenth-century textual register that emphasizes how the concept of race war mobilized the transference of colonial oppression into liberal state-building, they also have active projects on contemporary Yucatec Maya "literature", US Spanish-language "im/migration" literature, and feminist theory.

Robyn Wiegman is a professor in the Program in Literature and Gender, Sexuality and Feminist Studies at Duke University and the author and editor of numerous projects on racial formation, feminist and queer theory, US studies, and cultural studies.

DOI 10.1215/00382876-10840238

Keep up to date on new scholarship

Issue alerts are a great way to stay current on all the cutting-edge scholarship from your favorite Duke University Press journals. This free service delivers tables of contents directly to your inbox, informing you of the latest groundbreaking work as soon as it is published.

To sign up for issue alerts:

1. Visit **dukeu.press/register** and register for an account. You do not need to provide a customer number.

2. After registering, visit **dukeu.press/alerts**.

3. Go to "Latest Issue Alerts" and click on "Add Alerts."

4. Select as many publications as you would like from the pop-up window and click "Add Alerts."

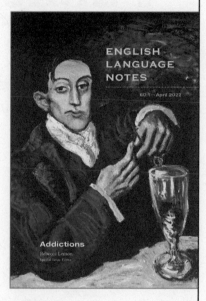